Getting to Heaven™

John Rosemond and Dr. Scott Gleason

Copyright 2018, John K. Rosemond, Scott A. Gleason

Getting to Heaven: A Guide for the Perplexed
By John Rosemond and Dr. Scott Gleason
Copyright© 2018 John K Rosemond, Scott A. Gleason
Homeless [song] Copyright John K Rosemond
All rights reserved

ISBN-13: 978-1984136749
ISBN-10: 1984136747
BISAC: Religion / Christian Education / General

Published by Tree of Life Books

Editing and art from Living Things Productions

Editing and illustration from John Rosemond and Dr. Scott Gleason

On the other side of that celestial river
There are places being kept for you and me
Close your eyes and just imagine
What it must be like to live eternally
We are homeless, we are homeless
And homeless through this broken world we roam
We are homeless, we are homeless
But we are going home

No need to pack your bags or withdraw money
When you get there you'll have everything you need
If you're in rags, you'll be in riches
If you're in bondage, you'll be set free
We are homeless, we are homeless
And homeless through this broken world we roam
We are homeless, we are homeless
But we are going home

We were made for Eden
Eden's where we're bound
Back to the tree of life
Back to paradise
We've been wandering for too long
Or long enough to know
We've been wandering
A long, long way from home

GETTING TO HEAVEN

Caveat

The authors do not pretend to be original thinkers on any of the subjects tackled herein. In every case, others have done the research, formulated the essential ideas, and reached the inescapable conclusions. We claim nothing except having connected the relevant dots for the purpose of convincing the reader that (a) God created and is sovereign over the entire Universe, (b) Heaven and Hell are real and *everyone* ends up in either the former or the latter, (c) you want to and most assuredly can end up in Heaven, and (d) as Jesus proclaimed, He is "the Way." We intend to kindle your desire for relationship with Christ Jesus, the Son of God, and put you on your journey to the Promised Land.

In the course of building our case for the Creator God of The Bible, Heaven, Hell, and Jesus as Lord and Savior of mankind, the authors tackle the most-common stumbling blocks to belief, including Darwin's theory of evolution, the discomforting issue of man's sinful nature, the Bible's reliability as both a historical document and source of unfailing truth, Jesus' bold claims to divinity, and His resurrection to life from a state of complete physical death.

Many people never get past even the first of those stumbling blocks. You may be one such person. You may have gone to a public or secular private school and been taught that Darwin's theory of evolution successfully explains every question concerning life on planet Earth and that the alternative is a pre-scientific myth that only ignorant and very gullible people still believe. Or you may have been raised by parents who either shoved religion down your throat, were indifferent when it came to spiritual issues, or were outspoken atheists. You may think that people who report seeing a man walk on water and perform instant cures of numerous dreaded diseases, including leprosy, are either wackos, hallucinating, or high on something (or all three). You may think that a man who claims to be God is either a lunatic or a cunning sociopath. Perhaps you think people only come back from the dead in Stephen King novels. If any of those portrayals apply, you're certainly not alone. In fact, and surprisingly enough, one of the authors' parents were outspoken atheists who taught Darwin's theory at the university level. Said author (JR) fit most of the preceding description until he was in his early fifties.

In developing our argument, we have used the best theological research and historical evidence. When we quote Scripture, we use several of the most widely-accepted and widely-used translations—the New King James, English Standard, or New American Standard Version. Likewise, when it comes to the somewhat tricky task of interpreting Scripture, we rely on interpretations that have been vetted and verified by reputable biblical scholars. Nonetheless, if it turns out that we are guilty of some error, the responsibility is ours and ours alone.

As you read, it is our most prayerful hope that you are enlightened, inspired, and moved to re-purpose your life. May the One Almighty and Trinitarian God, Yahweh, bless your journey!

Chapters

	Introduction	ix
1	Debunking Darwin	2
2	Saved from What?	31
3	Hell is for Real	51
4	The One-and-Only Way, Truth, and Life	69
5	Saved!	99
6	Heaven is Indeed for Real (as is Satan)!	119
7	Go to Church, But Not Just Any Church	141
8	Reading and Studying The Bible	163
9	Get Down on Your Knees (or stand if you prefer)	185
10	Spread the Good News!	209

GETTING TO HEAVEN

Introduction

An acquaintance of mine (JR) who struggles with faith once asked if I believed Heaven was a real place. I told him I thought it was. He then told me that as a child and up into his teen years he had believed in Heaven but that he had since concluded it was a fable.

"What caused you to change your mind?" I asked.

"I just can't wrap my head around the idea that a loving God would send a basically good person to Hell just because he doesn't believe Jesus is his Savior."

"Do you even believe in God?" I asked.

"Not really," he replied. "Not any longer."

I thought it best, on that occasion, to not pursue the issue. Suffice to say, the biggest reason for this individual's non-belief is that God doesn't make decisions he approves of. Like many non-believers (and contemporary liberal, progressive "Christians"), this fellow wants to create God in his own image. Rebellion often pretends to intellectualism.

Another friend told me he thinks a person gets to Heaven by "doing good things." In all fairness, he regularly attends a church that encourages that very wrong and even destructive notion (among others).

"How many good things?" I asked.

"Huh?"

"How many good things does a person have to do in his lifetime?" I asked. "And what if someone's life is fairly short? Does God determine who goes to Heaven on the basis of a certain average of good things per week, month, or year? And then there's the question of the *kind* of good things a person should or has to do? Do you get more Heaven-credits for certain things and less for certain other things? How does that work, exactly?"

He gave me a befuddled look for a moment or two and then said, "Uh, I guess I've never thought about those things. So, I don't know."

"You want to get to Heaven, don't you?" I asked.

"Of course!"

"Then you had better ask your priest if he can answer those questions."

Yet another acquaintance of mine unabashedly ridicules the very idea of God. Nonetheless, he believes in heaven—a lower-case heaven, that is. His heaven is a reflection of his very postmodern, progressive worldview. He thinks there's a place beyond this earthly life to which everyone goes when they die. It's a multi-cultural socialist utopia where no one has to work, everything is hunky-dory, necessities are plentiful, every request is granted, and everyone gets a "fresh start." Sort of a Country Club of the All-Is-One and Very Groovy Afterlife. Apparently even a Muslim terrorist who has beheaded a number of people who do not share his very sick, legalistic orthodoxy goes to this egalitarian paradise when he dies.

And then there's the atheist I know who thinks that when you die, you die, period. It doesn't matter what a person does or doesn't believe, what a person does or doesn't do during his or her lifetime, whether a person is "religious" or not, the cold blackness of death awaits one and all. Come to think of it, this fellow's afterlife is neither cold nor black. It's nothing. The lights go out and that's it. Quoting Tony Soprano of the eponymous hit HBO series, "Bada-bing, bada-*boom*."

Then there are the people I've known in my own past (pre-belief) life—I've stopped counting them—who believe in the "Ever-Turning Wheel of Reincarnation" on which we are all trapped, reincarnating again and again and again as bugs, birds, salamanders, porcupines, kangaroos, musk oxen and so on until we finally get it right and are able to get off this celestial merry-go-round and enter into a place called Nirvana where one floats around the universe like the cosmic fetus in the last scenes of the movie "2001: A Space Odyssey."

I can relate to all five of these notions concerning Heaven because at one time or another in my meandering journey to faith in Jesus Christ as my Lord and Savior, I believed in each of them.

It would appear that plenty of people, maybe most people, and including a fair number of Bible-believing Christians, are confused about Heaven. Some are confused about even whether there is such a place. Some are confused concerning the earthly price of admission. Others want Heaven (and God) to conform to secular notions of "fairness."

Based primarily on my own former muddle-headedness on the subject, I've come to the conclusion that some of the confusion concerning

Heaven is due to ignorance. Included in this category are people who've never taken the time to read the Bible from cover to cover. A fair number of the confused have been misled by people they trust, including church leaders and other very prominent people in the Christian world. That would include my friend who believes that one gets to Heaven by doing good things but has never paused to ask or even think about how many or what sort. And then there are those people who are confused in the sense of being just plain wrong. That includes, but is not limited to, atheists. Mind you, there are a good number of very smart people who are atheists. Personal experience leads me to say with certainty that they're just too smart for their own good.

This book is written for confused people everywhere. My esteemed co-author and I are aiming at atheists, agnostics, and people who believe in God but can't wrap their heads around the idea that some 2000 years ago God took human form, voluntarily died an *excruciatingly* painful death while nailed to a wooden cross, and then rose from the dead, fully healed, to offer us salvation and eternity in Heaven with Him. We're aiming at Catholics, mainline Protestants, Mormons and anyone else who would say they are Christian, attends a church, and professes belief in God and perhaps even Jesus as Lord and Savior but is not, in our estimation, being given proper instruction concerning either the Bible or the very important issue of Heaven. We're aiming at evangelical Christians who may not be receiving adequate pastoral teaching concerning this vital (literally) issue and might believe, for example, that every once in a while God randomly chooses someone—a preschool-age child even—to visit Heaven for a few hours and then come back and give the rest of us a full report. We are aiming at Jews, Muslims, Jehovah's Witnesses, Christian Scientists, Scientologists, Buddhists, Hindis, Confucians, Shinto, Sikhs, Wiccans and other pagans, tree-huggers, tree-climbers, tree-choppers, Democrats, Republicans, libertarians, conservatives, socialists, communists, nihilists, anarchists, vegans, carnivores, omnivores, and even people who are gluten-free. In short, this book is intended for everyone; therefore, it is intended for YOU.

We believe it is an important book with multiple purposes. First, it is a ministry to non-believers. One of us was an outspoken non-believer for the first fifty or so years of his life and knows, first-hand, the need for non-believers to understand what they will be missing if they don't change their erroneous and rebellious ways of thought and behavior. The other of us has been an equally outspoken believer for his whole life and pastors a large evangelical congregation. He knows, first-hand, the need for believers to have clarity on the issue of Heaven if for no purpose other than being better equipped to witness to others who for whatever reason do not possess that clarity.

After all, to possess clarity on the issue of Heaven is to possess clarity on Everything. Clarity on the issue of Heaven does not and cannot exist in a state of theological and intellectual isolation. It promotes and sits right alongside states of clarity concerning all of the following:

- the beginnings and nature of the Universe
- the one-of-a-kind significance of planet Earth
- the meaning of the human drama that ties all sixty-six books of the Old and New Testaments together into one cohesive story
- the nature of God
- sin—its origins and consequences
- The Bible as Divine Revelation
- Jesus—Who He was and is and what that means to each and every one of us
- salvation, repentance, renewal, and rebirth (but not in the sense of being reincarnated)

Like I said, Everything.

CORRECT QUESTIONS

In my college days and for many years thereafter, I pondered the question: What is the *meaning* of life? That single question caused me to wander, lost, over life's philosophical landscape, time after time thinking I'd found the answer and then eventually realizing that whatever answer I thought I'd found was wrong or certainly inadequate and beginning to wander, lost, all over again. It wasn't until age fifty-three, when I came to my senses and accepted Jesus Christ as Lord, Savior, Guarantor of my life, eternal, that I realized I'd been pondering the wrong question all those years. The proper question is not: What is the *meaning* of life. The proper question is: What is the *purpose* of life?

Once I knew the proper question, I also knew the answer: *The purpose of life is to glorify God the Father, to have a personal, intimate relationship with Him through faith in Jesus Christ His Only Son as one's Lord and Savior and in so doing, enjoy eternity in Heaven.*

In other words, getting to Heaven is the ultimate purpose of life; thus, the title of this book.

Now, bear with us for a moment because we are going to assert the following bold claim: The authors are confident that we know how to get to Heaven, and we are going to share that knowledge with you, the reader.

How do we know? Because God has told us. The Bible, His Infallible and Inerrant Word, says there is a very real place called Heaven and clearly spells out how to get there.

Some pastors, churches, and denominations make this issue very mysterious—complicated, even. The truth of the matter is: God makes *nothing, absolutely nothing*, complicated. Things only *seem* complicated if one does not believe in God and have saving faith in Christ Jesus. The moment one claims that belief and faith everything begins to become clear, including the fact that getting to Heaven is a very simple and straightforward matter. Here's how simple it is: Upon claiming that belief and faith (the details of which will be spelled out in Chapters 1 through 5), one possesses an irrevocable ticket to Heaven. You're automatically and instantly on the Heaven Train! Getting to Heaven does not require the performance of "good works," rituals, readings (one very old but timeless book is highly recommended, however), penances, mumblings, or the observance of numerous legalistic rules. Isn't that great!

Some of the people reading this book just need a little nudge to claim that belief and faith; some, however, will require a complete re-education program. They will need to wipe out the falsehoods currently stored in their heads and replace them with Truth. So even though getting to Heaven is a simple matter, for some people the steps they need to take to obtain that life insurance policy are not simple matters at all. They are not complicated, mind you. But for the people in question, those steps, spelled out in this book, are going to rock their worlds. Some of these currently lost folks[†] will even have to accept that their entire worldview—from the A to the Z of it—is in desperate need of replacement. We sincerely hope that a lot of the folks in question read this book and are moved to do exactly that.

As I discovered rather belatedly, to arrive at correct answers, one must ask correct questions. Where Heaven is concerned, the first such question is fairly obvious: "Does Heaven truly exist? Is it a real place?"

The answer is yes. How do we know? The Bible says so. I did not always believe that The Bible was an authoritative source for information or anything other than fantastic (as in, unbelievable) and somewhat entertaining (for children, maybe, but not for a smart guy like me) myths, but I have since come to the unshakeable conclusion that the Bible is the most authoritative source there is or ever will be. It is the inerrant, infallible Word of God Himself—His Revelation to us of Who He Is and what He wants us to know. It is The Truth. Not *a* truth as in one of many, but The One and Only Big and Final Overarching Truth About Everything Past, Present, and Future, Amen. Here, then, are some truths about Heaven according to the Bible:

- Heaven is not a charming myth. It is a real place.
- All roads do not lead to Rome and all religious beliefs or faiths do not lead to Heaven.
- Just because a person is "good" by some standard does not mean he is going to be admitted to Heaven.

[†] One can be completely lost and be thoroughly and blissfully convinced that one is not lost; such is the deceptive power Satan is able to exercise over our thinking.

- Some of the people you're going to meet in Heaven (assuming you really want to do what it takes to get there) did some really bad things when they were occupying earthly bodies.
- Some people who never did anything approaching the bad stuff the aforementioned folks did are not going to be in Heaven. (That, by the way, is perhaps the most difficult of all paradoxes to wrap one's head around, but we are going to make sure that happens).
- People who say they've been to Heaven and then returned to tell the tale are probably sincere (we happen to think, however, that some are not) but whatever they experienced, it was not Heaven. There is good possibility that Satan—who is also real and whose mission is to prevent Heaven from being populated—has misled them in order that they might mislead others. That would be consistent with one of his names: The Great Deceiver.
- Getting to Heaven is both very simple and very challenging.
- The idea that God loves all people but is not going to admit all people to Heaven is not a contradiction. God is not "fair" in the sense that many people expect Him to be. In The Bible, the word used to describe God is "just", not "fair." He will dispense perfect justice according to *His* criteria, not ours.
- When it comes to admission to Heaven, God is anything but arbitrary. It would be arbitrary for Him to admit people to Heaven based on good works they did while on earth. If that was the case, the questions "How many good works do I need to do?" and "What sort of good works do I need to do?" and "Do some good works earn me more Heaven points than others?" would be answered in Scripture. They are not. In Scripture, God is clear as to what it takes to get to Heaven. He says it takes ONE thing, and ONE thing only. That is hardly arbitrary.

The second question, following logically from the first, is: "What is Heaven like?"

The unsatisfying answer is that no one knows (not even folks who claim, sincerely or not, that they've been there). No one will know what Heaven is like until he or she gets there. One thing is certain: Heaven pre-existed the Universe. It is where God "lives." It is, therefore, outside of the spatial and temporal boundaries of the Universe—His creation. It is impossible for the human brain to conceive of a "place" that exists outside of space and time, a place that is eternal, which is why a word like "place," however inadequate, is nonetheless the best word at our disposal. We do know, because Jesus said so, that Heaven is a Paradise. The etymology of "paradise" equates it with the Garden of Eden. We know, therefore, that Heaven is more clean, abundant in all manner of goodness, and blissful than one can imagine. It is supremely peaceful, free of want, free of desire other than consuming desire for relationship with the Lord God, and full of wonder. In a word, Heaven is *perfect*, which is another word that challenges the human imagination. Because of our limited understanding, we use that word in sloppy ways. Someone will say, for example, that a certain performance of Handel's *Messiah* was "perfect in every way." Well, in fact, human beings cannot do anything perfectly. Humans employ the word "perfect" in the relative sense only, usually to mean—again using the *Messiah* analogy—something along the lines of "far better than I've ever heard before." Heaven, on the other hand, is the *quintessence* of perfect. Its state of flawlessness is beyond our comprehension.

In the first chapter of the Bible's first book—the Book of Genesis—God creates the Universe and everything in it: light, then stars and other Heavenly bodies, planet Earth, the sun and moon, plants, animals, and lastly, the first two human beings. At the end of every creation day, God pronounces that what He has done is "good." In that context, good means perfect. God does nothing less than perfectly. God also created Heaven; therefore, Heaven is perfect.

THE MOST IMPORTANT QUESTION OF ALL

When a person dies let's say he suddenly finds himself in a rather spartan room sitting at a bureaucratic-looking desk across from a bureaucratic-looking man who tells him to pay close attention to a movie screen hanging on one of the room's walls. The title "Heaven" comes up on screen and is followed by a continuum of amazing, indescribable images that induce a great sense of peace and happiness, so much so that the person begins weeping with joy. After "Heaven" plays for maybe five minutes, a second title comes up on screen: "Not Heaven." What follows are five minutes-worth of scenes so horrifying that words fail at describing them. These nightmarish images induce feelings of both immense loneliness and overwhelming terror, of unrelenting pain, as if one's body is being stung by wasps, and being trapped inside one's worst nightmare.

After the second video plays, the bureaucratic-looking man shuts off the projector, leans forward, folds his hands under his chin and asks, "Where would you like to go—Heaven or Not Heaven? Your choice, but remember, wherever you choose, you're going to be there for all eternity."

Would anyone in his right mind choose Not Heaven? No, and at least ninety-nine percent of people of unsound mind would choose Heaven as well.

The point is that the answer to the question "Do you want to go to Heaven?" is a no-brainer. That's true of you, too, isn't it?

Having established that you want to go to Heaven, we have also established that this book was written for you.

Enjoy your journey!

GETTING TO HEAVEN

Section One

The Way

GETTING TO HEAVEN

1

Debunking Darwin

In the mid-1800s, British naturalist Charles Darwin proposed that life on Earth could be explained without invoking God or any other supernatural cause. To explain how life began without a creator, Darwin asserted that a one-celled life form appeared spontaneously through some unspecified process involving chemicals (e.g. methane, hydrogen, carbon dioxide), heat, water, and perhaps lightning, and that from that auspicious beginning, over millions upon millions of years, random evolutionary processes (mutations) produced increasingly complex life forms until, finally, human beings walked forth on the planet. More than one hundred and fifty years later, it is relatively rare to find a person with *bona fide* scientific credentials who does not believe Darwin was fundamentally correct. Although polls find that most Americans either reject or have serious problems with Darwin's theory, it is taught in America's public schools and secular private schools (and even some nominally Christian schools) as if it is a done deal when in fact it is not. Over the past sixty-plus years, as more and more has been learned about how the universe began and the nature of life, Darwin's theory has been slowly unraveling. Much to the chagrin of his devotees in the scientific and academic communities who are scrambling as fast as they can to keep the unraveling from happening or at least slow its progress, the only plausible explanation, it seems, for everything—the universe and life on planet Earth, including us talking bipeds—is God.

THE LITMUS TEST

Science is not simply a body of information, although it is certainly that. Science also refers to a finite set of specific procedures with which information is gathered and fundamental questions are answered—questions that concern us humans, the planet we live on, the solar system in which said planet orbits, and the workings of the universe. It is through the means of science that theories concerning these issues are either confirmed or tossed into history's dustbin. The scientific method is one such means. Without going into detail that is unnecessary to our purpose, the scientific method governs the manner in which experiments are conducted. It is a research paradigm. Conclusions drawn vis-a'-vis an experiment that violates the rules of the scientific method are regarded as unreliable, even worthless. At times, however, circumstances prevent the use of the scientific method in its pure form. When that's the case, confirming or at least advancing any given theory requires pre-existing, verifiable, objective evidence of its accuracy.

With regards to any scientific means of verification, Charles Darwin's famous theory of evolution is a complete bust. Since astronomers have not found another planet like our own to use as a control planet, it is impossible to confirm or deny Darwin's theory using the scientific method. An analogy might be helpful: Since John Rosemond has no genetic twin from whom he was separated at birth, it is impossible to assess how growing up in another family would have affected John's life and worldview. One can *speculate* how growing up in a different family environment—one in which his parents did not divorce but enjoyed a long and happy marriage, for example—would have influenced his life, but since any such speculation is impossible to confirm, it does not constitute science. Rather, it is nothing more than an interesting (optimistically speaking) mental exercise.

So it is with Darwin's theory of macro-evolution: the notion that it is possible over a considerable period of time for one species to mutate into a completely different species—dinosaurs into birds, for example, as true believers in evolution insist was the case. Darwin's theory is speculation, and nothing more. Experimental methods cannot confirm it and no one has discovered even one iota of pre-existing objective evidence—as in fossils of so-called transitional species—that would even barely support it. It is a theory lacking any tangible evidence at all—none, zip, zero, nada. As a Darwinian proponent recently said, Darwinism is a "fascinating idea." He went on to say that this idea explains how life began and began diversifying. But that's not true. Ideas explain nothing. They are ideas, nothing more. And it is significant to note that after slightly more than one hundred and fifty years, Darwin's theory has not moved beyond being a mere idea. A fascinating idea, for sure, but a fascinating idea that lacks supporting evidence of any sort.

Furthermore, the existing fossil evidence, which is considerable, actually contradicts Darwin's theory. Fossils tell the story of complex creatures such as trilobites and fish that suddenly appeared fully-formed as opposed to having evolved in small incremental steps over long periods of prehistoric time. Darwin himself accepted and publicly stated that without supporting fossil evidence his theory was a failure. In that regard, Darwin seems to have been much more objective concerning his fascinating idea than are the thousands of college professors across the USA who preach his theory as if it was a scientific reality. Take, for example, a 2014 book by Bill Nye. From 1993 to 1998 Nye hosted the popular PBS children's program *Bill Nye the Science Guy*. In *Undeniable: Evolution and the Science of Creation*, Nye puts forth what he sees as—per his title—*undeniable* evidence for the veracity of Darwin's theory. In the process he lambasts leading figures in the creationist and intelligent design (ID) communities, characterizing the lot of them as backward-thinking and in denial. But the "evidence" he offers is not only very old news but also accepted as fact by creationists and ID proponents—to wit, micro-evolution.

Darwin actually proposed two theories of evolution: macro-evolution and micro-evolution. The latter proposes that over time changes *within* a species can and do occur as members of the species adapt to changes in the environment or maximize their performance within a relatively constant environment. So, for example, when the planet goes through a long period of cooling as occurred in the last Great Ice Age, the fur of mammals becomes thicker and darker from generation to generation, thus keeping them warmer. That process—known as adaptation through natural selection—has been confirmed. Therefore, Darwin's theory of micro-evolution is no longer a theory, a "fascinating idea." It is a fact.

The issue, therefore, is Darwin's theory of *macro*-evolution, the notion that small mutations in a species can accumulate over long stretches of time (millions of years) to the point where the species in question suddenly transforms into another completely different species—a fish into a salamander, for example. Said another way, Darwin's theory proposes that enough micro-evolutionary changes (adaptations) within a species can eventually produce a macro-evolutionary change into different species.[†]

From time to time, people who believe in Darwin's theory of macro-evolution have rejoiced over a newly-found fossil, claiming that it represents a so-called transitional species—a distinct "bridge species" between two more viable and possibly still-extant species. The fossil of the supposed reptile-bird Archeopteryx was initially heralded as such a find. So was the collection of hominid bones found by anthropologist Donald Johanson and others in Ethiopia in 1974 and which they named "Lucy." At both discoveries, Darwinists jumped for joy. Unfortunately, both fossils have been since debunked. If the bones Johanson found even come from one individual—and there is evidence that they do not—even many Darwinists now agree they are from a species separate and apart from the evolutionary line that supposedly produced modern human beings.

The fact that no one has yet to find confirming transitional fossils does not daunt committed Darwinists, however. They persist in their claim that as micro-evolutionary changes occur over long periods of time (millions upon millions of years) a point is reached where the sum total of said changes results in the sudden emergence (a spontaneous evolutionary "jump") of a new species. That's a worthwhile and, again, fascinating idea, but where is the supporting evidence? There is none. Again, there is only speculation, and speculation may lead researchers to facts, but speculation itself is not fact.

That doesn't daunt Darwin's devotees either. As "proof" that Darwin's theory of macro-evolution is fact, they point out that an overwhelming majority of academic biologists believe in it. That's undeniably true. But two things need to be considered:
- First, biologists who do not believe in Darwin's theory of macro-evolution are *persona non grata* in America's secular universities. They are even looked upon disparagingly by fellow faculty at some ostensibly Christian universities (e.g. Notre Dame). Biology professors who go public with their skepticism concerning macro-

---

[†] This hypothetical process is also known as *speciation*.

evolution put themselves in danger of not receiving tenure, and already tenured professors who express skepticism are dismissed as crackpots and find it nigh unto impossible to obtain funding for their non-Darwinian research. Indeed, Darwinists are in the definite majority in America's university biology departments, but that deserves a big "so what?"

- Second, a consensus is not proof of anything. Furthermore, it is often if not usually the case that no great and lasting scientific theory of anything enjoyed consensus when first proposed. Up until the mid-1600s, for example, the idea that the earth revolved around the sun (as opposed to the other way around) was considered ludicrous, even heretical and worthy of being burned at the stake. That's just one example of a scientific consensus being dead wrong. Where most great and lasting theories are concerned, a lack of consensus eventually evolves into consensus. With Darwin's theory, it's been quite the opposite. His theory of macro-evolution gained instant, nearly unanimous affirmation from other scientists when first proposed in the mid-19th Century. In recent years, however, as the lack of confirming evidence has become more glaring and evidence supporting the alternative theory has begun piling up, more and more scientists who previously believed in Darwinism have been jumping off that slowly sinking ship.

The alternative theory is creationism or intelligent design. Actually, they are two slightly (some say significantly) different theories:

Creationists believe God created the universe and everything within it in six 24-hour days. A literal reading of Genesis, Chapter 1, seems to confirm the creationist position. God does indeed perform the entirety of creation in six *yom*, the Hebrew word for day (as in *Yom Kippur* or Day of Atonement). A day, creationists point out, is a 24-hour period; therefore, God created the entire universe and everything in it in 144 hours. Some scholars point out, however, that *yom* can also mean an epoch. It is also relevant to note that every creation day ends with "There was evening, and there was morning." Yet God did not create the sun, by which evening and morning are defined, until the fourth day. Some Hebrew scholars, furthermore, point out that the Hebrew words for evening and morning also mean, respectively, chaos and order; in other words, they say, God is telling us that He created order from disorder and did so over the span of six distinct creation periods. And then, making matters even more confounding, Israeli astrophysicist and Old Testament expert Gerald Schroeder insists that God created the Universe and everything in it, including the first human beings, in six 24-hour days but that because time is constantly stretching as the Universe expands (one of Einstein's predictions, now confirmed [see Jeremiah 10:12]), those first six days (from God's perspective) presently measure 13.8 billion years (from the perspective of a person living today). Schroeder also maintains that consistent with Genesis arithmetic, after playing around for millennia with various humanoid forms, God created the first *homo sapiens* (Lt: intelligent man), Adam and Eve, a little more than 5000 years ago. Go figure. The only sure thing to be said about this ongoing debate is that human ability to understand the ins and outs of God's creation is limited, and permanently so.

Concerning the issue of the length of each of the six creation periods described in the first chapter of the Book of Genesis, it is relevant to note that The Bible clearly says that to God, a day is not necessarily a 24-hour period. In his second epistle, the Lord's disciple Peter writes "that with the Lord one day is as a thousand years, and a thousand years as one day" (2 Peter 3:8). In other words, from God's point of view, which is the point of view of Genesis 1, time is not measured as we humans measure it.

Intelligent Design theorists believe that the geological and astrophysical evidence points to a universe that was created approximately 13.8 billion years ago by an unidentified designer who was definitely a supreme being. Beyond that, most ID proponents agree with creationists on this fundamental point: The supreme being in question created every species fully formed. He did not create a one-celled life form and then sit back and watch life evolve or direct its development (known as theistic evolution). Some ID people believe humans have been around for forty thousand years or so; others, including Schroeder, believe that modern man—*homo sapiens sapiens*—has been around for only approximately 5000 years, the same period of time literal creationists maintain is the age of the universe as well as the age of mankind.

In the authors' view, the term intelligent design avoids, and consciously so, mention of the designer in question. It leaves unanswered the question of who he is (or they are) and it does so purposefully so as to persuade federal judges that teaching ID theory in America's public (i.e. government) schools would not violate the principle of separation of church and state. Darwinian activists claim ID theory is a stealth way of sneaking creation theory into America's public schools, which, let's face it, it is. It's an attempt to wrap an idea that a lot of highly educated people think is nothing more than a fable—to wit, a Supreme and Omnipotent Being known as God or Yahweh created the universe and everything in it from nothing—in sheep's clothing (even if a black sheep) in the hopes that judges will let it pass. The authors maintain that this attempt is counterproductive. We who believe that a Supreme and Omnipotent Being known as God or Yahweh created the Universe and everything in it in six *yom* of whatever length should be unabashed about our belief. God did it! Not the god of Muslims or Buddhists or even Mormons and not some unspecified "Source" either, but the Old Testament God of The Bible! The Almighty I Am!

Even the term "design" is somewhat disingenuous, an obvious attempt to disguise the fact that a design is meaningless without someone who creates the design (e.g. blueprint) and then makes it a reality—in the case at hand, a living organism. In other words, the ID folks simply replace "create" with "design" and "creator" with "designer." They do this so as to create the illusion that they are not creationists, when in fact they are. They deny that their reasoning leads straight to a Supreme Being when in fact it most assuredly does.

Granted, a few advocates of intelligent design maintain that earth's myriad life forms may have been designed elsewhere in the universe by highly advanced beings who then found a suitable planet (earth) and "seeded" it with their creations. That's a fanciful story indeed, but it begs the question: How did said advanced beings come about? Were they created by an even more advanced alien race and if so then how did that superior race come about? Obviously, the question can be asked infinitely with no successful answer. On the other hand, however, that specific question *cannot* be asked infinitely because current estimates of the age of the universe are no larger than 15 billion years. At some point, therefore, the answer to "how did this superior race come about?" runs out of time and one is then confronted with the only answer possible at that point: The One Omnipotent and Omniscient Creator who created the entire universe *ex nihilo*, out of nothing. That would be God—the God of the first chapter of the Book of Genesis.

In the final analysis, the problem with the "seeded by aliens" version of intelligent design theory is that like Darwin's theory, there is no supporting evidence. There is nothing but imagination, which humans sometimes confuse with reality. Many of the humans in question teach at secular colleges and universities.

THE BIG BANG AND THE BIG FLOP

The Big Stumbling Block for atheists and Darwinists is an event known as the Big Bang. It is "the beginning" referred to in the first sentence of The Bible. Two verses later, God speaks the Universe into being. He said "Let there be light!" and there was light. Wham! In one micro-instant of time, from one point so small it cannot be measured (known as a "singularity"), all the matter currently contained in the universe burst forth in a flash of light-energy so bright it cannot be fathomed. The fourth dimension of the universe—time—was also created at the Big Bang.

The Big Bang is not only what The Bible clearly describes; it is also the dominant view of science. In 1927, priest, astronomer and physicist Georges Lemaitre first proposed that the origin of the universe could be traced back to a single point, which he termed the *primeval atom* or *Cosmic Egg* (subsequently called a *singularity*). In 1950, British astronomer Fred Hoyle coined the name Big Bang Theory during a radio broadcast. Originally, it was just that: a theory. Since then, so much confirming evidence has been gathered that it is no longer considered a theory. The "Big Bang" is a fact.[†]

[†] Some creationists associate the Big Bang with evolution, probably because the scientists originally associated with Big Bang theory were also believers in Darwin's theory. Initially, it was thought that all of the matter in the universe had somehow become compacted into one microscopic point that then suddenly exploded at the speed of light--in other words, that matter pre-existed the universe. It is now known that the universe burst forth *ex nihilo*, or out of nothing. Not only is that consistent with the Genesis 1:3 account ("And God said 'Let there be light; and there was light'"), but it is also why the mainstream scientific

Now, here's something completely amazing, and if this doesn't light up your brain, then nothing will: *Moses, the fellow who authored the Book of Genesis, described the six-day creation sequence as it actually happened!* Consider: Moses had no telescopes; he'd never studied astronomy or physics; he had no knowledge of relativity, photons, dark matter, singularities, red shift, or any of the other aspects of the mathematics and physics of creation, yet he nailed it! How did he do that? How did he know that immediately after the initial mega-explosion of light, what is known as dark matter separated from light (photons)? The Bible says "God divided the light from the darkness" (Gen. 1:4). Some people think that Bible passage refers to separating daytime from nighttime (the words "day" and "night" are, in fact, used). No, it doesn't. It cannot, in fact, because the stars, sun, and moon were created by God on the fourth day. The fourth verse of the book of Genesis, refers to something Moses could not possibly have known because dark matter (i.e. "the darkness" of Genesis 1:3) was not discovered for another 3500 years! The ONLY POSSIBLE EXPLANATION is that God—the Supreme Being Who made it all happen—was telling Moses what to write (which has always been the contention of Orthodox Jews)! How else could Moses have known that God's creation began with an inconceivably immense burst of pure light? How else could he have known that the next stage in the sequence of creation involved the separation of light and dark matter? How did he know that the Earth was initially completely covered in water and that land masses appeared later; that sea life preceded terrestrial life; that birds appeared prior to mammals; that humans are the last species to inhabit the earth and that since our appearance no other species have appeared? We are told all that in the first chapter of Genesis. How did Moses know all this? The answer is simple, but mind-boggling at the same time: God told him. There is no other possibility. The idea that Moses simply guessed right that many times in a row is a complete and utter impossibility.

And here's another mind-boggler: God told Moses in language he and his fellow Hebrews could grasp. Without sophisticated Twenty-First Century knowledge of physics, Moses and the rest of God's people would have been bewildered if God had told Moses to write down the actual

---

community is scrambling to come up with an explanation for the beginning of the universe that involves pre-existing matter and, therefore, no Creator.

physics of creation. So God made the description of creation in Genesis 1 as understandable as possible to Moses and the people of his day and left it to future humans to discover the actual physics and put two and two together. That is exactly what parents do, after all. When a parent is explaining something to a very young child, he explains in terms the child is capable of understanding. In the process, the parent often uses words figuratively. That's what God, our Heavenly Father, did. Based on the chronology given in Genesis, the human race was around 1500 years old when God dictated the first five books of The Bible (circa 1448 BC) to Moses—less than that if one dates present-day human beings from the worldwide Flood (circa 2315 BC).

The facts of the Big Bang boggle atheists in the scientific community; which is to say, it boggles nearly all scientists, throws them into a tizzy. As a consequence, they are currently scrambling to figure out some means, however far-fetched, of denying that the only plausible explanation for the instantaneous creation of the entire universe out of nothing (*ex nihilo*) is the purposeful action of a Creator, the Beginner of "In the beginning..." (Gen. 1:1). The latest example of their scramble is the "multi-verse" theory. According to multi-verse proponents, our universe sprang into being from another universe, which sprang into being from another, which sprang into being from another, and so on. A universe develops a pimple of sorts on its surface and when the pimple bursts (sorry, but it seems like an apt analogy) part of the matter in the "mother universe" comes rushing out of the puncture and forms a new universe. When enough material has come forth, the puncture heals, or something like that. We are simply one of an infinite number of universes out there...or, if you will, out *here*.

The multi-verse theory is yet another "fantastic idea" from the proponents of Darwin's theory. It is not a serious, scientifically-minded attempt to explain the beginning of the universe. Rather, it is a blatant attempt to deny that there was, as The Bible tells us in the first lines of the Book of Genesis, a beginning out of nothing (ex nihilo). One of the world's leading Darwinists has admitted as much, in fact. In a 1999 review of *Demon-Haunted World* by fellow Darwinist Carl Sagan, evolutionary biologist, Harvard professor, and avowed Marxist Richard Lewontin writes:

> It is not that the methods and institutions of science somehow compel us to accept a material explanation of the phenomenal world, but, on the contrary, that we are forced by our *a priori* adherence to material causes to create an apparatus of investigation and a set of concepts that produce material explanations, no matter how counter-intuitive, no matter how mystifying to the uninitiated. Moreover, that materialism is absolute, for we cannot allow a Divine Foot in the door.

This is nothing short of startling. Lewontin—one of the leading figures in modern Darwinism—admits that the scientific method does not support Darwin's theory; nonetheless, scientists must come together in support of it *for the express purpose of denying God*—or, as Lewontin, in a burst of complete honesty, puts it, to prevent "a Divine Foot" from getting through the door of the scientific establishment's commitment to materialism, a commitment that forces Darwin's present-day adherents to turn a blind eye to any evidence that contradicts their worldview and to cut pro-Darwinist evidence out of whole cloth. Lewontin is saying that Darwinism is less science than ideology.

Lewontin and his materialist colleagues certainly realize that evidence supporting biblical creation (or, if one prefers, intelligent design) is winning the day. And that realization is driving increasingly desperate and absurd attempts to keep the "Divine Foot" from jamming the door. In fact, the Divine Foot has already stuck itself into the door and is slowly, inexorably, forcing it wide open to the truth, which is that the universe was created by a Supreme Being known as God. This Supreme Being did not make the universe out of already existing stuff as a potter would make a pot. Before "the beginning" of Genesis, Chapter One, verse one, there was nothing except God, the One Eternal Lord of All There Is, Was, and Ever Will Be.

WHAT ABOUT OTHER CREATION STORIES?

Creation-deniers argue that all aboriginal cultures have creation myths that are every bit as fantastic as The Bible's. They reason that since all these very different stories cannot be true, none of them are true. That's known as a logical or formal fallacy, by the way. At first hearing, it may sound vaguely valid, but close inspection reveals it to be bogus. In the first place, it does not logically follow that because creation stories abound they are all myths. One of these creation stories might be the real deal. The discriminating question: Is a certain creation story borne out with scientific findings? Concerning the creation story Moses wrote, the answer is yes; it is the one and only creation story that science confirms. Furthermore, the creation myths of other primitive cultures are far more fantastic than The Bible's. In the creation myth of ancient Egypt, for example, before time existed there was a dark, swirling chaos called Nu. Out of this watery chaos rose a god named Atum who created himself with sheer willpower. Okay, we can stop right there. The significant differences between this myth and The Bible's creation story:

- Before creation, stuff already existed.
- The god Atum is not eternal.
- Most significantly, unlike The Bible's creation story, none of the elements of the Egyptian creation myth line up with any known, scientifically-obtained, verifying facts.

In the Mesopotamian creation myth, a god kills his mother and uses half of her body to create the earth. What scientific finding does that line up with? None. The ancient Scandinavians (Norsemen) told of fire from the south and ice from the north clashing to produce the creator god who then births the first human from his armpit. No joke. Another dead-end. Notice that according to Norse mythology, matter pre-exists. There is no way to connect the elements of Norse myth to the known facts of astrophysics. The *one and only creation story* that fits the facts is the one set forth in the first chapter of the Book of Genesis in the Old Testament of The Bible.

The atheists then raise the question: Who created God? The Bible is clear on this issue: nothing, no one, created God. He did not create Himself, even. God is pre-existent, eternal, existing outside the boundaries of space and time. God does not "live" in the universe any more than a potter exists inside of and is therefore part of the material that forms his pot. The idea that God has always existed, that He existed prior to the Universe (His creation), may strike some readers as implausible, but its implausibility is a matter of the limitations of human thinking concerning space and time, nothing more. In fact, the *only* plausible explanation for creation out of nothing is a pre-existing, Eternal Being who, unlike the gods in the above creation myths, is not Himself created. If God was created, then we are faced with the question of who created the being who created God? And then, who created the being who created the being who created God. And so on, infinitely, *ad absurdum*.† Although an eternal, pre-existing God who was not created may stretch the mind, it is the only sensible, logical explanation. It is the only explanation that fits the fact of the Big Bang—creation out of nothing *(ex nihilo)*. More accurately, since the astrophysical facts were discovered long after the story was written down by Moses, the facts fit the story. Science confirms that the story of creation contained in Genesis is completely accurate (although simplified, for reasons discussed earlier). Moses didn't have facts and then seek to construct a story that would explain them. In effect, that's what ancient cultures—Egyptian, Mesopotamian, Scandinavian, and so on and so forth—tried to do. Those attempts to explain creation are by definition myths. By contrast, Western Civilization began with a story and as human science developed, facts were discovered that have fully confirmed it and clearly demonstrated that the story in question (Genesis 1) is most definitely *not* a myth.

THE BEGINNING OF LIFE

Darwinists have no plausible, testable explanation for the beginnings of life either. Once again, their desperation to deny the reality of God drives them to produce what are, in effect, creation myths. One such creation myth has it that when the earth first formed out of the chaos of the young universe, it

---

† Atheists employ this very absurdity to "prove" that God does not exist. They begin with the false premise that if God even exists then He, like everything else, has to be created; therefore, their conclusion is another example of a logical fallacy.

was covered with something Darwinists refer to as primordial soup. Many chemicals swirled around in this warm ooze. One day, a bunch of chemicals—just the right ones, mind you—happened to be in close proximity to one another and suddenly a lightning bolt came down and struck the ooze in the exact spot where these precisely correct chemicals had randomly congregated and—VOILA!—the heat and electricity of the lightning caused a chemical reaction that produced the first living cell. That cell then floated around, lonely, until one day it was in a part of the ooze that was hit by another lightning strike and the cell divided into two cells that mated and produced a third cell and this process, called evolution, continued in this random way for billions of years until one day, a human was born to something that wasn't fully human and from that first human...what? Actually, this entire theoretical scenario breaks down, comes completely undone, millions upon millions of years before modern humans supposedly were produced by the mindless, random evolutionary process.

First, there is not the tiniest shred of evidence that inert chemical compounds, even organic compounds (those consisting of carbon atoms), can spontaneously or otherwise combine to form a living thing. Life is not a matter of a certain combination of molecules. It is a quality, not a quantity. No one has ever succeeded—and many have tried—at infusing this truly miraculous quality that we take so much for granted into something inanimate and thereby bringing non-life to life. The reader may recognize that as the theme of one of the greatest works of 19th Century fiction: Mary Shelley's *Frankenstein*. The operative word in the previous sentence is *fiction*. Such speculations make for interesting fantasy, but man is incapable of creating life. Science cannot create life, not even one-celled life. That is God's work, and His alone.

The preposterous nature of these pseudo-scientific creation myths is exemplified by a conversation I once had with a Ph.D. biologist who held a coveted teaching position at an prestigious academic institution. As one would expect, he believed in Darwin's theory.

"Why?" I asked.

"Because it's the only explanation for life that makes sense," he answered.

"How did life first begin?"

"It was a spontaneous beginning involving heat, maybe lightning, water, and various hydrocarbons," he said. His answers sounded memorized, like he'd gone to a seminar titled "How to Respond to Those Dumb, Pesky God-People."

"So why don't we see life forms spontaneously arising today?"

He had not memorized an answer to that one, obviously, because he suddenly looked like the proverbial deer in the headlights. "Uh, well, I happen to believe, as do other researchers, that life is in fact continuing to arise spontaneously, but the phenomena in question are beyond the reach of our current technologies."

"Like?"

"Like in hot water vents at the bottom of the deepest undersea trenches."

"That's a very interesting speculation," I said, "but is there any evidence with which to support it?"

The deer was staring at me again. Finally, he said, "Well, not really, but it makes sense, doesn't it?"

"No."

"Well," he said, laughing, "I'm a biologist; you're a psychologist. If you had my training and background, it would make sense to you too."

I barely stopped myself from saying, "Well, being that I am a psychologist and you are not, I am uniquely qualified to inform you that your explanation qualifies as pure mumbo-jumbo." A much younger and brasher John Rosemond probably would have.

This fellow obviously believes that life is a relatively simple matter of composition and structure, but organic molecules and a shape do not make for life. Life is a quality. It's an ineffable force, a form of energy, but energy like no other. Unlike other forms of energy—light, for example—no one has ever isolated, measured, produced, or satisfactorily explained the nature of life's animating energy. That's because it is more accurately called spirit. In the first chapter of the first book of the ancient Scriptures, God creates human beings and breathes the "breath of life" into them. The Bible tells us that we were created in His image and brought to life by His very own breath, His Spirit. That's an amazing thing to comprehend, but no less mind-boggling than the notion of primitive life forms spontaneously appearing in deep-sea hot water vents.

But let us for the moment accept the Darwinian premise that due to some impossible combination of just the right circumstances, some one-celled living thing spontaneously appeared in the primordial soup. From there, one can further speculate that the first one-celled organism auto-reproduced, meaning it pulled itself apart into two separate one-celled organisms that then pulled themselves apart and so on. That scenario is implausible because it presumes that the first one-celled living thing contained, from its auspicious beginning, a highly complex biological mechanism for pulling itself apart, but for argument's sake let's accept that premise as well. One can then further speculate that some of these one-celled organisms failed to pull themselves completely apart and became two-celled organisms that failed similarly and became three- and four-celled organisms that began to evolve into more complex biological structures. We can even suspend credulity and go with that. But when one gets to the point in the evolutionary process where random forces produce the first thingy that could not auto-produce, but needed a mate of the opposite gender in order to reproduce, we have a big problem.

At that point, the question becomes: What are the chances that the unguided process of evolution-by-random-mutation (so-called "natural selection") would produce a male thingy and a female thingy—both representing the same hitherto unknown species—that would suddenly emerge at approximately the same time and within relatively close proximity of one another?[†] The answer: very, very small. But still not small enough to completely eliminate the possibility, so let's move on. Darwinists believe that the thingy species managed to survive and eventually evolved into the ting-um species. The question then becomes: What are the chances that the random process of evolution would produce a male ting-um and a female ting-um that would suddenly emerge at approximately the same time and within proximity of one another? Very, very small. At this point, we are adding the very, very small odds of the ting-um species surviving to the very, very small odds of the thingy species surviving. At every stage in this hypothetical process, we are dealing with very, very small odds that when the next species emerges, a male and female of the species emerge at around the same time in pretty much the same place and successfully

---

[†] A species is defined by a mating boundary that prevents the ability to produce fertile offspring with other species.

mate; thus guaranteeing the species' survival. At some point in the process, as the very, very small odds at every stage of the evolutionary process accumulate mathematically, the boundary of possibility is breached, at which point we have impossibility. Mind you, this breaching occurs millions upon millions of years before humans are said to have evolved. In other words, the chances of some random evolutionary process ever producing humans is zero. Not approximately zero, but *zero*. In fact, the chance of some random evolutionary process ever producing something as simple as an earthworm is zero. Planaria? Zero. We now know enough about the highly complex biological machinery inside something as simple as a one-celled bacterium to conclude that the chance of even so relatively simple an organism as that resulting from a floating bunch of gook struck by lightning is zero.

NO EXPLANATION NECESSARY?

As a college student in the 1960s, I had to take a certain number of semester hours of science. To satisfy part of this requirement, I took Introduction to Biology. Both my mother and stepfather held PhD's in life sciences and biology had often been a topic of household conversation. I figured, and correctly so, that I would ace biology with relative ease. At the time, mind you, I was an atheist who believed that evolution explained everything about life on Earth. My highly-educated and highly-intelligent parents had told me so, and I believed them.

I remember my biology professor saying things like "The first land animals evolved from fish that developed rudimentary legs along with the ability to breathe air" and "As evidenced by the anatomical similarity of their respective bone structures, the human hand obviously evolved from flippers such as one finds even today on aquatic mammals like dolphins, whales, and seals." These are examples of the sort of statements Darwinists have been making since, well, Darwin. Notice that neither statement explains the details of the biological process in question. The question of how fish develop legs and the ability to breathe out of water is not considered worthy of explanation. Neither is the question of just exactly how flippers developed into hands. Darwinists don't think they are obligated to explain such things because to them the truth of evolution is obvious, or should be. To the average Darwinist, if someone does not accept the obvious truth of Darwinism, the problem is not with the description, it is with the person. Specifically, the person in question is not intelligent enough to fathom Darwinism's depth. Sadly, this very anti-scientific intellectual arrogance is a hallmark feature of the Darwinian community.

A more contemporary example is found in an article that appeared in The Wall Street Journal on December 3, 2016. Titled "Our Noble Cousin: The Octopus," it was written by Colin McGinn, whom the Journal identified as a philosopher who has authored, among others, a book on evolution.

The article began: "Around 600 million years ago there lived in the sea a small unprepossessing worm, virtually eyeless and brainless. For some reason, this species split in two, thus seeding the vast zoological groupings of the vertebrates and the invertebrates."

No doubt the irony of starting a presumably scientific article as if one is writing a children's fairy tale escaped McGinn (and the WSJ). As is typical of Darwin's apologists, McGinn engages in what is known as an *appeal to authority*. In this case, he is an expert on the subject of evolution—having written a book on it—and therefore is not obligated to explain just how said unprepossessing worm species split into two species, one giving rise to animals with backbones, the other giving rise to animals without backbones. The closest McGinn comes to such an explanation is to say this bicameral transformation happened "for some reason."

In fact, the transformation in question occurs only in the imaginations of people like McGinn. But, paraphrasing French philosopher Rene Descartes (1596 – 1650), Darwinists think, therefore, they are correct. They feel superior to those of us who are too benighted to accept the supposed face value of such an outrageously absurd idea as a worm splitting into two different species, one with a backbone and one without a backbone, without demanding proof in the form of objective, verifiable evidence.

As said earlier, Darwin's theory lacks even a speck of objective (verifiable) supporting evidence. But the real problem for Darwinists is that over the past sixty years, along with dramatic advances in knowledge, methods, and investigative tools, evidence has been accumulating that refutes Darwin, and unequivocally so. It is only a matter of time—and a relatively short time at that—before those Darwinists who possess even an inkling of intellectual honesty are going to have to admit defeat. In the world of evolutionary theory, the bad words are fossils, DNA, irreducible complexity, time, and lack of even a shred of corroborating evidence. One at a time:

FOSSILS TELL THE STORY...OR NOT

The fossil record contains a stumbling block that Darwinists have repeatedly tried to circumvent and have consistently failed at doing so. This stumbling block is known as the Cambrian Explosion.

In the early Twentieth Century, geologists and paleontologists discovered that the geological strata of the Cambrian Period (estimated to be approximately 540 million years old) literally teems with fossils of new multi-cellular life forms, none of which have precursors in previous (Precambrian) geological deposits. Many of the species in question have since become extinct, but quite a number, including trilobites, are still around, unchanged for 540 million years. Let us emphasize: *Lots of animals that suddenly appeared during the so-called Cambrian Explosion more than one-half billion years ago are still with us, unchanged.* In more than one-half-billion years, not one of them has evolved into another species. Isn't that fascinating? Furthermore, not one of them is on the "brink" of evolving into another species. In other words, there are no fossils of so-called "transitional species" in the Cambrian strata either. Not one of the original body plans has changed in any significant way in 540 million years. Darwin's theory requires transitional species represented by vastly altered body plans. Are you getting this?

Various theories have been proposed to account for the fact that no transitional fossils have ever been discovered that would reconcile Darwin's theory to the Cambrian Explosion, but every one of these theories has been debunked by either a lack of supporting evidence or the discovery of refuting evidence. Thus, the Cambrian Explosion continues to be the Darwinian stumbling block, the factual event that Darwinists cannot explain. They make limp-wristed attempts to explain it away, to dismiss its significance by proposing that the fossil evidence is there—it just hasn't been found, they say. At first, Darwinists argued that the phantom fossils would be found buried deep beneath the seabed and would be discovered when drilling techniques improved to the point where deep-sea core samples could be obtained. But when drilling techniques improved to that point, still no fossils were found that would explain the Cambrian Explosion in Darwinian terms. And so, there it sits today, mocking Darwinism from a 540-million-year-old grave.

In the absence of a host of transitional fossils that would link the Cambrian fossils to the earlier geological record, the only sensible explanation for the sudden appearance of hundreds of multi-cellular life forms is a Superior Being who created the life forms in question, fully formed, as described in Genesis, Chapter One.

THE PROBLEM OF DNA

In 1952, Francis Crick and James Watson discovered that DNA (deoxyribonucleic acid), the genetic code that directs the assembly of all life forms, consisted of two strands of biologic code that curve gracefully around one another as a double-helix (Figure 1:1). Subsequent research has found that even the DNA of a one-celled bacterium contains over a million bits of genetic information! The biological code encrypted in DNA is more sophisticated than any computer code ever devised by a human being. It is far, far more complex even than the computer code (named Deep Blue) that beat world chess champion Gary Kasparov in 1997. Belief in Darwinism, therefore, requires that one accept that a mindless, random process—evolution—resulted in the mind-boggling genetic code that directs the assembly of a human being in its mother's womb—in biblical terms, "knits" the developing human together (apt terminology, for sure, found in Psalms 139:13). Obviously, DNA is another of Darwinism's stumbling blocks.

It is fanciful to suppose that the first life form was spontaneously created by a purely material process involving inert molecules, heat, and lightning, but that begs the question of how something as sophisticated and complex as the double-helix of DNA came about. DNA simply could not have been the product of that hypothetical lightning strike, and the idea that it assembled itself over billions of years means that early life forms had no DNA. If so, how did they reproduce? Quite simply, life requires DNA. A thingamajig that lacks DNA isn't a life form; it's just a thingamajig. It's not alive. It's a rock or a blob of "stuff."

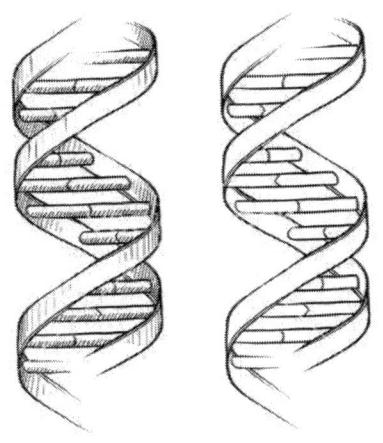

Figure 1:1 – The Double Helix of DNA
(Greatly simplified, of course)

The Cambrian Explosion is strike one against Darwinism; DNA is strike two. Strike three is irreducible complexity.

IRREDUCIBLE COMPLEXITY

In 1996 molecular biologist and university professor Michael Behe published *Darwin's Black Box* in which he set forth his theory of irreducible complexity. Some organic systems—he cites most prominently the eye and the blood-clotting mechanism—involve too many necessary working parts to have evolved over long periods of time. Keep in mind that Darwinists propose an evolutionary process that takes place in very small steps and took hundreds of millions of years to produce a human with binocular vision. The evolutionary process, Darwinists maintain, is mediated by the principle of natural selection. For a small mutation to be incorporated into the evolutionary drama it must be functional—it must work, in other words. If it doesn't work (render its host organism more "fit"), then it has no purpose and will be rejected by natural selection. Organisms with non-functional mutations are not selected as mates and so do not reproduce. In that event, the mutations in question are not passed on. They were doomed from the beginning.

For the eye to function properly, several hundred different parts and molecular particles must be present and working together. If one of them is missing, the eye can't see. It serves no function. (Likewise, remove one of a digital camera's parts or one aspect of its program code and it will no longer function.) Therefore, according to the rules of Darwin's theory, the human eye is an impossibility. Several hundred parts and particles could not have come together all at once. If the eye evolved, then proto-eyes were blind, they served no purpose. And they served no purpose, presumably, for millions of years. The only way all the parts and particles could have come together all at once to produce the human eye is if an intelligent being brought them together. Only creation can explain the eye. Creation requires a Creator. That is, God.

Behe applied the same argument to the human blood-clotting mechanism, which requires numerous molecular compounds to work. Without one of them, blood does not clot properly and a person who is bleeding dies. So how did the human species (or the pre-hominid species that supposedly preceded humans in the evolutionary chain) survive while the blood-clotting mechanism was evolving? The answer is that the first organisms with blood could not have survived unless blood clotted from the get-go. (First, blood clots; then cellular healing—another very complex process—begins.) Again, the only plausible explanation for the blood-clotting mechanism is a highly intelligent being. Again, God.

The next strike, the fourth, against Darwinism is time. Yes, the authors know that three is all the strikes a baseball player gets. The fact that we are giving Darwin four strikes is nothing less than an example of our magnanimous willingness to work with him and his true believers.

TIME IS OF THE ESSENCE

According to current astrophysical wisdom, the age of the universe is 13.8 billion years (give or take a few hundred million); that of the earth is approximately eight billion years. The earth cooled and stabilized enough to support life around 750 million years ago. For argument's sake, the authors will go with those numbers. The Bible says God created every living thing that has ever slid, crawled, swum, flown, or just been swept along. Some made it; some did not. That's life, as they say.

Even some Darwinists admit that 750 million years is not long enough for a one-celled thingy to evolve into a walking, talking, pipe-smoking, guitar-playing, Ferrari-driving, condo-dwelling human being who invents computer code. A growing number of scientists have accepted that even if the Absolutely Mind-Boggling did happen and a one-celled living thingy spontaneously appeared in the muck 750 million years ago, even that is not long enough for a one-celled thingy to evolve into something as simple as a worm. In the first place, for it to qualify as a living thing, that first theoretical cell had to contain deoxyribonucleic acid, DNA, and DNA is simply too exquisite, complex, and packed full of much too much information (genetic code) for it to have suddenly, spontaneously appeared, like a magician's rabbit out of a hat.

DNA screams CREATION! Again, the only explanation that makes sense is God. That is exactly what we are told in The Bible. That makes perfect sense. The Bible is His Word, set to papyrus and paper by His scribes, beginning with Moses. God has told us what He did. He is beyond amazing, and He wants us to know it.

UNVERIFIED ASSERTIONS

Darwinists say things like "a small dinosaur species first developed rudimentary feathers from hair-like follicles on its skin and then its feathers grouped together on its upper limbs which it flapped one day to beat away a swarm of mosquitoes and discovered it could fly, and from there it developed into the first bird." When a well-known proponent of Darwin's theory of evolution says something of that sort, other people who believe in Darwin's theory generally assume he is speaking fact. He is invited to speak on his dinosaur-to-bird theory at reputable scientific conferences. When he speaks, the people who attend these conferences are impressed. They give him standing ovations in recognition of his cleverness. They tell other people what he said. Scientific publications like *Scientific American* magazine write up what he said and make it widely available. And pretty soon nearly every gullible person in the world believes dinosaurs developed feathers, then wings, and then took off into the air at which point they were no longer dinosaurs—they were birds. Mind you, the supposed authority who first came up with this fanciful scenario presented no objective evidence with which to support his theory (other than feather-looking thingies do appear in certain dinosaur fossils, but shared physical characteristics do not prove evolution). He simply thought it up. He then convinces himself that his theory is correct and worth sharing with the world. In short, he becomes well-known, even famous, because he thinks of and impresses himself with ideas no one has ever thought of before.

To put that into proper perspective: Everyone has had unique thoughts. Ninety-nine-point-nine-nine-nine-nine percent of these thoughts are not worth sharing with others except perhaps as examples of the ability of humans to think strange thoughts. Such strange thoughts are called "what ifs."

The authors, for example, have produced strange thoughts, but if either of us ever related one of our strange thoughts to other people, those other people would either (a) laugh, (b) think perhaps we were suffering food poisoning, (c) be moved to share similarly strange thoughts of their own, or (d) be so concerned as to call the appropriate authorities. No one of sound mind would ever believe that one of the authors' strange thoughts was true. But in our case, the strange thoughts in question have nothing to do with either of our primary areas of expertise: theology and family psychology. Trust us, they are harmless.

But when an authority on a certain subject comes up with a novel idea concerning said subject, other people are likely to give his novel idea lots of credence no matter how strange it is. As a result, the expert's novel idea—in this case, the very novel and strange idea that a species of dinosaur miraculously changed into the first species of bird—spreads from person to person. These days, television talk shows and social media are very helpful in this regard. Soon, lots of people believe that dinosaurs turning into birds is an established fact when it is nothing more than a novel and manifestly strange thought produced by a person with too much time on his hands, which describes most university professors.

The dinosaurs-evolved-into-birds-theory is an example of what is called "arguing from authority." An argument from authority goes like this:

1. Dr. Billy Bubba is a celebrated authority on Darwin's theory of evolution.
2. Dr. Billy Bubba says birds evolved from a species of feathered dinosaur.
3. It has been established, therefore, that birds evolved from a species of feathered dinosaur.

Mind you, the only factual statements in the above syllogism are 1 and 2. Statement 1 establishes Dr. Bubba's authority. Statement 2 is Dr. Bubba's argument. One is supposed to believe that statements 2 and 3 are true because of statement 1. But statement 2 lacks proof; it is simply a proposition. Therefore, statement 3 does not logically follow from statements 1 and 2. It is a false conclusion, a "logical fallacy." Arguments based solely on the established authority of the individuals in question always, without exception, result in logical fallacies. Because it depends on arguments from authority, Darwin's theory of macro-evolution abounds in logical fallacies. For example, in his best-selling book The God Delusion (2006), esteemed Darwinist Richard Dawkins says that no intelligent person will admit to belief in the Virgin Birth. But both authors, if we do say so ourselves, are intelligent persons who firmly believe that as foretold by the prophet Isaiah seven hundred years prior to the event, Christ Jesus was born of a virgin. Like Dawkins' spurious claim, all of Darwinism depends on arguments from authority because no concrete evidence exists that would support it. Furthermore, as with strikes one through four above, the concrete evidence that does exist unequivocally contradicts it.

In short, Darwin was smart and a very inventive thinker. Nonetheless, he was wrong. Darwin could not have known he was wrong, however, because none of strikes one through five were discovered in his lifetime. So, Darwin can be forgiven for being wrong. But the scientists and professors who continue despite all the contradictory evidence to believe in macro-evolution cannot be forgiven. They should know better.

CONCLUSION

The problem with scientists who believe in evolution is they can't seem to accept that the creativity of a theory is no indication of its rightness. Indeed, the speculations of Darwinians and multi-verse proponents are highly creative. They write long academic papers that are difficult to understand. But when all is said and done, speculations are nothing more than ideas until someone finds tangible evidence with which to support them. And big words and complex theoretical formulations do not truth make. Hard evidence makes for truth and the rather sad (given the time that's been wasted) fact is that none of the speculations the authors have reviewed in this chapter are backed by even the slightest bit of hard supportive evidence. As opposed to the Big Bang (for which the evidence is conclusive), they are Big Flops.

The Big Bang, the lack of any hard evidence that would even hint at validity for Darwin's theory of macro-evolution, the sudden appearance in the fossil record of every animal group that currently exists (the so-called Cambrian explosion), the mind-blowing accuracy of the creation account in Genesis 1—all point to one inescapable conclusion: An eternal, supernatural, omnipotent, omniscient being whom we call God created everything...in the beginning...and it was all good.

RECOMMENDED READING

- Stephen C. Meyer, *Darwin's Doubt* (HarperOne, 2013)
- Stephen C. Meyer, *Signature in the Cell* (HarperOne, 2010)
- Gerald L. Schroeder, *The Science of God: The Convergence of Scientific and Biblical Wisdom* (Free Press, 2009)
- Gerald L. Schroeder, *Genesis and the Big Bang* (Bantam, 1991)
- Michael J. Behe, *Darwin's Black Box* (Free Press, 2006)
- Phillip E. Johnson, *Darwin on Trial* (IVP Books, 20th Anniversary Edition, 2010)
- Hugh Ross, *Why the Universe Is the Way It Is* (Baker, 2008)
- Hugh Ross, *Improbable Planet* (Baker, 2016)
- Hugh Ross, *Beyond the Cosmos* (Second Expanded Edition, NavPress, 1999)

QUESTIONS FOR PERSONAL REFLECTION AND DISCUSSION

1. What are some of the primary arguments from or appeals to authority used by Darwinists to support their belief in macro-evolution?

2. Hitler's Minister of Propaganda, Joseph Goebbels, asserted that if an influential person tells a lie often enough, people will begin to believe it. How does this propaganda principle apply to the teachings of Darwinists?

3. Is Darwinism a true science or is it more accurately termed an ideology? If the latter, what are the characteristics that qualify it as such? What is the ultimate purpose behind the strenuous attempt on the part of certain elements of society to instill unquestioning belief in a Darwinian worldview into children (*vis-à-vis* public education)?

4. Can you think of another currently or recently popular pseudoscientific belief that is not supported by any good evidence?

5. Darwinists propose that the elements necessary to life came together by random processes to form highly complex life forms. Can you think of an analogy that would demonstrate the absurdity of this claim?

2

Saved from What?

"Have you been saved, John?"

The question came from a slightly older fellow who approached me after a speaking engagement in Iowa in 1996. I must've looked like a deer in headlights because he immediately said, "Oh, I'm sorry. That was too forward, wasn't it? I really didn't mean to make you uncomfortable. Please forgive me." And as quickly as he'd shown up, he was gone. I hadn't said a word, but I had answered his question nonetheless.

Before I asked Jesus to come into my life in the year 2000, at age 53, I had no idea what terms like saved and born again meant. Since 1978 our family had attended a very proper Episcopal Church where such ideas were regarded as the bailiwick of people who lived out on religion's eccentric and maybe even nutty fringe. Never once did our pastor give a sermon on being saved. Never once had the subject come up in our very proper adult Sunday School class, where discussion centered less on Jesus and more on how to translate the New Testament into proper social action. The rather overt message was that being a Christian was all about engaging in work that advanced certain politically-correct causes. I was very comfortable being an Episcopalian. It didn't challenge me in the least. If I had any faith, it was in my fundamental goodness and willingness to do the right thing at the right time. I had heard people say that Jesus had died for my sins, but I had no idea what that meant. And after all, I wasn't so bad that someone should die for me...or so I thought (in my sin).

Undoubtedly, some people reading this book are where I was at prior to being saved. If you're one of them, the term "saved" is somewhat mystifying. Like the pre-2000 me, you probably ask: *Saved from what?* And like me, you may think: *I'm okay. I don't need saving, whatever that is.* When you see a billboard proclaiming that *Jesus Saves!* you may be immediately reminded of the standard joke: *At which bank?* If so, you're not alone. Been there, laughed at it.

In this chapter, Scott and I hope to convince you that you are indeed in need—dire, desperate, urgent need—of being saved. To come to that understanding, you must first accept that your life is in grave danger. Even though you may be and probably are living a reasonably comfortable existence, if you have not been saved you are in great and constant peril. Why? Because, as the Bible clearly and repeatedly says, you are an inveterate—which is to say incorrigible, entrenched, confirmed, habitual, and for all those reasons, hopeless—sinner. And if you are not saved from the natural consequence of your sinfulness by the only means available, and thereby forgiven and cleansed of sin, then when you die—and make no mistake, you could die within the next couple of days, hours even—you will *not* go to Heaven. The Bible, which is God speaking, clearly and repeatedly says this as well.

You may to this point in your life think that life begins at conception and ends when a person takes his last breath. That's not actually the case.

The Bible tells us that God created the first human being out of already existing physical materials which it refers to as the "dust of the ground" (Genesis 2:7). He then brought Adam to life in a completely unique fashion: He breathed into Adam's nostril's the "breath of life" at which time Adam became a "living soul" (Genesis 2:7).

In this regard, we are completely unique in God's creation. Like all living things, including plants, we possess the fundamental energy of life (which, as pointed out in Chapter 1, science has never successfully measured or explained). But we humans possess a quality that no other creature possesses: spirit, or soul. The soul is akin to a spiritual umbilical cord that connected Adam (and shortly thereafter, Eve) to God. That connection, that life-line, was broken by the sin described in Genesis, Chapter 3: At the urging of the serpent (aka Satan, Lucifer, the Evil One), Adam and Eve went over to the "dark side" and ate of the fruit of the Tree of Knowledge of Good and Evil, the fruit God had specifically forbidden them. When the God-to-human life-line was broken by our first ancestors' act of rebellion, human life became finite.

At the moment of death, the spirit departs the body. Lacking vitalizing energy, the body begins to decay, to revert back to its original state. Through the process of oxidation, the body is slowly transformed into carbon—the "dust" to which the Bible says we shall return. According to the laws of physics, however, the vitalizing energy of the spirit is not, cannot be, destroyed—it continues to exist. The Bible is clear on this as well (Luke 16: 21 – 29). For the purposes of this book, the pertinent question becomes: Does a person's soul/spirit continue to exist in a state of "death," which in the Biblical sense means eternal separation from God, or is the person's soul/spirit restored to God in a state of eternal life? The person in question is you!

WHAT IS "SAVED" AND WHY?

Let's just put it this way: Eternal death (separation from God) plus acute awareness equals Hell (ED + AA = Hell). Being saved simply means you have been rescued from that most unpleasant fate. You need to be rescued because you are a sinner and to put it in contemporary terms, a one-way ticket to Hell is the natural consequence of your sinfulness. How do we know that the reader—you!—are a sinner? Because sin is the human condition. To assert that you are a sinner is not a criticism. After all, it's not personal; it is simply irrefutable fact. All human beings (save one) have been, are, and will be sinners. Mother Teresa, in spite of all the good she did, was a sinner. Contrary to the teachings of the Catholic Church, Jesus' mother, Mary, was a sinner chosen by God for a single holy purpose. (If you are Catholic and are having difficulty with Mother Teresa and Mary being sinners, consider that the Bible clearly says—see 2 Corinthians 5:21--that Jesus is the one and only sinless person who has ever lived). Ghandi, Abraham Lincoln, Florence Nightingale, all good people by human standards, were sinners. We hope the following news doesn't burst your bubble, but so are you.

It doesn't matter how good you are in your own or other people's estimations, how many awards you've been given for your civic and charitable contributions, how polished your manners, or that you've never had an episode of road rage, you're a sinner. You can't help it. You were born that way. Sin is the spiritual DNA all humans have inherited from Adam and Eve, who when given a choice between believing and obeying God or believing Satan and disobeying God, chose Satan. The Bible says they ate of the fruit of the Tree of Knowledge of Good and Evil. Then, even though they were experiencing great shame and guilt (because they now possessed knowledge of good and evil and, therefore, a conscience), they made matters much worse by denying responsibility for what they had done. Because they had defiled the perfect place—the Garden of Eden—God had provided for them, He had no choice but to turn them out into a state of exile. That's where we are today. We are exiles. We are homeless.

The same situation exists with regards to Heaven, our true home. Just as God would not allow two unrepentant sinners to continue living in the Garden of Eden, He will not allow unrepentant sinners into Heaven. But remember, if a person doesn't go to Heaven, he goes to Hell. There's no third option. And let's be clear, even though the popular rock 'n' roll band AC/DC in their hit song "Highway to Hell" portrays Hell as a great big party where people can do all the bad things they've ever wanted to do, Hell is a really bad place. It is not a party, and Satan is not a cool DJ who plays all your favorite dance music. You don't want to go there. That's why being saved is so important. Until a person is saved, he exists in a state of sin. Now, it's important to understand that a person who is saved is not saved from *sinning*. A saved person still sins and always will. Rather, he is saved from the natural *consequence* of his sinfulness. He is saved from Hell. Jesus has paid the penalty for the sin of all who accept Him as Lord and Savior.

At this point, an analogy may be helpful: Remember when you were a child and your mother wouldn't let you come into her clean house because you'd been playing outside and become covered with dirt? You may have had a great need to come in the house. You may have become thirsty and were desperate for a drink of cool water. You may have endured the cold or the heat for as long as you could and longed for the temperature-controlled comfort of your home or you may have held your bladder for too long and were going to wet yourself if you didn't get to a toilet quickly. In this analogy, God is your mother, the dirt that's covering you is the filthiness of your sin, the inside of your home is Heaven, and having to remain outside is Hell. When the time comes, the one thing you do not want is for God to refuse you entry to His house forever. You need to get clean, and time's a-wasting.

Again, you have no more control over being born a sinner than you do the color of your eyes. You inherited a sinful nature from Adam and Eve. But you also inherited from Adam and Eve knowledge of good and evil—right and wrong. That knowledge constitutes your conscience. So every time you sin you know, however deep down inside, that you are doing something wrong (Romans 2:14-15 describes this as having the law "written in their hearts" and that "their conscience bears witness" to their sinfulness). You may and probably do in many cases rationalize and justify your sins, but you rationalize and justify precisely because your conscience—your sin detector—goes off like a smoke alarm. Over time, you can turn your conscience down, but you can never shut it off completely. When you sin, you know it even if you deny it. Because you possess a conscience, you are completely, one hundred percent responsible for your sins and God is going to hold you accountable for them when you die. You may blame someone else for your sins—your parents maybe (that's a very popular blaming these days)—but God is going to hold no one responsible but *you* for them. From God's point of view, you have no excuses. You will either die with ugly blotches of sin—a spiritual rash of sorts—all over your soul or you will die with your sins forgiven and washed away (more on that in Chapter 5).

It bears repeating: Heaven is God's Perfect Place, and God is not going to allow you to dwell there with Him if you are not completely clean. Your mother wanted you to use a hose to wash off the dirt before you came in her house; God wants to wash off your sin with His Living Water before you come in His house.

Sin is never free, in other words. Even if you get away with lots of sins during your earthly life, you are going to be held accountable for them when you take your final breath. And there's no A, B, C, or D in God's grading system. It's either pass or fail, thumbs up or thumbs down.

LINKED-IN TO SIN

Some sin is overt, obvious, and unambiguous. In that category one finds burglary, rape, murder, embezzling, adultery, lying, child abuse, spouse abuse, animal abuse, and other obvious evils. But evil can wear a very respectable face. Using one's talents (gifts freely given by God) solely for the purpose of self-enhancement (to obtain riches or fame) is sin. So is performing charitable work primarily for recognition or to feel righteous. Bragging or even having private feelings of pride about one's accomplishments or possessions is sin. And sin is not limited to things people do—their behavior. Sin includes improper *thoughts*. Jesus said, for example, that a man who merely *looked* with lust upon a woman was guilty of adultery (Matthew 5:28). You don't have to actually commit murder, you only have to *wish* someone was dead or fantasize about hurting someone, to qualify as a sinner. You don't have to actually steal someone's else's diamond bracelet, you only have to be jealous of the person and wish the bracelet was yours, to qualify as a sinner. And so forth.

The Bible—the validity and complete, unequivocal truthfulness of which the authors will establish in Chapter 7—says that human beings are sinful before they are born (Psalm 51:5). That means that sin comes naturally to us humans. It's as close as we come to having instinct. The goose cannot resist the instinct to fly south as winter approaches, and the human cannot resist the inclination to sin—to do that which puts gratification of self above love of God and neighbor. To not sin requires constant vigilance and equally constant effort, and the authors do not use the word *constant* in any figurative sense; we mean during a person's every single waking moment, which is, of course, utterly impossible. The vigilance and effort theoretically required is *prima facie* evidence that sin is the dominant aspect of human nature. Furthermore, we are completely incapable of the vigilance and effort required, which is why people who attempt this degree of vigilance and effort (thinking that salvation is a matter of not doing bad stuff and doing good stuff instead) always, without exception, end up dealing with perennial feelings of inadequacy, despair, and guilt. They can't help but fail. Despite their obsessive watchfulness and effort, they go right on sinning—screaming abuse at other drivers or cutting them off in traffic, treating restaurant waitpersons as if they are underlings, laughing at vulgar jokes, disrespecting their parents, contemplating revenge on someone who's done them wrong, ignoring someone who's in obvious distress, being jealous of someone else's lifestyle, and so on. Living the sinless life is the Impossible Dream. Furthermore, the vain attempt to perfect one's self is in and of itself sinful because it presumes that one can become like God (see Genesis 3:5). It is a subtle and seductive form of self-idolatry.

It may be difficult for the reader to accept that sin qualifies as an instinct—that you are human; therefore, you sin. In my previous life, that concept was very difficult for me to wrap my head around. I could readily accept that I *occasionally* sinned because when that realization surfaced, I simply did something good to balance the scales again and cancel out the sin. I apologized, for example. Or I just shrugged it off, reassuring myself that when all things were considered, I was a pretty good guy. After all, I'd just contributed a significant amount to my Rotary Club's toys for underprivileged kids Christmas fund. Or I rationalized my sin—whatever it was—as the inevitable consequence of stress. If I hadn't been under so much work pressure, I wouldn't have snapped at my wife. But accepting that sin was not just something I occasionally let slip, but my very condition, *that* was difficult. It seemed so self-abusive, self-demeaning; stupid, even. I associated the idea with ignorant, easily manipulated people living in the backwaters of Appalachia who'd fallen under the sway of preachers who grunted every five words or so, yelled a lot, and made generally no sense—people who handled snakes and stuff of that sort.

Then Jesus came into my life and I began reading the Bible. As I read, my denial concerning my sinfulness began to melt away—the Bible refers to this as scales falling off one's eyes (Acts 9:18). It was either that or deny Jesus. The choice was a no-brainer. Jesus told His disciples that he was "the Truth," and the evidence is overwhelming that God had given Him the authority to make that claim (John 14:6). Jesus even said sin is a master to whom we become enslaved (John 8:24). I had to admit that certain sins, as if they were addictions, had taken over my life. Jesus said that only knowing the Truth—Him—can set us free (John 8:32). Without Him, we have no hope. Jesus said that sin blinds us (John 9:39 – 41). The author of the Epistle to the Hebrews says sin makes us deaf to the reprimands of the conscience (Hebrews 3:12 – 13). In the Apostle Paul's letter to the fledgling Christian community at Ephesus, he describes the unsaved sinner as being in a state of spiritual death (Eph. 2:1). The unsaved sinner is already dead, in other words. To use a popular movie title, the unsaved sinner is a "dead man walking." Paul goes on to say that unrepentant, unsaved sinners are bent on "fulfilling the desires of the flesh and of the mind, and (are) by nature children of wrath" (Eph. 2:3).

I came to this point of reckoning: Either I was correct concerning myself—I was a good guy who only slipped up occasionally—or Jesus and the Bible were telling me the truth about myself, giving me a much-needed wake-up call. I made the correct choice and discovered the paradox of all paradoxes: It is liberating to accept that you are a sinner. One would think that this acceptance would send a person head first down a deep black hole into clinical depression, but it doesn't. It's somewhat akin to finally, after months spent consulting one mechanic after another, learning why your automobile's engine sometimes makes a loud knocking noise. Knowing the source of the knocking means a mechanic can fix it. What a relief! In this case, the intermittent loud knocking is your conscience and Jesus is the Master Mechanic. And indeed, the Truth does set a person free (John 8:32).

John Newton was the captain of a ship that carried slaves from Africa to the Caribbean and the American colonies. After a brush with death at sea, Newton became a Christian, repented of his former life, became a minister, and began writing hymns, the most well-known of which is Amazing Grace. The familiar words of the first verse attest to the spiritual healing and liberation that accompanies being saved:

> Amazing grace, how sweet the sound
> That saved a wretch like me.
> I once was lost but now I'm found
> Was blind but now I see.

THE CUTE LITTLE FACE OF SIN

Psalm 51:5 tells us that we are "sinful from birth" from the moment we are conceived. After the Flood, God promises to never again "curse the ground because of humans, even though *every inclination of the human heart is evil from childhood* (italics added)." These are but two of many scripture verses that refer to man's inborn iniquity. If the Bible is true concerning sin, there must be hard evidence of its truth—irrefutable proof—and sure enough, there is. In fact, the evidence is ample and should be obvious to anyone who has spent any time around very young children.

At some point during early toddlerhood, the real human being awakens from the relative slumber of infancy and realizes that he's an autonomous individual, a person with an identity, a "me." It is at that point that human nature begins to show itself for what it is. Parents unwittingly attest to this awakening with story after story of adorable little cuddle-bugs who suddenly begin to act as if possessed by demons. Like a switch has been thrown, the former cuddle-bug begins to do precisely what his parents tell him *not* to do, obstinately refuses to obey the simplest command, sets out to willfully destroy whatever he can get his little hands on, and instantly becomes a raging homicidal maniac whenever something, the slightest thing, does not suit him. Homicidal? Yes, homicidal. During said rages, he scratches, bites, kicks, and hits anyone who comes within striking distance, even someone trying to calm him down, even the very people who have done nothing but shower him with love, love, and more love since he was born.

It is a sure sign of God's mercy and grace that He has distinguished human beings from animals in one unique and significant way: Unlike any other species, God does not allow humans to grow to full size in one or two years. Anyone who's ever tried to deal with the rage of a toddler will appreciate the implication.

The homicidal tantrums of a toddler are unique among God's creatures. My wife and I are raising a Toy Schnauzer, Mazie, who loves to play fetch. It is accurate to say that fetch, to Mazie, is the Meaning of Life. But as important as fetch is to Mazie, if I refuse to play she does not begin barking threateningly and try to bite me. She just drops the fetch ball and finds herself a comfortable cushion on which to spread out and resume the proverbial dog's life. Mazie, you see, is not a sinful creature. She is just cute. By contrast, human toddlers are both cute and sinful. And to paraphrase the old nursery rhyme, when toddlers are cute they are very, very cute, and when they are sinful they are horrid.

The *enfant terrible* behavior in question, traditionally referred to as the "terrible twos" (even though it generally begins three to nine months before the second birthday), is the province of the child regardless of how responsible, patient, and loving his parents are. A toddler's often outrageous behavior—the defiance, rages, and obviously deliberate provocations—is what raw, unbridled human nature looks like. Without a doubt, the toddler believes that

    a. what he wants he deserves to have;
    b. because he deserves what he wants, the ends justify the means;
    c. no one has a right to deny him or stand in his way;
    d. rules do not apply to him (but whatever "rules" he invents definitely apply to everyone else)

In short, the toddler's mindset is the same mindset as that of an adult criminal. Not a petty criminal either, but the sort that's locked away for life in a maximum-security prison. If anyone needs further convincing, ask: Does one need to teach a toddler to hurt other children to get what he wants? Answer: no. A toddler who has never seen or heard described an act of violence, even so much as cartoon violence, if he wants a toy another toddler is playing with, will hit, push, slap, and bite to get it. Does one need to teach a toddler the ins and outs of not being truthful for the toddler to lie? Again, no. As soon as a child begins to talk, he begins to lie. And the first lie a child—every child—tells is a variation on the first lie recorded as having been told (see Genesis 3:11 – 13): *I didn't do it! It wasn't my fault! I'm not responsible!*

When I'm asking an audience this series of questions, I will sometimes throw in this one: Does one need to teach a toddler to steal? People have no difficulty correctly answering the first two questions, but at this one, people look confused. Finally, someone will say, "But when toddlers take things that don't belong to them, they really don't know that they're stealing."

To which I ask, "Why, then, does the toddler hide what he has taken? And why, when asked if he has taken it, does he insist that he has not?"

Adults have difficulty conceiving of toddlers being covetous, devious, conniving, and acting with malice aforethought. They're so cute, after all! But the overwhelming preponderance of evidence confirms that they are capable of being quite disingenuous. The 10th Commandment says "Thou shalt not covet" for a reason: Human beings are, by nature, covetous. Likewise, the 8th Commandment instructs us not to steal because we are, by nature, thieves. And I can't stress it enough, human nature emerges full-blown and in full force during toddlerhood. And for this reason, God keeps us small enough that even a petite woman can exert physical control over a toddler when all else fails.

Psychology has no explanation for the sudden, volcanic eruption of sin-behavior from the young toddler. No psychological paradigm explains it. It's a direct contradiction of the humanist creed that humans are inherently good.[†] Behaviorism and learning theory also fail. By what process involving rewards, punishments or modeling did an eighteen-month-old child develop the behaviors in question? Which of the adults in the child's life modeled throwing oneself on the floor and writhing about, shrieking, in a fit of pique (or gave the child ice cream when he did so)? Who modeled or rewarded scratching and biting other people? Who modeled or rewarded slapping people when they don't give you what you want? Who modeled or rewarded snatching things away from other children? In every case, the answer is no one. Such behavior comes naturally—*instinctually*, if you will—to a young child.

Freudian theory also comes up empty-handed. The raging, homicidal toddler is usually several months away from the supposed traumas of toilet training and much too young to have developed an Oedipal complex (another of Freud's many fanciful fictions). The complete failure of any psychological theory to account for the toddler's sin-eruption is irrefutable evidence of psychology's bankruptcy when it comes to explaining human nature. If psychology cannot understand and explain the behavior of a young toddler, then psychology cannot claim to correctly understand *any* human behavior, no matter the age of the human in question. Beginnings are everything.

It all boils down to this: You don't need to teach a child to be bad. Being bad comes naturally. Adults need to teach a child to control his or her bad, self-centered impulses and instead be compassionate, helpful, and responsible. This teaching requires *force* because sin is one of the most powerful forces in creation and to teach a child to control it and overcome it requires even greater force, known as firm, consistent, unwavering discipline. The "terrible twos" is all the proof necessary that sin is hard-wired into us.

Secularists have great difficulty accepting that the young child is bad. Their religion—humanism—posits that humans are by nature good. Furthermore, secular-humanists are pride-fully convinced that believing the best of human nature is indication of their own moral superiority. In their view, mean-spirited people believe human beings are fundamentally bad.

[†] Humanists, by definition, do not believe in God, the source of all that is good. As the label implies and their creed makes clear, humanists believe in man, the individual. Therefore, man is good. Humanism is, literally, an anti-Christ.

GETTING TO HEAVEN

Good people believe human beings are fundamentally good. Human beings do bad things, secular-humanists believe, not because of an inborn sin-nature but because of early abuse, neglect, trauma, or some other malfeasance on the part of their parents, other caretakers, or something called "society." In some cases, those dots certainly can be connected, but what explanation is there for the child raised by loving parents who protect him from all harm who grows up to be a clever, manipulative sociopath, rapist, or even a murderer? Yes, a bad childhood can make an already bad person much worse. But a good and happy childhood with responsible, loving parents is no guarantee that a person will grow up to be responsible and loving toward others. He may, during late adolescence, take the wrong road and never find his way back to the civilized path. That story, hardly rare, is testimony to the power of human nature, the power of sin.

Because they believe human nature is essentially good, secular-humanists must somehow explain why young children and other supposedly good people do bad things. In this regard, they claim that people simply make what they call "bad choices," as if life, like the old game show "Let's Make a Deal," is a matter of constantly choosing between doors A, B, or C, never really knowing the consequences of a choice until it's been made and the door is opened to reveal what's behind it. A person makes the wrong choice simply because he didn't know better, didn't know what the consequences were, wasn't paying attention, or just plain old made a rather accidental (and certainly innocent) mistake—he chose the wrong "door." Surely he'll do better next time, thinks the secular-humanist. He just needs love, understanding, and patience. In any case, note that the individual in question was not fully aware of the fact he was doing something wrong. He was not premeditated, deliberate (he cannot be because that would contradict the secularist myth that he is fundamentally good); therefore, what he did was not malicious. The notion that he simply made a bad choice neutralizes his action. Suddenly, it carries no moral value. The term "bad choices" is an example of how secular humanists manipulate language in order, in this case, to preserve humanism's central tenet.

Secularists must now account, however, for the misbehaving child who persists in making bad choices and eventually becomes a misbehaving, even criminal, adult. They accomplish this by positing forces that are supposedly beyond the control of the adult in question, the top six of which are (in no particular order), bad parenting, poverty, race, gender, ethnicity, and sexual orientation (or a combination thereof). The misbehaving child is simply making bad choices; the misbehaving adult is acting out his bad childhood or his perpetual victimization at the hands of a society that has stacked the deck against him because of something about himself that he (supposedly) cannot help. Once again, the humanist myth is preserved. It's a fairy tale that ends happily ever after when the handsome prince (secular humanism) triumphs by defeating the powers of darkness (conservative Christianity) and brings about the restoration of the perfect kingdom (a socialist utopia). In other words, secularists refuse to admit that (a) sin is a reality, (b) sin is universal, and (c) sin is a primary feature of human nature. Instead of being embedded in our natures, secularists believe sin is nothing more than a pesky monkey that sometimes jumps onto and grabs ahold of people's backs—some people's backs more than others. With the right social engineering (enforced by various government agencies such as child protective services), the monkey can be tamed, will release its grip, and life will be perfect. Like most secular-left ideas, this is nothing more than sounds-good mega-baloney.

THE *ENFANT TERRIBLE* UNMASKED

The Judeo-Christian Bible—God's Holy Word—is the only reference work that explains the sudden outpouring of sin-behavior that occurs in toddlerhood. The third chapter of the first book of The Bible, Genesis, recounts our first ancestors' temptation, sin (disobedience), lack of repentance (denial of responsibility, absence of remorse), and fall from grace. The rest of the Old Testament consists of one story after another of how that original sin affected human history. And then, when all seems lost, Jesus walks on stage. He came for one purpose and one purpose only: to offer each of us the opportunity to restore relationship with God (the lifeline spoken of earlier) and obtain a one-way ticket to Heaven, regardless of how many or what kind of sins one has committed. He offers cleansing through the suffering and blood of His redemptive sacrifice on the Cross. He reaches out His hand to you and me and all the rest of us drowning souls and asks, "Would you like to be saved?" But we get ahead of ourselves.

All sin is self-gratifying, and all self-gratification, because it either offends God or is at the expense of others (or both), is sin. This is the overarching theme of the Ten Commandments. They are not mere "don'ts." Each prohibition corresponds to a self-gratification to which our sinful nature predisposes us. They are, in order:

NO.	COMMANDMENT	CORRESPONDING SIN(S)
1	You shall have no other gods before Me	Duplicity, Treachery, Rebellion
2	You shall not make idols	Idolatry (see Romans 1:25)
3	You shall not take the name of the LORD your God in vain	Blasphemy, Vanity
4	Remember the Sabbath Day, to keep it holy	Irreverence, Worldliness, Materialism
5	Honor your mother and your father	Disrespect, Disobedience
6	You shall not murder	Violence, Homicide, Suicide, Hatred
7	You shall not commit adultery	Lust, sexual immorality
8	You shall not steal	Theft, cheating, dishonesty
9	You shall not bear false witness against your neighbor	Deceit, Lying
10	You shall not covet	Jealousy, Greed

Note that they are in two groups. The first four commandments pertain to our relationship to God; the last six to our relationships with others. Jesus summed up this dichotomy in his answer to a Pharisee (Jewish noble) who was challenging his religious credentials: *"'Thou shalt love the Lord thy God with thy whole heart, and with thy whole soul, and with thy whole mind.' This is the greatest and the first commandment. And the second is like it, 'Thou shalt love thy neighbor as thyself.' On these two commandments depend the whole Law and the Prophets."* (Matthew 22:35-40). In short, when all is said and done, the Ten Commandments and Mosaic Law *(set forth in the Torah or first five books of the Old Testament) boil down to loving God and loving your neighbor at least as much as you love yourself.* That's quite a tall order.

Catholics believe that sins can be forgiven by priests sitting in dark confessionals and remitted by donating money to the church (indulgences) or repeating certain phrases (e.g. "Hail Marys"). Make no mistake, there is not one shred of biblical support for such legalistic *practices*.

Members of the Church of the Nazarene believe they can achieve complete sanctification, or personal holiness, in this life. This is not supported biblically, supposes that it is possible for a sinful person to save himself from sin (an apt analogy here would be the absurdity of believing that a non-swimmer can save himself from drowning), and denies the sufficiency of Christ's sacrifice on the cross.

Christian Scientists believe that by properly connecting with God's love, a person can be made sinless (similar to Nazarene doctrine, above). As CS doctrine puts it, *"God, our all-powerful, ever-present, tenderly loving Father-Mother, maintains our wholly spiritual identity and relationship with Him as forever perfect, made in His image and likeness"* (see http://christianscience.bc.ca/faq/). That's an appealing idea, for sure, to believe that God, being Pure Love, maintains those who believe in Him in a state of spiritual perfection. Once again, there is no biblical support for this fundamental CS belief.

Mormons do not believe that children are capable of sin until they reach the age of accountability which Mormon doctrine *determine*s as *age* eight. This is inconsistent with the fact that children as young as two are clearly premeditated in their misbehavior. If premeditated, then accountable. It is also contradicted by a straightforward reading of God's Word, notably Psalm 51:5: "Surely I was sinful at birth; sinful from the time my mother conceived me." *This Mormon doctrine implies that punishment is not appropriate until a child has reached the age of accountability (determined arbitrarily). That begs the question "So what is a parent to do about misbehavior for the first eight years of a child's life?" Ignore it? Simply talk to the child in the hope that words will suffice?*

These are but four of many examples of how certain non-Christian *sects misrepresent the nature of sin and misrepresent what is required of a person to be saved from the eternal consequences of sin. As the reader will discover in Chapter 6, false teachings abound in Christianity—or, more accurately, false teachings abound in churches that falsely claim to represent valid Christianity.*

THE TWO-FOLD NATURE OF REPENTANCE AND FORGIVENESS

Just as the Ten Commandments boil down to loving God and loving one's neighbor, a sin can be forgiven at the same two levels: it can be forgiven by God and by the individual against whom the sin was committed. Taking them in reverse order: One person can forgive another person's sin, but the forgiver cannot be a third party. He or she must be the person against whom the sin was committed. If you have stolen from your employer, for example, asking for and receiving forgiveness from a priest is worthless. You've wasted your time. The only human being who can forgive you is your employer. To obtain his forgiveness, you must confess to him in full and ask for it.

Likewise, forgiveness is worthless without confession. In other words, for an offended person to forgive someone who has sinned against him in the absence of a full and honest confession on the part of the sinner doesn't count. It is a seemingly gracious thing to do, but it actually lets the sinner off the hook without acceptance of accountability and therefore, graciousness aside, it is not in the best interest of the person who committed the offense. As such, "forgiveness" of that sort, while it may seem to repair a relationship (but only creates the illusion of repair), is itself a sin.

But here's the further catch: The person against whom you sinned can forgive the sin, but that person cannot cleanse you of the stain of that sin. That can only be accomplished by repenting—making full confession and asking forgiveness—before God in the name of His Son, Jesus Christ. That can't be done through any third party either. If you have sins to confess, get down on your knees and confess to your Heavenly Father and ask His forgiveness in the name of your One and Only Savior, Jesus Christ His Only Son. And then go make confession to the person or persons against whom you sinned.

In his letter to the Christians at Galatia, the apostle Paul writes that the law—of which the Ten Commandments are the foundation—"was our tutor to bring us to Christ" (Galatians 3:24). This "tutor" holds up the mirror of the law and allows us to see our true reflection in it.

With proper discipline, a child learns to control his sin nature. But does a person ever conquer it? The greatest Christian who ever lived could not. Paul laments that despite his personal encounter with the risen Jesus, despite the sea-change that encounter wrought in his life, despite his self-sacrificial ministry, despite his willingness to die for his Lord, he continues to do that which he should not do and does not do the things he should do (Romans 7:15 – 20). Despite his desire to do otherwise, despite his concentration and best efforts, Paul continues to sin and even says his sinful nature acts contrary to his will. In other words, and as said before, sin is a human instinct. When Paul writes that "all have sinned and fallen short of the glory of God" (Romans 3:23), he is including himself. Earlier, Paul quotes the Psalmist, writing that "There is none righteous, no, not one...There is none good, no, not one." (Romans 3:10, 12 ref. Psalm 14: 1 - 3), the "none" includes himself. Paul does not place himself above the rabble, but down on their level. It is highly doubtful that anyone has or is ever going to do any better with sin than did Paul.

The older man in Iowa (it has occurred to me that he might have been an angel—he certainly functioned as one in that moment) asked me, and now I will ask you: Have you been saved? If you haven't, what are you waiting for? Time's a-wasting!

RECOMMENDED FOR FURTHER READING

- Spring, Gardiner, "Human Sinfulness," http://www.gracegems.org/SERMONS/Spring_sin.htm

- Burroughs, Jeremiah; *The Evil of Evils: The Exceeding Sinfulness of Sins.* Soli Deo Gloria Ministries, 2008 (Originally published in 1654)

- Venning, Ralph; *The Sinfulness of Sin.* Amazon Digital Services (Originally published circa 1650)

- Morgan, Christopher and Robert Peterson, eds.; *Fallen: A Theology of Sin* (Crossway; 2013)

- Mack, Wayne; *A Fight to the Death: Taking Aim at Sin Within.* P & R Publishing, 2011.

QUESTIONS FOR PERSONAL REFLECTION AND DISCUSSION

1. Identify times when you have acted or continue, as an adult, to still act like a toddler. Do you still throw "tantrums" when you don't get your way? Do you still take opportunities to rebel against authority, however subtly?

2. Using the Ten Commandments as your guide, identify the continuing sin issues in your life. For example, do you have a bad temper? Jesus said that when a person gets angry at someone else, he might as well have committed murder. Do you become jealous when you hear of other people's successes or things they've acquired that you don't have?

3. Is there a sin issue in your life that you just can't seem to get away from, no matter how hard you try? Can you accept, at this point in your struggles against sin, that you cannot save yourself? The fact is that one sinner (you) cannot be saved from the consequences of his or her sin by another sinner (you, priest, therapist, guru). What is the only option that remains?

4. Why is Jesus referred to in the New Testament as the "Lamb of God"? To what Old Testament ritual does that term refer? What was the precondition required of the Old Testament sacrificial lamb?

5. When the apostle Paul referred to himself as the worst of all sinners (1 Timothy 1:15), what was he trying to say to his readers? What was he trying, by using himself as example, to get his readers to confront? In what ways are YOU the worst of all sinners?

GETTING TO HEAVEN

3
Hell Is for Real

In September of 1994 media mogul Ted Turner offered these thoughts on life after death to a gathering of journalists who laughed at all the appropriate moments:

> Heaven is going to be a mighty slender place. And most of the people I know in life aren't going to be there. There are a few notable exceptions and I'll miss them. Remember, Heaven is going to be perfect. And I don't really want to be there...Those of us that go to Hell, which will be most of us in this room; most journalists are certainly going there. But, when we get to Hell we'll have a chance to make things better because Hell is supposed to be a mess. And Heaven is perfect. Who wants to go to a place that's perfect? Boring. Boring."

One can reasonably assume that Turner's intent was not to lay out a thoughtful theological perspective on Heaven or Hell. In fact, the flippant nature of his comments indicates a lack of belief in traditional conceptions of either.

Like Turner, many people are confused when it comes to their understanding of Hell. Look in any bookstore or browse Amazon and you'll find a good number of books written by or about people who've been pronounced clinically dead, (supposedly) gone to Heaven, and come back to tell about it. After some time spent perusing these "I went to Heaven and returned to tell the tale" offerings, one can easily get the impression that these folks are competing for who had the most far-out near-death experience. It is interesting, and pertinent to this discussion, to note that only one person has ever written a (rather ludicrous, and perhaps intentionally so) book in which he claimed to have gone to Hell and back.

Heaven is a pleasant subject. It's even suitable for the dinner table or the parlor. But Hell? Not! Besides, no small number of people—including no small number of evangelical Christians—are simply unwilling to believe that such a place exists. The rhetorical question, "How could a loving God send anyone—especially a fundamentally good person—to such a horrible place?" has been asked many, many times. And even if Hell-skeptics reluctantly acknowledge that a supremely horrible place called Hell actually exists, they believe that only the worst of the worst offenders will end up there—Nero, Hitler, Stalin, Charles Manson, Pol Pot, Saddam Hussein, Mao Zedong, Osama bin Laden and other evil-doers of that ilk. Hell-skeptics just can't wrap their brains around the possibility that ostensibly "good" people might end up there as well. They ask: How could a person who's done a lot of good works in his lifetime and is a highly-respected member of the community end up in the same place as Adolph Hitler? Even people who realize that sin is a huge problem and deserves some form of divine judgment are really hoping that God will just overlook their sins—they aren't that big, after all (or so they think)—and let them into Heaven.

"I think," said one such person, "that when St. Peter looks over my entire life, he'll see I've done more good than bad and he'll let me in (to Heaven)."

Unfortunately—and ignoring the error of thinking that St. Peter has the final say in the matter—that's not even close to what the Bible says. It clearly says that one does not get to Heaven by doing good things (the authors will cover this topic in depth in Chapter 5), and if you don't wind up in Heaven, there is only one alternative. The Bible also makes it perfectly clear that Hell is a real place or state of being. It's not myth. (Remember, the Bible is God talking. It is downright dangerous to dismiss anything God says.) Hell is referenced in both the Old and New Testaments. Jesus tells some people, to their high-and-mighty faces, that if they don't change their high-and-mighty ways, they are going to Hell.

The Bible is unequivocal on the subject: Hell is not just a tad uncomfortable. It's *Hell*. What more can be said? But no one really knows precisely what Hell is like. Suffice to say, it's indescribable for a reason.

It is important that the reader understand one thing: You do not want to end up in Hell; you want to end up in Heaven. While the purpose of this book is to show you, the reader, how you can know for certain you're going to Heaven, the path requires understanding some very difficult albeit non-intellectual truths. In the previous chapter you were confronted with one of the most difficult of these truths: to wit, every person ever born was born into a state of sinfulness and no one can solve that problem for themselves. In other words, everyone begins life headed straight down AC/DC's highway to Hell. That is everyone's destiny on day one, right out of the womb. But the news gets worse. If that sinful condition goes uncorrected in a person's life, then that person is going to fulfill his or her day-one-destiny. In this chapter, we're going to work through how the Bible describes those consequences.

The reader may question why we would insert this kind of chapter into our discussion in the first place. Why don't we just get to the point of how to get to Heaven? That would be nice, wouldn't it? Just avoid the unpleasantness altogether. The reality, however, is that the Bible does not avoid the subject of Hell; therefore, the authors cannot avoid it either. Furthermore, it's difficult to provide you the solution to your day-one-destiny if you're not aware of the problem in the first place. Think of it this way: You're on an airplane flying through the great blue yonder at 30,000 feet and suddenly someone offers you a parachute, saying, "You're going to need this."

"Why?" you ask.

"We're going to crash," your benefactor says.

You look around you. No one seems the least bit upset. People are dozing, talking to their seatmates, reading, on their laptops. The plane's ride is and has been smooth. You hear no rattles, no sounds of metal grinding on metal. No alarms are going off. You look out the window and see no smoke pouring off the engine.

"What do you mean?" you ask. "Everything's fine!"

"Trust me," says your good Samaritan. "You need this."

At this point in our hypothetical scenario, you have a choice. Trust and believe...or not. Likewise, the authors are trying to give you a parachute. First, however, we must convince you that your "plane" is going down. Let's face it, you might not even be reading this book if you were one hundred percent certain that your ultimate destination was Heaven. So, let's take a good look at what The Bible says Hell is, and isn't.

SIN AND THE CONSEQUENCE OF DEATH

If you recall, God was very specific with Adam concerning the punishment for violating the one thing he told Adam not to do. God said Adam would die—not *might* die, mind you, but *would* die.

"Die?" Adam probably thought. After all, he had no understanding of death. To add to Adam's likely bewilderment, he did not die right away when he ate of the fruit of the Tree of Knowledge of Good and Evil. He continued to live—physically, that is. But when he ate of the forbidden fruit,[†] when he chose Satan over God, when he rebelled against his Creator, Adam died spiritually. He died "inside." His mate, Eve, had died inside only moments before. She looked no different to Adam, but she had changed in the most fundamental of ways. That condition of spiritual death is the spiritual equivalent of DNA. For some five thousand years, it's been passed down from one generation to the next. Because of Adam and Eve's rebellious choice, every human being born since has been born spiritually dead (except one, but we digress). No longer do human beings enjoy a deep and meaningful one-on-one relationship with God. Adam and Eve's sin severed that relationship and sin keeps it severed today. In order to get to Heaven we need God to bring our original, unsullied spirit back to life. That's why you hear Christians talk about being "born again"—the very language Jesus uses to talk about being made right with God (John 3:3).

Let's review:

1. When you came into the world, you were physically alive but spiritually dead.
2. You were, on day one of your life, headed down the highway to Hell.
3. Jesus Christ is your only hope, your only salvation. Only by trusting Him and surrendering without qualification to His Lordship will the Holy Spirit begin to indwell you and your spiritual being come alive for the first time and for eternity and your sanctification (sin-cleansing) begin. That's what being "born again" means. That's what Jesus freely offers anyone who follows Him.

[†] The popular myth is that the "fruit" in question was an apple. Not so. If it was an apple, God would have said "Don't eat the apples from that apple tree over there." The fact is that no one knows what the fruit in question was, only that it was forbidden.

But if you never receive the gift of life from God through His Son Jesus Christ and you die physically in that life-less state, you will face the worse consequence imaginable—eternal separation from God. The Bible has one word for that state of existence—Hell!

You may wonder how separation from God can be so horrifying, why it's described in The Bible using words such as excruciating, agonizing, tormenting, tortuous, and the like. Up until this point in your life or at some past time in your life, you may have had no relationship with God and, well, that wasn't so bad, or so you think. You weren't (or aren't) in discomfort, much less agony. You know a good number of other people who don't recognize Jesus as their Lord and Savior and they seem to be okay too. They're not constantly down in the dumps and some of them are really good-hearted folks. What's the big deal? Could it be that concerning this Hell business Christians make much ado about something that isn't much of anything at all?

If those are your thoughts, then please, please believe us: The answer to that question is an unequivocal NO. While you are on planet Earth, your needs are earthly. They can be counted on one hand: food, water, air, and protection from the elements. So, you have, count them, four earthly needs and the overwhelming likelihood is that you've never really suffered for lack of any of them at any time in your life. You've been hungry, thirsty, cold, hot, and you've gasped for breath on occasion, but you always knew that your discomfort was temporary. But imagine being hungry and knowing that you're never going to taste food again, that your state of hunger is forever. And then imagine being thirsty and knowing that you're never going to have even a drop of water, ever again—that your state of thirst is forever. And then imagine the same concerning being cold or hot and never being able, ever again, to take a satisfying deep breath. Finally, imagine perpetual hunger, thirst, extreme temperature, and oxygen depletion, together, forever. That analogy is probably as close as one can get to imagining what Hell is like. It's certainly consistent with Jesus' description of Hell as a place where "their worm does not die and the fire is not quenched" (Mark 9:48).

In this life, there is no greater torment imaginable than a state of prolonged separation from the sources of your earthly needs, the things necessary for life. Likewise, torment in the afterlife is a matter of being permanently separated from the Source of Life itself—God. When you die, your earthly, material needs will cease and be replaced by the spiritual need for direct relationship with God. Separation from Him in the afterlife will no doubt be as excruciating as it gets. You won't need food, water, air, or protection from the elements after you die. You will need God, and God only. If you have not yet submitted your life to His Son, there's no time like NOW.

SIN AND ITS CONSEQUENCE

These days, many people regard traditional belief in Heaven and Hell—the latter, especially—as a sign of ignorance, even downright stupidity. Some of the folks in question might concede the possibility of some tranquil state of being after death, akin to the Buddhist concept of Nirvana, where the former person is now "one with the universe," but they probably believe everyone—the good, the bad, and the in-between—enters this transcendent state when they die. The notion of Hell offends their sense of fairness. A place of fire and brimstone akin to painter Hieronymus Bosch's famous representations—replete with horrors of every description—is, as was Bosch, downright medieval. The notion is antiquated; therefore, the notion is absurd.

Among those folks who allow the possibility of Hell being a real place to which some are assigned after death, one finds various levels of belief.

- Some believe in the stereotypical, fire-and-brimstone Hell to which all unsaved sinners are condemned to spend eternity.
- Others think Hell is only for really evil people—serial killers and child molesters, for example—but they have difficulty with a Hell that is also occupied by basically good people who just couldn't wrap their heads around the idea that Jesus was their only means of salvation.
- For some, Hell is a post-mortem reform school, a place for people to get things right after death (e.g. the Catholic notion of Purgatory). At some point, at God's discretion, these folks will suffer enough to earn forgiveness and be taken up to Heaven.

- And some may even think of Hell as a type of a party—thus the popular quip that one would rather party in Hell with sinners than hang out with the saints (i.e. tediously boring and irritatingly self-righteous) in Heaven.

These various positions all have one thing in common: they are based on the thoughts and opinions of people. They do not reflect accurate Biblical teaching. They are not even close to God's word on the subject.

ANNIHILATIONISM

Even among evangelical Christians there are varying positions concerning Hell. One such belief is called annihilationism (an-aye-ill-a'-shun-ism). Adherents to this position believe that when an unsaved sinner dies, his or her life is simply snuffed out like a candle flame. They believe that's what God meant when He told Adam that if he ate from the Tree of Knowledge of Good and Evil, he would "certainly die" (Gen. 2:17). To an annihilationist, references in the Bible to Hell and eternal punishment are merely poetic or symbolic. Certain people may spend a certain amount of time in Hell after which a merciful God will simply erase them and "poof," they'll be gone. Jehovah's Witnesses believe the traditional concept of Hell is merely a hold-over from pagan beliefs. The mainstream annihilationist, however, argues that at his or her physical death the unsaved, unrepentant sinner simply ceases to exist—his consciousness dies along with his body.

The problem with annihilationism is three-fold:

- First, it hardly seems like a fitting form of justice for those who have committed heinous sins. Justice consists of dichotomies, as in good/bad, not guilty/guilty and reward/punishment. Therefore, the opposite of Heaven is not nothing. The opposite of paradise is a place that is the antithesis of paradise.
- Second, annihilationism flies in the face of passages in the Bible where the promise of an eternal reward is placed alongside warnings of eternal punishment (Matt 25:14-30, 46; John 5:28-29; Rom 2:7-8).

- Third, annihilationism is based on the red-herring argument that a truly loving, just and merciful God would never create and assign a person to a place of eternal suffering just because he did not accept Jesus as his Lord and Savior. But that is no more valid than the notion that a truly loving and merciful God would not allow evil and suffering to exist and affect all people, good and bad (an argument often raised in defense of atheism).
- Fourth, according to the New Testament, Christ Jesus suffered horrible torment on The Cross in order to pay the price for mankind's sinfulness. That clearly means that the price of unrepentant sin is horrible torment, as in Hell.

In the final analysis, annihilationism consists of an appeal to sentiment that distracts from the real issue, which is simply what the Bible says and does not say about Hell. The pertinent question becomes, "Why would God, in His inerrant Word, say that Hell exists if Hell does not exist?"

PURGATORY

Annihilationism is not the only doctrine concerning Hell that does not enjoy even one shred of biblical support. According to official Roman Catholic doctrine, Hell is a very real place in which lost souls will suffer eternal punishment of an unspecified nature. But Roman Catholic theology also allows for Purgatory, which is a sort of "Little Hell" where certain individuals will have the opportunity to atone for sins they did not repent of in this life. Purgatory provides final sin-cleansing to make one ready to enter into God's presence. Catholics also believe that a deceased person's friends and relatives can accelerate this final cleansing process through fervent prayer (asking Jesus' mother Mary and/or other Catholic "saints" for intercession). Such a position, however, is impossible to square with a straight reading of Scripture and seems to suggest a type of "second chance" after death about which The Bible says nothing. The notion of Purgatory also means Christ Jesus' atoning sacrifice on the Cross was not sufficient for mankind's salvation—it was close, but not quite close enough.

Obviously, the concept of a Hell of eternal damnation and suffering is uncomfortable for some folks. It doesn't fit nicely with the orthodox Christian belief that God is full of mercy and grace. It is a troubling concept that begets questions the authors cannot answer with absolute certainty. Although some theologians claim certitude, no one really knows what Hell means or its actual characteristics. The only certainty is that The Bible speaks of such a place in rather vivid language. The doctrine of Hell reminds us that our choices in this life have potentially serious, lasting ramifications in the next. If everyone, no matter their life-choices, went to Heaven, this entire discussion would be moot; there would be no purpose to a book of this sort. But that is not what The Bible teaches, and ultimately that would mean God wasn't both loving *and* righteous, a God who dispenses not just mercy and grace, but justice as well.

Let's turn our attention at this point to what The Bible—God's Word—says about Hell.

THE BIBLE TELLS US SO

The Bible uses three words that are either translated as "Hell" or thought to be references to Hell. Two of these words, Sheol and Hades, are used to refer to death, the grave, or the place of the dead. However, certain references to the afterlife obviously refer to a state of eternal exile from the holy presence of God. The psalmist declares, for example, "But God will redeem my soul from the power of Sheol" (Psalm 49:15). Elsewhere in Psalms, a song of hope is offered: "For Your lovingkindness toward me is great, And You have delivered my soul from the depths of Sheol" (86:13). Then there's Psalm 16:10: "For you will not abandon my soul to Sheol." Obviously, Sheol, also known as Hell, is not a desirable place.

In the New Testament, the words "Hades" and Gehenna are used as references to an afterlife of pain and suffering. Jesus makes several significant references to both. Interestingly, Gehenna was an actual location just outside the walls of ancient Jerusalem that was essentially a garbage dump containing not only refuse but also the bodies of certain animals and people too poor to afford a proper burial. To keep the accumulation of garbage under control and the stench from becoming overwhelming, fires burned day and night. Because it was an unclean place of death, decay, and constant burning, Gehenna was the quintessential metaphor for Hell. Some theologians argue, however, that when Jesus speaks of Gehenna He's not referring to an actual place of eternal suffering. And yet a comprehensive overview of the term's use in Scripture supports the contention that it does indeed refer to a place of eternal judgment for the wicked. For example, Jesus' use of the Hebrew word Gehenna in Mark's Gospel translates as Hell (9:47-48). He then strings together quotes from Isaiah and Jeremiah to describe it as the place where "their worm does not die, and the fire is not quenched." Jesus is obviously describing a place of perpetual suffering in the afterlife.

The above passage is but one of many instances where Jesus refers to Hell as a real place. In fact, no biblical character—prophet or otherwise—talks more about Hell than Jesus. That may shock some folks, especially those who think Jesus goes around with a perpetual beatific expression promoting love and peace, blessing little children and healing the sick. The reality is that in His day Jesus was a confrontational, controversial, and quite unsettling figure. Yes, He was the paragon of love and charity, but He also turned over the tables moneychangers had set up on Temple (holy) ground, told people discomforting truths about themselves, and gave his audiences vivid and discomforting descriptions of Hell.

Jesus' most graphic teaching on the subject is found in the parable of the rich man and Lazarus (Luke 16:19-30). Of Jesus' approximately thirty-three parables—scholars do not agree on the actual number—most are relatively simple stories that refer, metaphorically, to spiritual principles. The only parable in which Jesus refers to His characters by name involves a beggar named Lazarus and the patriarch Abraham (in a minor role). It is unlikely that Jesus would have used proper names arbitrarily, which leads some theologians to posit that this little story may be true.

As the scene opens (Luke 16), Jesus is preaching on the sins of wealthy individuals who pursue money as an idol. He tells his audience, which includes a group of wealthy Pharisees, "No one can serve two masters...You cannot serve both God and money" (v. 13). He then begins telling the story of an unnamed rich man and the beggar Lazarus.

The rich man enjoys the good life: a large and richly-appointed home in a highly desirable location, finely-woven clothes, slaves, and so on. Lazarus, a filthy, diseased beggar, sits at the rich man's gate, perpetually hungry and sick. Lazarus hopes for nothing more than the crumbs and leftovers that fall from the rich man's table. Suddenly the scene fast-forwards. Both men have died. Lazarus, the beggar, ends up in Heaven at "Abraham's side." The rich man, on the other hand, is sentenced to Hades. He's in torment and pleading for relief. He is also acutely aware that Lazarus is in Heaven. He even tries to speak to some of Heaven's residents. In other words, Jesus portrays Hell's denizens as being acutely aware that they now exist outside of the manifest presence of God.

Some argue—annihilationists, for example—that Jesus is simply retelling a Jewish fable that would have been familiar to his audience; that He did not intend for people to take literally the story or its reference to Hell. This explanation—what is referred to as an *argument from a conclusion*—simply doesn't add up. First, no such story in Judaic folklore has ever been identified. Its existence is therefore nothing more than speculative. Second, if Hell is not a real place, then Jesus is engaging in deceptive hyperbole—akin to a parent who uses a made-up story about ghosts and monsters to frighten a child into obedience. Given Jesus' claim to being "the Truth," that is simply preposterous. Jesus is God Incarnate. God is incapable of deception; therefore, so is Jesus. Third, even accepting for the moment that Jesus did use elements from a story already familiar to a Jewish audience; that does not mean He was engaging in mere story-telling. Folks who want to believe that Jesus was not referring to a real place called Hades are making the mistake of reasoning from their previously-held conviction that Hell is a fiction. They cannot accept that a just and merciful God would consign unsaved souls (especially "good" souls) to a place of eternal torment; therefore, they reason that Jesus's story of Lazarus and the rich man is nothing more than a metaphor—for what and for what purpose, however, remain a mystery. The authors, along with an overwhelming majority of orthodox New Testament scholars, maintain that the only sensible take on Jesus' description of the rich man's afterlife experience is that it is dead-on, no pun intended.

With this disturbing story, Jesus makes two powerful points, the first of which concerns the wickedness of self-possessed and wealthy people. During his life, the unnamed rich man enjoyed God's blessings (without recognizing from whence they came). His wealth and social prestige were idols that blinded him to the plight of those less fortunate, those whom he could and should have helped. To him, they were no more significant than the ants he stepped on walking from his villa to the Temple. To the rich man, Lazarus is despicable. To Jesus, however, it is the rich man who is despicable.

Jesus' second point concerns the eternal consequences of such a lifestyle: to wit, when they die and pass from this life to the next, the greedy money-worshippers of this world will receive their just deserts. Ironically, Lazarus is now in Paradise while the rich man has exchanged his paradise-on-earth for the eternal longing and suffering of Hell which, Jesus makes perfectly clear, is a place of unrelenting agony. Jesus says the rich man is in "torment." He pleads for just one drop of water because he is in "anguish in this flame." In other words, there is no respite from Hell's tortures.

Jesus' story of the rich man and Lazarus also tells us that Hell is forever and inescapable. God offers no Hellish equivalent to Monopoly's "Get Out of Jail Free" card. Abraham tells the rich man that between Heaven and Hell there is "a great chasm" that "has been fixed." In other words, there is no possibility that those dwelling in Hell can cross over to the other side. Hell is all there is ever again going to be for its inhabitants. The slow dawning of realization that the torment is forever, inescapable, is perhaps Hell's most unbearable aspect.

In this story, Jesus' description of Hell is consistent with remarks of His found elsewhere in the Gospels. Hell is, Jesus says

- a place of "unquenchable fire" (Mark 9:43)
- a "furnace of fire" and a place of "wailing and gnashing of teeth" (Matthew 13:40-42)
- a place of "eternal fire prepared for the devil and his angels" (while making it clear that this is also where the "accursed" of the earth are headed) (Matthew 25:41)
- "eternal punishment" (Matthew 25:46)

Those who want to insist that Heaven is eternal while Jesus' references to Hell in the Gospels are merely metaphorical must answer the following two questions:

1. If Jesus' descriptions of Hell do not pertain to a real place, then why does He describe this supposedly fictional place in such vivid terms?

2. If Hell is not a place of torment and eternal punishment where the accursed of the earth are headed, then what is Jesus' purpose in saying that it is?

One other Scripture passage worth considering comes later in the New Testament. The apostle Paul, in his second letter to the church in Thessalonica, comments on those "who do not know God" and "do not obey the Gospel of our Lord Jesus Christ" (2 Thessalonians 1:8). He says, "These shall be punished with everlasting destruction from the presence of the Lord and from the glory of His power" (1:9). In this context, the Greek word meaning "destruction" does not speak to soul-annihilation. Instead, it means "ruin" and implies the permanent loss of everything that makes life worth living. Note also that Paul says the people in question will be "punished." Punishment is not an abstraction; rather, it is a conscious, tangible experience. One who is no longer conscious, who no longer even exists in any sense of the term (i.e. has been annihilated) is not being punished. He is experiencing nothing. He simply isn't, period. Rather than affirming some form of annihilationism, this verse reinforces the meaning of the story of the rich man and Lazarus. Paul describes a time after life on this earth where non-believers will face eternal consequences for their sin.

The bottom line is this: If the Bible's representation of Hell is not truthful, then one can begin to question the validity, the truth, of anything and everything The Bible says.

GOD'S LOVE, MERCY, AND JUSTICE

Some people just can't accept that a just and merciful God could be so unforgiving. Some folks are even convinced that someone who takes Jesus at His word and believes in an afterlife of unrelenting torment of every description must be mean-spirited by nature and certainly lacking in the smarts department.

How, they rhetorically ask, can a loving, merciful God condemn to the same horrific fate both a monster like Hitler and, say, an atheist who is a caring employer, a doting family man, and gives millions of dollars every year to worthy causes? The error in this reasoning is the assumption that God's justice should reflect man's justice. In effect, they reverse the fifth line of the Lord's Prayer—they believe that *as it is on earth, so it should be in Heaven*. On earth, the punishment is matched with the crime; therefore, God should do the same.

But a God who graded crimes on a scale of one to one hundred and matched each crime to an equivalent punishment would be a very arbitrary God indeed. That would also require a Hell that consisted of one hundred floors, each one less punitive than the one before, the second-to-the-last floor being almost like Heaven but without the same quality food perhaps, or not as many palm trees, or palm trees that only produce the occasional coconut. No, God is anything but arbitrary and capricious. Whether one goes to Heaven or Hell is definitely not a matter of tallying up the number of happy faces a person has earned for doing good stuff and then deducting the number of frowny faces received for bad stuff. God gives us one choice and *one choice alone*: either one accepts His Son Jesus as his Lord and Savior and surrenders his life to Him, or not. A person says either "yes" or "no" to Jesus. As Jesus told his disciples during the Sermon on the Mount, there is nothing righteous "between" yes and no—no sorta-kinda, maybe, or sometimes (Matt. 5:37). For those who accept His Son (say yes), there is eternal reward; for those who refuse to do so (say no), there is eternal punishment. That is, in fact, the all-time purest, most perfect example of justice.

The Hell-is-inconsistent-with-a-God-of-love argument, furthermore, assumes that we mortals possess the ability to accurately recognize and evaluate sin. But the concept of sin is of God's authorship; therefore, whether something is or is not a sin is something only God determines. The first sin is recorded in Genesis, Chapter 3. Adam and Eve ate something God told them not to eat. How is that a sin? But the fact that someone might think that sneaking a certain food doesn't sound like a big deal is irrelevant. The issue was disobedience, not the nature of the rule Adam and Eve disobeyed. God might just as well have told them they were not to venture beyond a certain point on a path in the Garden of Eden. Had they done so, the consequences to them—and us—would have been the same. As further indication that only God can define sin, the word *sin* was first used by God in Genesis 4 where He warns Cain that "sin is crouching at the door," wanting to ensnare him (4:7). Where sin is concerned, God and only God has the final say, not us. We do not possess the ability to know how grievous our sins are to Him. Most of the time, because it comes *naturally* to us, we do not even recognize sin in ourselves. Because only God can determine sin, only God can decide what is just punishment for sin. *Therefore, if a perfectly just God has decreed that eternal torment is the just punishment for one's sins then eternal torment is perfectly just, period. End of argument.*

This position can be defended by examining what The Bible tells us about sin. When we talk about sin we're not talking about some minor mistake or lapse in judgment. As noted in the previous chapter, The Bible describes people who insist upon living in denial of and rebellion against God even when creation and their senses give unmistakable evidence of Him (see Romans 1). In other words, human beings are totally and utterly warped in their depraved sin condition. Because we are not capable of seeing ourselves from God's perspective, we cannot fathom the depth of our depravity, how egregious our sinful condition is to Him. We do not have the capacity to understand the evil behind just one sin from God's perspective. The best example of this would be the consequences brought to bear on Adam and Eve and the entire human race with just one sin. For one seemingly innocuous act (from a certain perspective, no more egregious, perhaps, than a toddler disobeying his mother and pilfering a cookie from the cookie jar), Adam and Eve were expelled from Paradise, no longer to enjoy unimpeded fellowship with God. They also faced the curses of painful childbirth and the need to work inhospitable ground to scratch out a meager existence. And to top it off, Adam and Eve now had to confront the reality of death. All that for but one sin! (In fact, eating of the Tree of Knowledge of Good and Evil was not just "a" sin or "one" sin—it was THE BIGGEST SIN POSSIBLE because in so doing, Adam and Eve chose Satan over God, rebellion over obedience, relativism over truth. It's been downhill ever since.)

But God has thrown us a lifeline and given us a choice: Grab hold of it and live forever with him in a Paradise that is beyond our comprehension, or refuse to take it and live forever in an agonizing state of exile that is beyond our comprehension. When all is said and done, it all comes down to yes or no.

CONCLUSION

There's one other truth about Hell that for the purposes of this book is the most important truth of them all. Furthermore, it's a very positive and happy truth about Hell: *You don't have to end up there*. The reader holds in his or her hand a message of hope. God has provided you with the means of attaining eternal life with Him in Heaven. If you want to know what that is then stay with us!

RECOMMENDED FOR FURTHER READING

- Edwards, Jonathan. "Sinners in the Hands of an Angry God." Sermon preached on July 8, 1741 at The Church of Christ in Enfield, CT. DigitalCommons@UniversityofNebraska-Lincoln. http://digitalcommons.unl.edu/cgi/viewcontent.cgi?article=1053&context=etas

- Fudge, Edward William and Peterson, Robert A. *Two Views of Hell: A Biblical and Theological Dialogue* (Intervarsity Press)

- Peterson, Robert A. *Hell on Trial: The Case for Eternal Punishment|*

- Morgan, Christopher and Peterson, Robert A. (eds.) *Hell Under Fire: Modern Scholarship Reinvents Eternal Punishment.*

- Ramsey, Thor. *The Most Encouraging Book on Hell Ever.* Cruciform Press, 2014.

- Donnelly, Edward. *Heaven and Hell.* Banner of Truth, 2012.

QUESTIONS FOR PERSONAL REFLECTION AND DISCUSSION

1. Given that many people today prefer to believe in Heaven but reject the notion of Hell, what are the ramifications of such a position? What would be some reasons why the reality of Hell would be an important doctrine to uphold?
2. What are the main objections to the doctrine of Hell? Are those objections valid? Why or why not?
3. Some people suggest that Hell is incompatible with God's love. Are there any attributes or qualities about God that are compromised if Hell does not exist? If so, what are they?
4. Are there attributes or qualities of God that are compromised if Hell as described in The Bible does exist? If so, what?
5. Knowing what we know about Hell, why would anyone consciously choose Hell over Heaven?
6. Since so many Christian teachers are denying the existence of a literal Hell, is belief or non-belief inconsequential? Is consensus a reliable means by which we can determine the truth of an idea?

4

The One-and-Only Way, Truth, and Life

In the preceding three chapters, the authors established that:

- God exists, created the universe and everything within it, and is all-powerful (omnipotent) and all-knowing (omniscient).
- We humans, created by God for relationship with Him, corrupted ourselves right off the proverbial bat, thus requiring God to deny us the Tree of Life by putting us into a state of exile from the paradise of Eden, a state of exile in which we have languished for some 5000 years.
- We cannot cure our own sinful nature, which is indeed "original"—as in, going back to the very beginning. In other words, because we have stained and continue to stain ourselves with sin, we cannot save ourselves from sin's consequence—Hell. Therefore, to regain eternal life and restore relationship with God, we require a Savior, a sinless mediator-redeemer who will take our sin and pay the penalty we are incapable of paying on our own.

The choice every person faces, whether he faces it consciously or not, is simply this: Is Jesus that Savior and if so, how so? Concerning this issue, there is no maybe, no grey, no relativistic middle ground on which to stand (an example being the postmodern contention that Jesus was one of many so-called "Christs"—including Buddha and Muhammed—that have appeared throughout history). In fact, the answer "maybe" is equivalent to no, as is seeking any other politically-correct middle ground.

Buckle your seatbelts because we're headed into some very turbulent subject matter, stuff that has, as Jesus Himself said it would, divided many families and ended many friendships. Up until now, your understanding of who Jesus was may correspond to the image found in many Christian churches of an immaculately bearded, white-robed fellow holding a shepherd's staff in his left hand while blessing a group of children with his right. But the Jesus we all need to contend with is the Jesus who spoke these words to his disciples:

> Do not think that I have come to bring peace to the earth. I have not come to bring peace, but a sword. For I have come to set a man against his father, and a daughter against her mother, and a daughter-in-law against her mother-in-law. And a person's enemies will be those of his own household. Whoever loves father or mother more than me is not worthy of me, and whoever loves son or daughter more than me is not worthy of me. And whoever does not take his cross and follow me is not worthy of me. Whoever finds his life will lose it, and whoever loses his life for my sake will find it. (Matthew 10:34-39)

Yes, Jesus was a peacemaker, healer, and insightful spiritual teacher, but He was also the most controversial and intimidating figure of His time. Furthermore, He is without doubt the most controversial and intimidating figure of *all* time. Orthodox Christianity is founded on the most outrageous claim ever made: that some 2000 years ago, in what is now Israel, God descended to Earth and became a man named Jesus who willingly sacrificed His life in order to save *you*, dear reader, from the most horrible fate imaginable—Hell.

THE LAMB OF GOD

To put what it means that God/Jesus gave His life for you into perspective, consider the following hypothetical scenario: You are a solder hunkered down in a foxhole with another soldier whom you hardly know. A ferocious battle is raging all around your small refuge. Bullets are whizzing through the air just above your heads, artillery shells are bursting all around, and above the din you can hear the despairing cries and agonizing screams of the wounded and dying. Your fear is palpable. All you can think of is surviving this hell-on-earth and going home. Suddenly, a hand grenade falls into the foxhole. You and your comrade look at it, then look at one another with panic-stricken expressions. As your mind goes blank and your body freezes in horror, your fellow soldier throws himself on the grenade just as it goes off, protecting you from the blast. His body convulses, then goes perfectly still. You crouch down into a fetal position, shaking, disbelieving, unable to think about anything but the fact that you're still alive because of a young man about whom you knew nothing except his rank and name. When the battle is over and the shock of what happened in that foxhole begins to settle in, you experience an incredible upwelling of gratitude toward the stranger who purposefully sacrificed his life so that you might survive. You begin to tell everyone who will listen. You visit his family and thank them for raising such an incredibly humble human being. Later in your life, you establish a university scholarship in his name.

In that hypothetical story, your fellow soldier saved your life, but he did not, could not, save you from *death* itself. You're still going to die someday, right? You may be surprised to learn that the correct answer to that question is maybe yes and maybe no. And that, right there, is where Jesus comes in. Two thousand years ago, Jesus willingly suffered the most agonizing execution ever devised so that you can live forever with Him in Heaven. That—eternal life—is what it means to say that Jesus is your LORD and Savior.

If that is in fact true, then consider: In the hypothetical story, your gratitude toward the soldier for his sacrifice is immense. But he only made it possible for you to live a *longer* life. As incredible as it may sound, Christ Jesus offers you respite, pardon from death itself. He has made it possible for you to live forever in an indescribable state of happiness and joy. How much gratitude, then, do you owe to Him?

The question thus becomes: Why should you believe that Jesus is your LORD and Savior? You certainly should *not* believe simply because we, the authors, believe it and want you to do likewise. You should begin your Christian journey from a position of skepticism. You should want, even demand, proof—irrefutable evidence. And if the authors cannot provide such evidence, then you should not go on reading this book. It's as simple as that.

In fact, and contrary to what secular spokespersons want you to believe, compelling evidence that Jesus was, as He Himself said, God-in-person, the promised Jewish Messiah, and Savior of mankind does in fact exist. But Jesus didn't just *say* those things; He *proved* them to be true, and the proof is undeniable. Make no mistake, there are plenty of folks who deny the proof, who say that the evidence in question is myth, hearsay, wouldn't hold up in a court of law, and appeals only to simple-minded people who, like children, believe in fairy tales. You can take this to the bank: Those nay-sayers have not examined the evidence dispassionately, if they have examined it at all. That's indisputable because an impartial, intellectually-honest consideration of the evidence leads but to one rational conclusion: Jesus was who He said He was. (That describes, by the way, the very process that led author John Rosemond to belief. A skeptic by disposition, he dispassionately examined the evidence both pro and con and became a committed believer. A desire to share that experience led to the writing of this book.)

The evidence consists of (a) prophetic Old Testament passages concerning the Messiah that Jesus fulfilled to the letter, (b) startling claims He made concerning who He was, (c) numerous remarkable miracles He performed that were witnessed and attested to by many, and last but certainly not least, (d) His resurrection from death, attested to by hundreds if not thousands of reliable witnesses.

NOT A NEAT AND TIDY MESSIAH

Two thousand years ago, Jesus caused a schism in First-Century Judaism. From the beginning of His ministry (circa 30 – 33 A.D.), He threatened the two most powerful elements of the Jewish establishment, the Pharisees and Sadducees—the groups that made up the priestly, judicial, and political classes. The controversy concerned the concept of the Messiah—literally, the Anointed One—a deliverer (Savior) whom God had promised to the Jewish people. Jesus, to the consternation of the elites, was performing public miracles and generally conducting Himself in a manner consistent with messianic prophecy, causing rumors to fly that He was, in fact, the Promised One of prophetic writings such as found in the Old Testament Books of Isaiah and Zachariah. The problem was that Jesus was not of noble birth, as many—especially the Pharisees and other Jewish elites—expected. Rather, He was low-born; essentially a nobody who'd come out of nowhere and almost instantly attained celebrity status among the common folk. None of His disciples were people of rank and there's no indication that anyone of status—at first, at least—thought Jesus was anything other than a fraud, and a heretical, blaspheming fraud to boot! The elites were also afraid that Jesus would become popular enough to lead a revolt against Roman rule and in so doing not only threaten their status but also bring about the destruction of Jerusalem, Jewish culture, and perhaps even Judaism itself by the invincible Roman legions.

Two thousand years have passed and Jesus is still a source of bitter controversy among Jews. To begin with, persons of the Jewish faith argue that only seminary-trained rabbis are qualified to properly interpret what Christians refer to as the Old Testament. According to orthodox rabbinic interpretations, Jesus does not satisfy messianic criteria. But concerning this issue, rabbis are and have been for some 2000 years committing the common error of reasoning from a foregone conclusion. They begin with the doctrinaire conviction that Jesus was *not* the Messiah and then look for historical and Old Testament evidence that would support that supposition. And seeking, they find, as flimsy as the evidence may be.

A prime example of this is *Twenty-Six Reasons Why Jews Don't Believe in Jesus*, written by attorney and self-defined Old Testament scholar Asher Norman. In Norman's book, facts and timelines are modified and the New Testament is consistently misquoted and misinterpreted to suit Norman's purpose, which is to completely discredit the Jewish Messianic movement that combines Christianity—most importantly, the belief that Jesus is the Messiah—with elements of Judaism and Jewish tradition (e.g. messianictimes.com). Norman is obviously relying on his Jewish readers' credulity when it comes to the New Testament. For example, despite the fact that First-Century Jewish historian Josephus refers to Jesus, His crucifixion and resurrection; despite the fact that people who witnessed Jesus' many miracles were still alive when the Gospels were written and would have protested if the accounts were not accurate, much less cut from whole cloth, Norman casts doubt on Jesus' existence and is adamant that the Resurrection is a fable. Anyone who relies on Norman's "scholarship" is being led astray, but his book is a testament to the threat Jesus continues to pose to the Jewish establishment even though two millennia have passed since He walked the dusty roads of Judea.

I (JR) have spoken to Orthodox Jews about Jesus, trying to persuade them to at least look at the evidence dispassionately. It is, I've discovered, a very difficult thing for them to do. Jesus evoked strong emotional reactions among the Jewish elite 2000 years ago, and He continues to do so today. One Orthodox Jew told me, with a straight face, that Jesus was anti-Semitic. That's an indication of the power of the emotions (and collective brain-washing) in question. When I asked for an explanation of that rather perplexing idea, I honestly could not make heads nor tails of the individual's reasoning, and the person in question is intelligent and generally logical.

There is no doubt but that Jesus was a real, flesh-and-blood historical figure. There is no doubt but that He was Jewish. His disciples were Jews. With rare exception, the common people who followed Him during his ministry were Jews. Until Paul began spreading the Gospel throughout the Middle East and into southern Europe, most of the first Christians were Jewish. Furthermore, said Jewish Christians absolutely believed Jesus was the Messiah. Most of the hundreds of believers upon whom the Holy Spirit descended at the Feast of Pentecost, fifty days after Jesus' crucifixion, were Jews (Acts 2:1 – 31).

The Jewish elites of Jesus' day expected a Messiah who was noble-born, even though the prophets clearly said He would be of unremarkable birth. The elites expected a priest-warrior Messiah who, like Moses did in Egypt, would lead them out of bondage (in this case, to Rome). Most of all, however, the Pharisees and Sadducees wanted a Messiah they could control or at least bargain with; a neat and tidy establishment-friendly Messiah who wouldn't do anything to threaten their prestige and power. The Messiah they got just didn't fit the bill. Not only wouldn't He play their hypocritical games, but His popularity diminished their influence. So, as the Gospels tell us, the Jewish establishment began conspiring early on in Jesus' ministry to have Him arrested and executed by the Roman authorities.

It has become politically-incorrect to assert that the upper crust of Jerusalem's Jewish community was responsible for Jesus' execution, but to arrive at any other conclusion requires a twisting and denial of facts. Were it not for the Pharisees' and Sadducees' agitated accusations, it is highly unlikely that the Roman authorities would ever have arrested Jesus and put Him to death. So we encounter a paradox: A privileged group of First-century Palestinian Jews were definitely responsible for Jesus' death—albeit they cleverly arranged matters such that Roman prefect (governor) Pontius Pilate actually sentenced Him to die and Roman soldiers carried out His execution—and yet all of Jesus' disciples and nearly all of the first Christians were Jews. So, and to be very specific, significant responsibility for Jesus' death falls at the feet of Jews, but only a small minority, not all Jews, and certainly not all Jews since. Furthermore, when all is said and done, one must keep in mind that God took human form for the specific purpose of making himself a sacrifice for *mankind's* sins. From that perspective, the Pharisees, Sadducees, and Romans were mere actors in a Divine production.

MESSIAH OR MESHUGGENEH?

Jesus clearly said that He was the Promised One, the Messiah, the fulfillment of the law and the prophets, equal to and one with God. In fact, He made those claims on numerous occasions, making sure no one misunderstood (nonetheless, they did). But a good number of nutcases and narcissists before Him had made similar claims (as have a good number of nutcases and narcissists since). How, then, can one separate wheat from chaff on this point? And by the way, if you are still skeptical, you have every right to be. After all, not even Jesus' disciples knew for sure that He was the Messiah, the Christ, God Incarnate, God's One and Only Son, until He appeared to and spent time with them on numerous occasions after His resurrection in a fully-healed body (having suffered, just days before, prolonged beatings with iron-tipped whips followed by the most physically agonizing and horrifying form of execution ever devised). When Jesus appeared to the disciples after His resurrection, the disciple Thomas was unable to believe his eyes until he had probed Jesus' healed wounds with his fingers to make sure he was not suffering from an extreme case of wishful thinking.

Consider also that after Jesus' crucifixion and prior to His first post-resurrection appearance to His disciples, they were in hiding, trying to figure out what to do now that their Master was apparently dead. For good reason, they feared for their lives. Suddenly, Jesus appeared amongst them (having walked through either a locked door or a solid wall, thus demonstrating his complete command of space and time—something only God can do).

Concerning that and subsequent encounters, all of which are recorded in the New Testament Gospels, some have argued that the disciples were experiencing group hallucinations. That's a fanciful theory, and has instant appeal to those who do not want to accept the evidence. The problem with that theory is that there is no such thing as a *group* hallucination. Hallucinations are highly personal, individual experiences. So, for example, if two people in the same room at the same time are both hallucinating, they are not hallucinating the same thing, even if they are identical twins. It follows that a group of people who all agree as to the specific content of a supposed "hallucination" (in this case, the eleven remaining disciples) are most definitely *not* hallucinating. They are confirming and giving absolute proof of what they are all simultaneously seeing and experiencing. After Jesus' first two post-resurrection appearances (which took place within days of one another), the disciples came out of hiding and began publicly testifying to the risen LORD, thus putting their lives at grave risk. In fact, all but one or two of them were eventually put to death by various means for their bold public evangelizing. People do not willingly put their lives on the line for anything less than what they are absolutely convinced is the truth, the whole truth, and nothing but the truth. That is, after all, what Jesus himself claimed: "I am the Way, the Truth, and the Life" (John 14:6).

What was it about Jesus that was so convincing to these first believers (and which should convince you!). What was it that caused thousands of First-Century Jews to suddenly and joyfully reject much of what they had been taught since childhood, alienate their families, provoke the religious leaders of the day, provoke the Roman authorities, and invite execution by stoning or crucifixion in the process? Such boldness speaks to irrefutable evidence. What was it?

First, Jesus plainly said He was the Messiah. Once He began His public ministry (circa 29 A.D.), Jesus wasted no time making His identity known. He knew that, after all, time was of the essence. The first occasion upon which Jesus revealed that He was the Promised One is recorded in the Gospel of Luke. As Jesus was ministering in His home town of Nazareth He went to the synagogue he had attended as a youth. The rabbi honored

Jesus' homecoming by asking him to read from Scripture, a customary aspect of Jewish Sabbath worship. Jesus chose verses from the Book of Isaiah that prophesied the coming of the Messiah. Jesus had already made a name for Himself by performing miracles and teaching with authority and Luke tells us that "the eyes of all who were in the synagogue were fixed on Him (4:20)." In other words, the atmosphere was charged with anticipation. When He completed the reading, Jesus looked up and declared, "Today this Scripture is fulfilled in your hearing (v. 21)." There was no misunderstanding His words. Jesus was identifying Himself as the Messiah. This was the worst of heresies, punishable by death!

The indignant congregation rose to their feet, forced Jesus out of the synagogue and tried to throw Him off a nearby cliff. Demonstrating His mastery of the physics of space and time, Jesus made Himself momentarily invisible (or so the reader is led to conclude), walked through the angry crowd, and then, once He was safely beyond their reach, made himself visible again and walked calmly away (Luke 4:28 – 30). At that point, the lynch mob was too stunned to come after Him. Nonetheless, the congregation's reaction to Jesus' bold assertion was a sure sign He'd hit a nerve—the Biggest Nerve possible, in fact.

Other recorded occasions upon which Jesus proclaimed that He was the Messiah, Christ, God Himself in the flesh, include:

- Jesus asks His disciples "Who do you think I am" and Peter answers "You are the Christ, the Son of the Living God," Jesus says, "Blessed are you, Simon Bar-Jonah! For flesh and blood has not revealed this to you, but my Father who is in heaven" (Matthew 16:16).
- The disciple John, an eyewitness, records an exchange between Jesus and His disciples in which Jesus has just told them that He is soon going to leave them but will return someday to take them with Him. He tells them that they already know where He is going and how to get there (but simply refuse to accept the full implications of what they have seen and heard). When Thomas expresses puzzlement Jesus says, "I am the Way, and the Truth, and the Life. No one comes to the Father except through me. If you had known me, you would have known my Father also. From now on you do

know Him and have seen Him" (John 14:6 – 7). History records no bolder statement.[†]
- During one public discourse that begins with John the Baptist's disciples asking Him if He is the Messiah, Jesus says, "All things have been handed over to me by my Father, and no one knows the Son except the Father, and no one knows the Father except the Son and anyone to whom the Son chooses to reveal him" (Matt: 11:27).
- While addressing a group of people, including some Pharisees, who had gathered to hear Him teach, Jesus tells them that He is "the door of the sheep." When some folks complain that they don't know what He is talking about, Jesus replies, "I am the door. If anyone enters by me, he will be saved and will go in and out and find pasture" (John 10:7 and 10:9).
- After Jesus' arrest, Pontius Pilate asks Him if He is the King of the Jews. Jesus answers, "My kingdom is not of this world. If my kingdom were of this world, my servants would have been fighting, that I might not be delivered over to the Jews. But my kingdom is not from the world" (John 18:36).

In each of these passages, Jesus unequivocally affirms that He is God, that He is the Messiah, Savior of the world, that His kingdom is Heaven and that it is through Him and Him alone that one obtains salvation. Jews like Asher Norman prefer to believe that if Jesus was even an actual historical figure (which Norman seriously doubts), statements such as these clearly indicate that Jesus was either crazy as a loon—in Yiddish (a Hebrew dialect spoken by European Jews prior to World War II), "meshuggeneh"— or a manipulative sociopath. Indeed, those are two explanations, but there is a third. As Oxford professor and Christian author C.S. Lewis famously put it, Jesus is either a lunatic, a liar, or He is our LORD.

One of the most well-known people in America and even the world is Oprah Winfrey. Since the mid-1980s, Oprah has been a shaper of popular opinion. Her imprimatur turns otherwise banal books into best-sellers, for

---

[†] Please note that Jesus is being unequivocal and absolute. Contrary to prevailing political correctness, Jesus is saying He is the ONLY means by which one can become reunited with God the Father in Heaven. In other words, a religion, sect, or denomination that teaches otherwise is wrong, false, an impostor.

example. On one of her television shows, Oprah responded to a person in her audience who boldly proclaims Jesus to be the One and Only Way to Salvation (as He Himself asserted) by saying, with a somewhat bemused expression, "That makes no sense." Indeed, it makes no sense to people who are desperate to believe about themselves and have everyone else believe that they are open-minded, non-judgmental, and everything else held up by the world as right and proper. Oprah can't bring herself to say Jesus was either a lunatic or a liar—that would be closed-minded and judgmental. She believes in the relativistic notion that one religion is as good as any other. If, and only if, there is a God, one can get to Him on any spiritual path one chooses. A nice idea, for sure. There's even a name for it: universalism. But the reader can be assured: not all food is equally healthy and not all beliefs are equally valid.

When the full body of evidence is considered, neither Jesus the lunatic nor Jesus the liar makes any sense. If He was merely projecting delusions of grandeur, He was a raging narcissist. If He was a cunning, manipulative liar, then He was, again, a raging narcissist. But narcissists are not capable of self-denial, much less self-sacrifice, to the complete benefit of others. Everything—every *single* thing—Jesus did during His three-year ministry, He did for others, not Himself. He even told some of those He had healed not to tell anyone. On more than one occasion, He told His disciples that He was going to be killed, yet He did nothing to prevent His arrest, knowing full well what lay ahead.

Some contemporary secularists are fond of saying that the Dalai Lama and Jesus are pretty much the same—as in, nothing more than great moral teachers. That both of them are moral teachers is true, but that is where the comparison ends. Their differences far exceed their similarities, but perhaps their greatest difference concerns the fact that when the Dalai Lama heard that he was about to be arrested, he took off running for his life. When Jesus knew that His arrest was imminent, He stayed put and did nothing to prevent His whereabouts from becoming known to the Roman authorities. Furthermore, on the Dalai Lama's own website, he clearly states that he promotes "*secular* ethics in the interest of human happiness" (ital. added) and that his ministry fosters "inter-religious harmony." In other words, as reflected in the numerous Hollywood celebrities he counts as close friends (e.g. Oprah), the Dalai Lama is a secular relativist. Make no mistake, the Dalai Lama is not in the same league as Jesus—not by a very, very long shot.

The notion that Jesus was narcissistic—one way or the other—just doesn't fit the facts. If the alternatives are truly limited to lunatic, liar, or Lord (and the authors, among many others, believe they are), then the only alternative that makes any sense, that fits the facts, is LORD.

Second, Jesus fulfills the Old Testament requirements for the Messiah. Jesus' claim was founded on fifteen messianic requirements, all of which were laid out in the Old Testament. As you read the following list, consider that the odds of even three of these prerequisites being true of one person are astronomical. Yet Jesus fulfills them all!

Old Testament Prophecy Concerning the Messiah	Old Testament Reference	Prophecy Recorded as Fulfilled in New Testament
Born of a Virgin	Isaiah 7:14	Matthew 1:18; Luke 1:26-27
Born in Bethlehem	Micah 5:2	Matthew 2:1; Luke 2:4
Preceded and Proclaimed by a Prophet	Isaiah 40:3, Malachi 3:1	Matthew 3:1-2; Mark 1:1-8; Luke 3:1-6; John 1:19-23
Of the Tribe of Judah	Genesis 49:10	Luke 3:23, 33; Matt 2:5, 6
Of the Lineage of King David	Jeremiah 23:5	Luke 3:23, 31; Matt 1:20
Taught with Parables	Psalms 78:2	Matthew 13:34; Mark 4:33, 34

Entered Jerusalem on a Colt	Zechariah 9:9	Matt 21:1-5; Mark 11:1-3; Luke 19:35-37; John 12:14-15
Betrayed for Thirty Pieces of Silver	Zechariah 11:12	Matthew 26:15; 27:3
Forsaken by His Disciples following His Arrest	Zechariah 13:7	Matt 26:31; Mark 14:50
Silent Before His Accusers	Isaiah 53:7	Matthew 27:12-14; Mark 15:3-5
Spit Upon and Beaten Prior to Execution	Isaiah 50:6	Matthew 27:30; Mark 15:18-19
Cried "My God, My God, Why Hast Thou Forsaken Me?" During Execution	Psalms 22:1	Matthew 27:46; Mark 15:34
Bones Not Broken During Execution	Exodus 12:46, Psalms 34:20	John 19:32-33
Executed with Thieves	Isaiah 53:12	Matthew 27:38; Mark 15:27; Luke 23:32-33
Buried in a Rich Man's Tomb	Isaiah 53:9	Matthew 27:57-60; Mark 15:42-47

No one before Jesus had fulfilled these Messianic requirements. No one since Jesus has come even close to fulfilling them. And furthermore, no one yet to live will ever fulfill them. They have been fulfilled, once and for all, some 2000 years ago, by Christ Jesus, LORD and Savior of mankind!

Third, Jesus demonstrates His identity through miracles and healings. More than simply connecting the life of Jesus with the promised Messiah, all four Gospels record Jesus' miraculous and divine power. He changed water into wine, walked on water, instantly calmed a raging storm at sea, healed numerous people of diseases and afflictions ranging from leprosy to congenital blindness, healed a person who had been born crippled, exorcised demons, multiplied several loaves of bread and a few fish to feed five thousand people, and brought three dead people (at least we are only told of three) back to life. Furthermore, the disciple John says that the miracles recorded in the four Gospels only scratch the surface; that thousands upon thousands of books would be needed to record all of Jesus' miraculous deeds (John 21:25). Also, the variety of Jesus' miracles is an unequivocal demonstration of his sovereignty over the whole of creation: human and non-human life, the demonic realm, and even its inorganic aspects (water, wind, gravity). The only being who can so thoroughly control every nuance of creation is the Creator Himself. It logically follows that just as Jesus claimed, He is that Most Supreme Being.

Fourth, Jesus demonstrated that He was both fully God and fully man. Such an assertion is the logical conclusion of the previous point. As the one who demonstrates mastery over creation, yet also walks and talks, eats and sleeps, Jesus is both divine and human. This is the most fundamental reason why Jesus is the one and only means by which one can obtain forgiveness of sin, salvation, and get to Heaven. Reversing the curse of the Garden of Eden—thus making it possible, once again, for people to enjoy direct relationship with God—would require God Himself, in the flesh. Only God can remove the curse that He pronounced upon humankind. Human beings require a Savior who has both (a) the power and purity of God and also (b) possesses the ability to fully identify with humanity and suffer on its behalf. One creative way this has been described is that for humans to obtain salvation, we need someone who can take both the hand of God and the hand of man and bring us together—someone who is qualified to act as mediator between the Divine and His Creation. And that is precisely what the Bible tells us about Jesus. In his letter to Timothy the apostle Paul says, "For there is one God and one Mediator between God and men, the man Christ Jesus, who gave Himself a ransom for all" (1 Timothy 2:5 – 6). Being both one hundred percent God and one hundred percent human, Jesus and only Jesus is capable of acting as the Mediator of whom Paul speaks.

Both the Old and New Testaments refer to this paradox. The prophet Isaiah, for example, says that the Messiah, born of a virgin, will be called Immanuel (v. 7:14). In the New Testament Gospel of Matthew, we are told that Immanuel means "God with us" (v. 1:23). In other words, the Messiah will be a human child, miraculously born, who will be the Incarnation of God Himself.

The virgin birth, related in both Matthew's and Luke's Gospels, is one of the more problematic Biblical events for nay-sayers. They reason that "virgin birth" is a contradiction of terms; that it is nonsense to assert that a virgin gave birth to a child. Actually, nay-sayers start at the very beginning, from the premise that the God of Judeo-Christian scripture is a fiction. Indeed, if God does not exist then a virgin birth is impossible. Miracles require a supernatural miracle worker. But as the authors established in Chapter 1, God *does* exist. He is real, and He is most assuredly a miracle worker! To begin with (pun intended), He created the entire Universe out of nothing! He didn't start with stuff that was already existing, like a potter begins with clay. God began with nothing and spoke the Universe into existence (Genesis 1:3). After He created the "stuff" of the Universe, He used it to form the sun, the moon, the stars, and every other heavenly body. He created every form of life that inhabits or has ever inhabited the earth, including human beings. Given that context, for God to cause a virgin young woman to become pregnant and give birth to a healthy child is small potatoes. In fact, as recorded in the Book of Genesis, on more than one occasion God intervened in the life an apparently infertile woman to enable her to give birth to a child (see the stories of Sarah, Rebekah, Rachel, and Hannah in the Book of Genesis, which is essentially a telling of the early history of humanity and the Jewish people). Furthermore, the Bible presents these stories, including that of Jesus' virgin birth, as factual events witnessed and attested to by multiple people. Keep in mind that when the four New Testament Gospels were written, witnesses to the events described therein were still alive. These documents were copied many times over and distributed throughout the Roman Empire (Europe, North Africa, and the Middle East). If the Gospels are fiction, credible individuals would have stepped forward and levied the charge of perjury, yet there is no historical evidence of anyone ever doing so. The proof that no one ever did so lies in the fact that the Christian movement grew like wildfire in spite of official persecution. Had a credible witness stepped forward and denied the veracity of the Gospels, Christianity would have been a non-starter.

Matthew's Gospel tells about the birth of Jesus from the perspective of Joseph, the older man to whom Mary was engaged. The text does not say how Joseph knows that Mary is pregnant—perhaps it was obvious or perhaps Mary told him so as to give him opportunity to withdraw his promise of marriage. In any event, Joseph knows something because Matthew tells us he wants to "put her away secretly" (1:19) rather than make a public example of her. The Bible tells us that an angel of the Lord appeared to Joseph in a dream and said, "Joseph, son of David, do not be afraid to take you Mary your wife, for that which is conceived in her is of the Holy Spirit" (Matt 1:20. The angel then tells Joseph about the purpose of this child: "And she will bring forth a Son, and you shall call His name Jesus, for He will save His people from their sins" (1:21). Such a statement indicates both Jesus' nature and mission. He is conceived of the Holy Spirit, destined for the single greatest purpose of all time.

Wouldn't a normal conception have been good enough? Not at all. Remember, Jesus was sent by His Father for one purpose: to give Himself as a redemptive sacrifice for the sins of mankind. To do so, He had to be the completely sinless "Lamb of God." Of necessity, that state of spiritual purity (lacking in sin or a sinful nature) had to include the nature of his conception. Jesus had to come into the world in a state of complete moral purity—even His conception had to be absent fleshly indulgence.

The angel's statement to Joseph affirms that Jesus, born of the Spirit and not of the flesh, is thus qualified to be humanity's Savior, to save God's children from their sinfulness. In fact, the name Jesus (Hebrew: Yeshua)—the name the angel instructed Joseph to give the child—means "Savior."

Mary has a similar encounter with an angel (probably the same angel whom Joseph encountered) that backs up this same message. After a rather startling appearance, the angel tells Mary, "And behold, you will conceive in your womb and bring forth a Son, and shall call His name Jesus. He will be great and will be called the Son of the Highest; and the Lord God will give

Him the throne of His father David. And He will reign over the house of Jacob forever, and of His kingdom there will be no end" (Luke 1:31-33). Not only do we have the same language related to the unique manner of Jesus' conception, but we also have the same testimony about His dual nature. Also, notice that the angel says Jesus will rule forever over a kingdom that will never end. Who else enjoys such sovereignty but God? How can a mere human rule an eternal kingdom?

It is in the virgin birth that the humanity and divinity of Jesus is expressed and protected. Jesus is born as every other human is born. However, since Jesus does not result from human conception then the corruption of man's sinful nature is not handed down to Him. This is not to say that sin nature comes from the father's side of the family. However, Genesis 5 does make it clear that while Adam and Eve were created in God's own image, their children were born in *their* image (Genesis 5:3). And so, instead of God's perfection being passed along from generation to generation, the sin-depravity of human nature is passed along. To protect Jesus from that same human corruption, His conception was by the miraculous power of the Holy Spirit rather than by normal biological means.

Philippians 2:5-11 is yet another New Testament poetic witness to Jesus' nature. It not only testifies that Jesus is divine but that He also "made himself of no reputation taking the form of a bondservant, and coming in the likeness of men" (7). The passage then goes on to stress the fact that Jesus came as He did so that He might die on the Cross. Understand: God cannot die. Only a human being could serve in this sacrificial role. This passage in the Apostle Paul's letter to the Christian community at Philippi illustrates the important connection between the nature of Jesus (divine) and the work of Jesus (human). The reason He can save us from our sins is because He is both fully God and fully man.

It is fair, by the way, for skeptics to ask how a person who is fully human can also be fully divine. The answer is that God is omnipotent—all powerful. He can do whatever He pleases. That we have a problem with an individual being both one hundred percent man and one hundred percent God is only because that defies mathematics. But God is not bound by the laws of mathematics. They are, mind you, His laws. They govern the workings of His creation, the Universe. But as the authors have already established, God is not part of His creation (as a potter is not part of his pot); therefore, He is not restrained by its laws. This is the precise reason that God is omnipotent. Therefore Jesus, being God incarnate, can die on the Cross as a human being and walk on water as God. He can shed tears of sorrow as a human being and raise the dead to life as God. He can drink wine as a human being and make wine out of water as God. He can eat bread as a human being and as God, He can multiply five loaves of bread to feed five thousand people. Is all of this mind-boggling? Absolutely, but that is the very nature of God. Because we do not, cannot, share His nature, everything He does is, to us, mind-boggling.

Jews like Asher Norman insist that Jesus—if He was a real historical figure—was merely human and that by worshiping Him, Christians are guilty of pagan idolatry. They also maintain that the Christian belief in a triune God—Father, Son, and Holy Spirit—is an example of polytheism.

"How can the One God be three separate beings?" they ask.

Answer: the same way one cardboard box has three dimensions—height, width, and depth. Mind you, that's an analogy, not a literal description. God is in fact dimensionless, which is why Jesus could walk on water and through walls. Again (because it cannot be over-stressed) God is not subject to the laws that govern the mechanics of the Universe—His creation. As a man, Jesus submitted to the pull of gravity and the physics of concrete objects. As God, He could transcend these limitations whenever He chose to do so.

It is also fair for the nay-sayer to assert that the New Testament's authors are also guilty of arguing from their own conclusion—in this case, that Jesus is God-in-the-flesh. Skeptics and nay-sayers maintain that the NT's authors simply constructed a creative and alluring myth around that belief. That simply isn't so. Remember, Jesus fulfilled fifteen Old Testament prophecies concerning the Messiah, the Christ. That Jesus is God is the *only* conclusion that can be reasonably drawn from that congruence. The purpose of OT prophecy was to help a future generation of Jews identify the Messiah. It was not enough that someone claimed to be the Promised One; he had to qualify himself by fitting the prophetic description. Jesus did precisely that, but as predicted by the prophets, he was rejected and executed by his own people. The Jewish elites of early First Century Palestine completely ignored the evidence that was staring them, literally, in the face.

SUBSTITUTIONARY ATONEMENT

There are situations in life where it's helpful to have someone mediate on your behalf—a go-between. Whether it is a lawyer trying to obtain justice on your behalf, a negotiator trying to get you a better contract, or a counselor attempting to heal a broken marriage, a mediator can be invaluable. The Bible uses this imagery in terms of our relationship with God—since the Fall, we have needed a go-between, someone to advocate on our behalf to God. In the Old Testament, this mediator was a priest. And the primary function of that priest was to offer sacrifices to God on behalf of the people. Therefore, for Jesus to be able to save us from our sin-nature He had to be not only both God and human, He had to also be both a perfect priest *and* a perfect sacrifice.

To fully appreciate how Jesus is both a perfect priest and a perfect sacrifice, one must turn their attention to the Old Testament. Remember that the consequences of sin included, ultimately, death. Every sin deserves God's judgment. However, rather than empowering the early Israelites to simply kill anyone who sins—in essence, self-genocide—God allowed them to substitute an animal—a bird or a lamb. The death-by-proxy of the animal satisfied the righteous judgment of God against human sin. In this regard, two sacrifice days were especially important to the Hebrew people: Passover and the Day of Atonement (Yom Kippur).

On both occasions, a lamb without blemish was offered as a sacrifice to God by a priest who had gone through an intense ritual of cleansing, symbolically purifying himself. Through the death of this spotless (perfect) lamb at the hands of a symbolically sinless priest, the people of God were reminded that Yahweh is a gracious and loving God who forgives sin and saves people from sin's consequences. Both the Passover and Yom Kippur lambs had to be spotless and the priest had to be ritually cleansed.

Jesus took the lamb's place as a perfect, final sacrifice for the sins of mankind. Thus, He is called the "Lamb of God." Since Jesus was fully divine He was an unblemished sacrifice. Since He was fully human He could physically die for our sins. All of this adds up to a startling statement: *Jesus accepted the penalty for the sins of mankind so that those who place their full trust in Him do not have to pay that penalty (death) themselves.* Jesus stood in our place. This is the constant witness of Scripture. John 1:29 identifies

Jesus as the "lamb of God who takes away the sins of the world." Jesus Himself recognizes this role when He says that He will give His flesh "for the life of the world (John 6:51)." Jesus knew all too well that His purpose was to offer His life for sinners. He is the only person who has ever lived whose ultimate purpose was to die.

The Bible's plain and simple teaching is that without a mediator, the only thing man can do with his sin is die—not just physical death, mind you, but an eternal condition of separation from God, a condition known as Hell. Because humans do not simply sin but carry a sin nature—making it entirely impossible for them *not* to sin—a human being cannot, on his own, cleanse himself of sin or save himself from its consequences. Mind you, the human being in the previous sentence is you, the reader. Read the following sentence slowly and carefully: *Because you are incapable of willing yourself to be sinless and incapable of bearing the full penalty for your sinfulness, God sent His one and only Son to be the necessary mediator, the go between, the one who would stand in your place and take your punishment.* That, right there, is the incredibly good news of the New Testament: Because of the substitutionary death of Jesus Christ, you do not have to die (go to Hell) for your sins. Romans 5:8-9 says, "But God demonstrates His own love toward us, in that while we were still sinners, Christ died for us. Much more then, having now been justified by His blood, we shall be saved from wrath through Him." Then verse 18 continues this idea by saying, "Therefore, as through one man's offense *judgment came* to all men, resulting in condemnation, even so through one Man's righteous act *the free gift came* to all men, resulting in justification of life." Paul's point is simple. Sin entered the world through the disobedience of Adam. The penalty, as God warned Adam, was death (eternal separation from relationship with God, also known as Hell). God reversed this death sentence by allowing His Only Son to take our place and receive His wrath. Therefore, through the ultimate sacrifice of one man God made it possible for the sins of all mankind to be forgiven—including *your* sins.

But it's not just that Jesus is a perfect sacrifice. He can offer it in a perfect way. Hebrews 2:17 tells us, "Therefore, in all things He had to be made like *His* brethren, that He might be a merciful and faithful High Priest in things *pertaining* to God, to make propitiation for the sins of the people." The word "propitiation" is not used very often in Scripture; rather, it is reserved for unique situations, of which Jesus' death on the Cross is one. In that context, propitiation means that Jesus was an acceptable sacrifice to appease God's wrath against sin—the one and only acceptable sacrifice in fact. On the Cross, God the Son was separated from God the Father so that *you* could be reunited with God and have the assurance of Heaven.

Understand, please, Jesus was not a martyr. The New Testament Gospels are not the story of a good man caught up in political intrigue and executed for crimes against Rome. Although they arrested Jesus, tortured Him, erected the Cross and nailed Him to it, the Romans, although culpable, did not actually kill Jesus. Neither did the Jewish elites (although culpable). It was God's plan to redeem mankind and restore us to Him. On the cross, the Father poured out His judgment and wrath against sin onto His Only Son (Rom 3:24-25; I John 2:2). The judgment and wrath *you* deserve was taken by Jesus. On the cross, the divine Son of God, fully God and fully man, endured the suffering of sin and its fate. On that cross God sacrificed His Only Son. For us. For you!

RESURRECTION!

No evidence of Christ Jesus' Lordship over all creation is more telling than His Resurrection. After dying on the Cross—and make no mistake about it, all of the evidence confirms that He did in fact expire and was physically dead for more than twenty-four hours—Jesus came back to life, fully healed, thus conquering death on our behalf. He not only told His disciples that He would do so—which they failed to comprehend until they saw Him, risen, with their own eyes—but was also seen on numerous post-resurrection occasions by upwards of several hundred witnesses. The modern mind is inclined to reject resurrection as a physiological impossibility. So what is the proof that Christ Jesus did in fact rise from the dead?

First, Jesus was actually dead. Some historians and biblical scholars have explained the Resurrection by suggesting Jesus did not actually die on the Cross, but only seemed dead because he had been given a powerful narcotic. This was, in fact, the central theme of *The Passover Plot*, a 1965 best-seller by Jewish biblical scholar Hugh J. Schonfield, later turned into an Oscar-winning film of the same title. It is a compelling notion and one, furthermore, that satisfies those who (a) simply cannot wrap their heads around the notion of someone coming back to life after being dead for some time and (b) are probably biased against Christianity to begin with. Yet the Gospels provide compelling evidence to that very startling effect. For example, it is inconceivable that trained Roman executioners would have been unable to determine if Jesus was truly dead or not. To make such a mistake would have cost them their own lives.

Scripture says that when the Roman soldiers came to break Jesus' legs and thereby hasten his death they discovered He had already expired. To ensure that He was in fact dead one of the soldiers stabbed Him through the lungs and heart with a spear, releasing a flow of "blood and water" (John 19:34)—the latter word referring to the semi-clear fluid that separates from blood cells after death. A short time later, Joseph of Arimathea and Nicodemus—Jewish nobility—ask for and receive Jesus' body, quickly prepare it for burial (they had to be finished by sundown on Friday in order to remain in good standing with Jewish law, so their preparations were incomplete) and then lay it in the tomb. If Jesus had not been dead, Joseph and Nicodemus would have noticed and would not have interred Him. Finally, the Jewish leaders requested that the tomb be formally sealed (an official imprint into a waxy substance affixed to the approximately one-ton stone that was rolled over the tomb's entrance). At least one Roman official and perhaps several Jewish ones as well would have entered the tomb to verify Jesus' demise before rolling the stone over the opening and placing the Governor's seal upon it.

Furthermore, in the course of researching his best-seller *The Case for Christ*, investigative journalist Lee Strobel interviewed physicians and physiologists who verified that all of the evidence presented in the Gospels points to one inescapable conclusion: when Jesus was taken down from the Cross, He was really and truly dead.

Second, the stone was rolled away. Matthew 27:60 and Mark 15:46 record that after Jesus' dead body was placed in the tomb a great stone was rolled in front of the opening and sealed with wax (Matt 27:63, 64). As final insurance and to fully satisfy the Jewish elites, Pilate ordered that the tomb be guarded by a cadre of battle-trained Roman soldiers (Matt 27:65). Four would stand guard for three hours and then rotate to the next four and so on. This pattern would have continued for twenty-four hours a day for the next three days, until the body had begun to decompose.

But all four Gospel writers tell us that the women who came to the tomb early Sunday morning—approximately forty hours after Jesus was pronounced dead by trained Roman executioners—to finish what Joseph of Arimathea and Nicodemus has started, found that the stone had been rolled away from the entrance. Matthew indicates this was caused or accompanied by an "earthquake"—whatever the actual event, it was certainly a force of great, earth-shaking power. This was no small stone, mind you; rather, it had been hewn from an immense boulder. The Gospel reader is told that on their way to the tomb, the women worry that no one will be available to roll the stone back for them (Mark 16:4). Why does this one fact matter so much that it is found in all four Gospels? Because it proves that the disciples did not steal the body. Keep in mind, this was the prevailing theory that Jerusalem's Jewish leaders later used to explain the empty tomb (Matt 28:11-15). But for this to happen you must believe that a group of women along with a group of very frightened disciples somehow mustered up the courage to overwhelm more than a dozen trained Roman soldiers and move a huge stone all by themselves. It is significant to note that such tombstones were set into inclined channels hewn into the surrounding rock. The incline was such that one man could close the tomb but three or more very strong men were required to roll the stone away from the tomb's opening. This refutes any theory that Jesus did not actually die but only lost consciousness and once regained, rolled the stone away Himself.

The possibility that a group of men stole back to the tomb after nightfall and performed the deed is eliminated by the fact that no group of men, however quiet they might have been, could have accomplished this without being noticed by the Roman guard. Nay-sayers counter by contending that the guard must have been asleep. That requires accepting that twelve trained Roman soldiers disobeyed orders that had probably come down from Pilate himself. Mind you, Jesus was no ordinary criminal. He had greatly threatened the security of both the Jewish elites and Roman officials. It was not typical to post a twelve-man guard—or any guard at all for that matter—at the tomb of a recently crucified criminal. The powers-that-be feared that Jesus' followers would attempt to steal the body and claim that He had come back to life. That rumor might have caused widespread rioting, even full-blown revolt, so the powers-that-be took every possible precaution to prevent tomb-robbing. The soldiers understood the gravity of their assignment. They were not going to fall asleep.

When all is said and done, one is left with the story presented by the four Gospel writers: Jesus died on the Cross following which He was taken down, prepared for burial and interred in a cave that was then sealed with a huge stone. Two nights later, God brought Him back to life in a fully healed body. Jesus then removed a wrapping of tightly wound grave linens from His own body (it is doubtful that even Houdini could have performed such a feat), folded them neatly, caused the stone to roll back (after causing the Roman soldiers to either fall asleep or be completely oblivious), and calmly waited for the appearance of the women who came on Sunday morning to complete what Joseph and Nicodemus had started.

Third, the tomb was empty. All four Gospel writers tell us that when the women get to the tomb, it's empty. They go back—presumably to the Upper Room—to inform the disciples. Perhaps skeptical (Jewish law forbade men from accepting the testimony of women), Peter and John return to the tomb with Mary Magdalene (John 20:1-10). Sure enough, it is empty and Jesus' body is nowhere to be found. This, by the way, is a fact that neither Jewish nor Roman authorities disputed. The reality of the empty tomb led the Jewish religious leaders to bribe the soldiers guarding the tomb to say the disciples stole the body while they slept (see Matt 28:11-13)—as the authors have already established, a preposterous notion. So not only do we have consistent testimony of an empty tomb but we also have evidence that this was a baffling mystery at first. Something unusual had taken place that no one could explain.

Fourth, the linen cloths used to wrap Jesus' body were unwrapped and folded. One of the most curious and yet enlightening facts involves the wrappings used in the preparation of Jesus' dead body. Consider the disciple John's own eyewitness testimony. "Then Simon Peter came, following him, and went into the tomb; and he saw the linen cloths lying *there,* and the handkerchief that had been around His head, not lying with the linen cloths, but folded together in a place by itself" (John 20:6-7). Notice how Peter not only saw that the linen cloths used to wrap the body were lying on the floor of the tomb, but that the particular cloth used to wrap Jesus' head was neatly folded and placed in a separate location.

You may wonder why this matters. The authors have never tried to carry a dead body, much less steal one, but commonsense says that if someone is going to carry off a body that's wrapped in linen cloths, they aren't going to unwrap it much less take the time to neatly fold the wrappings. A wrapped body is going to be easier to transport than an unwrapped one; furthermore, the wrappings would mitigate the smell of decomposition. Most important, however, is that Jewish law forbade touching a dead body. Bottom line: No one stole Jesus' body. The only possible explanation is that Jesus came back to life from a state of complete bodily death (as opposed a "near-death" experience), caused a troop of Roman soldiers to fall asleep (small potatoes for God), moved an immense stone away from the tomb's opening (which only a single man with supernatural strength could have accomplished), and emerged, fully healed.

Fifth, there were numerous eyewitnesses who were moved by Jesus' resurrection to put their lives on the line. At first, the disciples were bewildered by the empty tomb (including that Mary Magdalene subsequently claimed to have seen and spoken with the risen Jesus, but keep in mind that women were not regarded as credible witnesses). Several days later, Jesus suddenly appears to the disciples in the Upper Room, which they had locked out of fear for their lives. Mind you, He does not open the door and walk in; He simply appears, again demonstrating His complete mastery of the laws of physics. His body shows evidence of the crucifixion but the wounds in his hands, feet, and side are fully healed and this is but several days after he was taken down from the cross. That, as any physician will attest, is a medical impossibility. He speaks with them, eats with them, and lets them touch him. Immediately after this amazing experience, the disciples go out into the streets of Jerusalem proclaiming the risen LORD. Keep in mind that just hours earlier, they were huddled in seclusion, afraid for their very lives—and for good reason! In summary, we have personal verification of Jesus' Resurrection from the women who went to the tomb, Peter, John, and eventually the rest of the disciples (minus Judas of course), all occurring within several days of the crucifixion. Over the next month or so, Jesus appeared to more than five hundred people in all—not an apparition, mind you, but a flesh-and-blood, walking, talking, fully healed Jesus! (1 Corinthians 15:6). Hoo-hah! If that doesn't rock your world, nothing will.

The apostle Paul uses these very facts to argue for the reality of the resurrection in I Corinthians. He says that Jesus was seen by Peter, then the other disciples, then five hundred other people "at once" and then by His brother James (15:5). But what's striking is how Paul, in talking about the five hundred says, "of whom the greater part remain to the present (Paul is writing some twenty years later)." With those words, he throws down a challenge: "If you don't believe what I'm telling you then you can go on down to Jerusalem and find several hundred witnesses who can back up everything I'm saying."

No, the resurrection of our LORD Jesus was not staged, faked, made up, or hallucinated. It happened! It was as real as real can be! It was so completely, utterly, and unarguably real that a small group of men who were hiding in fear of their lives suddenly began doing the very thing that would (and eventually did) draw the homicidal ire of both Jewish and Roman authorities. The only explanation for this astounding turn-around, for them to completely cast aside all fear of death, is they had witnessed the most significant event, before or since, in human history. The only comparable event is the Creation itself.

Sixth, the resurrection caused his disciples to do an immediate and complete one-eighty. The initial depiction of the disciples found in the Gospels is not very flattering. They exhibit childishness, disobedience, ignorance, arrogance, pettiness, petulance, jealousy, and cowardice on a variety of occasions. This really comes to the forefront in the stories surrounding the crucifixion of Jesus. Rather than rush to the defense of their beloved Master, the disciples flee when confronted with a contingent of Roman guards. After Jesus is arrested and is on trial for His life, Peter denies knowing Him. And after the crucifixion these fellows were hiding behind locked doors. Fast forward a few weeks later and these same men are boldly proclaiming the Gospel of Jesus Christ in the streets of Jerusalem. They are standing before large crowds and confessing Jesus as the Messiah, the risen LORD of All. When taken before the religious leaders and threatened with bodily harm they do not hesitate to declare their unflinching allegiance to their Lord and Master (Acts 4:8-12, 19, 20). What can account for such a change? Only the Resurrection of Christ Jesus along with His promise of the Holy Spirit accounts for such a dramatic change. It defies credulity really believe that such a drastic reversal could have come about as the result of a plot to steal the body of Jesus and then lie about Him being alive?

And such a change is found not only in the disciples but other important figures as well. Consider the example of James, the half-brother of Jesus. We know from an earlier Gospel account that the family of Jesus, including his mother Mary, had grave concerns about His ministry (Mark 3:21). They were obviously discomforted by the attention He was attracting to Himself and, by association, the family. However, this all changed when James had an encounter with the resurrected Christ (I Cor. 15:7). Not only does James become a follower of Jesus, he goes on to become the leader of the church at Jerusalem. He even describes himself not as the brother of Jesus but a "bond servant (James 1:1)." And church history tells us that James was eventually martyred because of his commitment to Christ.

And then there is the example of Paul. Many people know the story of Paul who was originally called Saul. He was on the fast track to a position of power and influence in the religious culture of Jerusalem. He had the best possible training and education and possessed all the right credentials. One day, he might have become leader of the Sanhedrin—the governing Jewish council. His zeal was so intense that the book of Acts identifies him as a key player in the persecution of the early church. He is even identified as being in the crowd—perhaps its instigator—that stoned the disciple Stephen to death. But then everything changed for Saul while on the way to Damascus to arrest some Christians. A blinding light appeared before Saul, knocking him to the ground. Then Jesus spoke directly to him and confronted him with his sin (Acts 9:1-9). Saul surrendered his life to Christ that very day. Later, his name would be changed to Paul and the rest is history, as they say. That powerful confrontation with the resurrected Jesus produced the greatest missionary in church history. And following his miraculous conversion, Paul himself faced extreme forms of persecution. Why would Paul give up his heritage and tradition, his unyielding commitment to the ways of Judaism, his wealth and his promising career? He even gave up his name. Surely not for a hallucination. The only possible explanation is that he encountered, face-to-face, the resurrected Christ.

Again and again we find examples of the followers of Jesus exhibiting a complete turn-around. They were willing to die for their faith in Christ because they believed Jesus was alive, that He had conquered death on their behalf, and that they would enjoy life eternal with Him in Heaven. It is impossible to suppose that such a large number of people would be willing to die for something they knew was not true. It is incomprehensible that eleven frightened men could all be persuaded to go along with a ruse of this sort, risking their lives in the process. Keep in mind that most of them were eventually put to death. Facing death, none recanted, none begged for mercy. As Jesus had given His life for them, they willingly gave their lives for Him, knowing they would be reunited with one another and with Him in the glorious afterlife. Whether people today believe in the Resurrection or not, one thing is certain, these first followers of Jesus had no doubt but that He rose from the dead.

CONCLUSION

The facts about Jesus seem straightforward. All the evidence points to one undeniable truth: Jesus is the Son of God and the one and only way to salvation. While the material above presents objective facts about Jesus, God's motivation for sending Jesus in the first place is important. God is always motivated by His own glory. To save people from Hell is an expression of the greatness and glory of God. Second, God loves us. We are His most special creation. Imagine that for just a moment. The sovereign, holy, all-powerful God of the universe loves the human beings that He's created. We are not mere amusements; we are so special to Him that He died on a cross in order that we might live forever in His Presence. John 3:16, perhaps the most referenced verse in The Bible, bears witness to this love: "For God so loved the world that He gave His only begotten Son, that whoever believes in Him should not perish but have everlasting life." And that's the next step we need to explore. God, out of an act of immense love, has made it possible for us/you to have our/your sins forgiven and the assurance of life in heaven. That's been accomplished through Christ Jesus. In the next chapter, you'll find out what you need to do next.

RECOMMENDED READING

- Habermas, Gary and Michael Licona. *The Case for the Resurrection.* Kregel Publications, 2004

- Hanegraaf, Hank. *Resurrection.* Thomas Nelson, 2002

- Limbaugh, David. *Jesus on Trial.* Regenery, 2014.

- MacArthur, John. *The Murder of Jesus.* Thomas Nelson, 2004.

- Sproul, R.C. *The Unexpected Jesus.* Christian Focus, 2005.

- Sproul, R.C. *The Work of Christ: What the Events of Jesus' Life Mean for You.* David C. Cook, 2012.

- Strobel, Lee. *The Case for Christ.* Zondervan, 2013.

QUESTIONS FOR PERSONAL REFLECTION AND DISCUSSION

1. What are some of the common ways people describe Jesus? What are the problems associated with some of these descriptions?
2. Why is it so important for Jesus to be both fully God and fully man?
3. Many people today assume that there is more than one way to get to Heaven. What are some of the options offered by other religions? Are these means in any way compatible with Christian teaching? If not, what does this tell us about these "other means?"
4. What are or have been some of your personal struggles concerning the resurrection of Jesus?
5. How does the fact of Jesus' resurrection influence one's view of death and life after death?

5

Saved!

Oh happy day (oh happy day)
Oh happy day (oh happy day)
When Jesus washed (when Jesus washed)
When Jesus washed (when Jesus washed)
When Jesus washed (when Jesus washed)
He washed my sins away (oh happy day)
Oh happy day (oh happy day)

—*Oh Happy Day, The Edwin Hawkins Singers, 1969*

Sometime around 50 A.D. the apostle Paul and his missionary aide Silas were imprisoned in the small Greek town of Philippi, where they had been preaching and teaching about Jesus. Their enemies—Jews, mostly—had accused them of being disrupters (i.e. disturbers of the peace) and so the local Roman authorities had put them in what amounted to a filthy cave. But despite their unsanitary habitat, Paul and Silas were undaunted.

In the middle of the night, chained to a rock wall, these two apostles and church planters began singing praises to God. As they were singing, an earthquake shook the ground, the prison doors opened, and their shackles fell off, offering them blessed freedom. Upon being jarred awake, the jailer saw the open doors and assumed his prisoners had escaped. He was moments away from using his own short sword to take his life (because death would have been his sentence anyway) when Paul's voice called out to him from the dark, "Do not harm yourself, for we are all here." One can only imagine the man's relief, but the story, told in Acts, also indicates the man trembled with fear and fell down before Paul and Silas, asking, "What must I do to be saved (16:30)?" He thought that only the power of a Supreme Being could have opened locked prison doors and released captives from heavy iron shackles, but he was also overcome by the fact that despite their chance at freedom, Paul and Silas stayed put, demonstrating no fear of death.

The jailer's question is key. What must a person do in order to be saved? Many if not most folks want a "get saved" check list consisting of rituals, prayers, assignments, and maybe a book or two to read. But the answer to the jailer's question does not involve anything religious or ritualistic. Instead, being saved is a matter of an inner transformation of mind and heart (spirit) that produces an outward transformation in one's priorities and behavior. This transformation is known as being "born again."

If the reader is not yet saved, it is the authors' intention to convince you to get cracking and do so. Why? Because salvation through Jesus Christ opens Heaven to you. Two thousand years ago, Jesus paid the penalty for your sinfulness. Because of Jesus' sacrifice on the Cross, salvation is yours for the claiming. As He said, He is the door for the sheep (John 10:7). You are one of the sheep in question. To open the door, all you need to do is knock on it and ask to be let in. That simple act of humility is all it takes.

If you die without having knocked on the Door of Salvation, you will find yourself behind Door Number Two—Hell—with no way out. It's either Heaven or Hell, and it's one or the other for all eternity. According to The Bible, God's very own Word, there is no third option. At the end of the Introduction to this book, the authors described a hypothetical situation involving the reader and a bureaucratic-looking man whom you encounter immediately after you die. He shows you two short videos, one representing the chaos and agony of Hell, the other representing the eternal bliss and joy of Heaven. The bureaucrat then asks you to choose: Will it be Hell or will it be Heaven? We established that no sane person would choose Hell. It being reasonable to assume that the reader is sane, you would surely choose Heaven.

At this point it may be helpful to deal with some salvation terminology, prominent among which are the phrases "saved," "born again," "becoming a Christian," "getting right with God," and "trusting Jesus". The Gospels record Jesus using only the first two. He said that He had come to save the lost (Luke 19:10) and that to obtain paradise, one had to be born again (John 3:3). Nonetheless, all five of these phrases are valid ways of referring to the transformation from being a sinner separated from God—as it is expressed, "dead in sin and trespass"—to a *bona fide* Christian who has his or her sins forgiven and, therefore, the assurance of Heaven.

Since it was first used by Jesus Himself, the term "born again" is worth looking at in some depth and detail. In the third chapter of John's Gospel Jesus is talking with a man named Nicodemus whom John identifies as a Pharisee, a "ruler of the Jews." Because Nicodemus does not want to be seen with Jesus, he comes to Him under the cover of darkness. Using the honorific "rabbi," Nicodemus tells Jesus that the Pharisees know He must be a man of God "because no one can do these signs that you do unless God is with him." Jesus tells Nicodemus that "...unless one is born again, he cannot see the kingdom of God," and goes on to say that being born again is a work of the (Holy) Spirit (John 3:5). Jesus thus lays the foundation for understanding the process by which someone moves from being dead in sin to forgiven and alive with God. There must be a new birth, a change of heart and mind, a work in the spirit of man by the Spirit of God.

Back to the jailer's question: What must a person *do* to be born again? As was the case with Nicodemus, the term raises lots of questions. What does being born again *feel* like? Does it require witnesses who can attest to the experience? How does one know he's been born again? Can one be a Christian without being born again, and if so, is that good enough?

The most important thing that can be said about being *saved* or *born again* is that one doesn't have to "do" anything, at least not in the sense of doing certain good things. There's no required list of works one must perform, no rituals in which one must participate; there are not even any personal reforms one must accomplish before one qualifies as a saved Christian. The mental/spiritual process of being saved begins with something called "being convicted."

CONVICTED

To become a saved, born-again Christian means that God has done something for you and in you, not the other way around. As the authors have already noted, everyone, from the moment of birth, is spiritually dead in sin. For someone to confess his sins and trust completely in Jesus for salvation, God must first grant that person the ability to see (a) his sinful, depraved condition for what it is and (b) Jesus for who He is. God uses His Spirit—the Holy Spirit, who along with the Father and the Son, is one aspect of the Holy Trinity—to accomplish this work. Jesus, in telling His disciples about the Holy Spirit says, "And when He has come, He will convict the world of sin, and of righteousness, and of judgment" (John 16:8). It is the Holy Spirit who opens an individual's mind and heart and makes him aware of his sinful condition. Being convicted is something only the Holy Spirit can bring about. However, that should not be taken to mean that the individual in question bears no responsibility. Indeed, the person who is dead in sin must unconditionally accept the truth of his sinful condition in both his heart and his mind. From that point, it is the Holy Spirit who causes the now-convicted individual to realize that he is subject to God's judgment. This first step toward salvation is often associated with feelings of guilt and profound regret. The secular world regards guilt as a hindrance to living the good life, but in this case, guilt is helpful, even necessary. Scripture tells us that Godly sorrow leads to repentance (2 Corinthians 7:10).

CONFESSION

Once a person has accepted unconditional conviction, the next step on the short road to salvation is confession—coming clean about one's sinfulness. This doesn't mean a person must name every sin he's ever committed. That would be an impossible task. Confession simply means that you admit, to God (although you might want your pastor or best Christian friend to be present), your sinful condition. In effect, you agree with God, unequivocally and without reservation, that you are a recalcitrant sinner. Consider some statements in the Bible that instruct us in this matter.

- "If we confess our sins, He is faithful and just to forgive us our sins and to cleanse us from all unrighteousness" (1 John 1:9).
- "He who covers his sins will not prosper, but whoever confesses and forsakes them will have mercy" (Proverbs 28:13).
- "Therefore, confess your sins to one another and pray for one another, that you may be healed" (James 5:16).
- I acknowledged my sin to You, and my iniquity I have not hidden. I said, "I will confess my transgression to the Lord," and You forgave the iniquity of my sin. (Psalm 32:3 – 5)

In these verses, the words sin, iniquity and transgression refer not to specific acts of wrongdoing but rather to our general condition, our sin nature. The adage says, "Confession is good for the soul." But confession is not just good; it is absolutely necessary to the health of one's soul. You could, if you feel so moved, put this book down right now, bow your head in submission to God, and pray something like this:

"Heavenly Father, Lord God, I confess to you that I am a sinner, and not just occasionally, but that sin is my condition, my burden, that it weighs down my soul and causes me great sorrow in knowing that I have failed to honor you in all that I do, that I have often acted out of love for myself rather than love for you and my neighbor. I humbly commit myself to you and ask that you forgive me through the life-saving work your Son, Jesus Christ, did for me on the cross. I make this confession and ask this forgiveness in His name, Amen."

REPENTANCE

Confession is essential to true salvation, but simply confessing bad "stuff"—bad things one has done in his or her lifetime—falls short. Doing good things won't get you into Heaven, so confessing bad things avoids the real issue: to wit, that the bad things in question are simply manifestations of a much deeper spiritual problem. To simply confess one's bad works, an item-by-item confession, is superficial. In fact, a confession of that sort is a paradoxical form of sinful rebellion and denial because it implies that you're not really and truly an incorrigible sinner; rather, you simply sin every now and then. That, in turn, implies that you are, deep down inside, a basically good person who simply messes up on occasion. The discomforting truth is that you mess up—in thought, word, and deed—numerous times a day. Maybe even numerous times in an average hour. Remember, every time your actions are motivated primarily out of self-interest rather than love of God or neighbor, you are sinning, and let's face it, no amount of mental effort can prevent you from being the number one priority in your life.

At this point, you may ask, "But doesn't God want me to be successful and doesn't that require that I be Numero Uno in my life?"

The answer is no, and no. Contrary to the sick and sickening (in the sense of making people sick) message of the so-called prosperity preachers,

God does not care whether or not you are successful in the eyes of the world. His number-one desire is to have relationship with you, which is only possible if you have been cleansed of your sinfulness by subscribing to the redemptive work Christ Jesus did for you on the Cross and submitting to His Lordship in your life. That requires that Christ Jesus be Numero Uno in your life. That's the New Testament message in a nutshell; to wit:

1. You are an incorrigible sinner.
2. Your sins, unforgiven, are taking you slowly but surely down the highway to Hell.
3. You cannot save yourself from that horrible fate.
4. Jesus—God Among Us—paid the price of your sinfulness by willingly going to the Cross and suffering agony and death on your behalf.
5. Only by thanking Jesus for what He did for you and submitting your life to Him can you escape the natural consequence of your sinfulness and be assured of going to Heaven when your physical body stops working.

It is through relationship with Christ Jesus—remember, He is the one and only Mediator between you and God—that you can be restored to relationship with Father God in Heaven. That's God's one desire for you. It is a desire for your heavenly salvation, not your earthly success. Truly, no success in this life is possible without God, because He is sovereign over all things, but God sometimes gives material success to bad people. Don't be fooled by material success into thinking that you have God's blessings. Remember the parable of Lazarus the beggar and the rich man? Believing that his riches were proof he was superior to Lazarus was the rich man's grave mistake.

The apostle Paul, the greatest Christian who ever lived, was living a very successful life as Saul the Pharisee, persecutor of Christians. In one blinding flash of light on the road to Damascus (where Saul was headed to persecute another group of troublesome believers), God put a permanent end to Saul's chances of further earthly success and turned him into Paul, an instrument of His will. Saul was well-to-do. Paul had no money. When Saul became a Christian named Paul, he lost all claim to his prestige and wealth. From that point on, he relied on charity from the various Christian communities to which he ministered. Saul was destined to be one of the elites of Jerusalem. Paul was eventually executed (or so it is generally thought) for being a troublemaker, a threat to Rome. As was the case with Saul, if God grants you earthly success, He does so for His purposes, not yours.

Furthering your journey to Heaven requires that you understand the difference between confession and repentance. The two are often confused, but they are not synonymous. While repentance is a word you find frequently in Scripture, it isn't often used in everyday conversation. Yet repentance is essential for being made right with God. Jesus Himself centered His primary message on repentance. The Gospel of Mark describes the earliest days of Jesus' ministry as "preaching the Gospel of the kingdom of God." Mark goes on to say that Jesus' basic thesis was "The time is fulfilled, and the kingdom of God is at hand. Repent, and believe in the Gospel (Mark 1:14-15)." Translate: "I am the fulfillment of messianic prophecy. I am God's representative on earth. The time to *repent* of your sins and believe in me has come!" The apostle Paul described his own teaching as including "repentance toward God and faith toward our Lord Jesus Christ (Acts 20:16)." Clearly, the issue of repentance was central to the earliest teaching of the church.

What does it mean to repent? It means more than just feeling bad about your sin-condition and the sins you have committed, although sorrow should be a part of the equation. To repent is to change direction. It is the spiritual equivalent of a making a U-turn. Whether wittingly or not, every person on the planet who has not accepted Jesus Christ as Savior is living in rebellion to God. Therefore, they are living in accord with their own selfish desires. To repent is to turn from that life and toward a life of faith in Christ.

This is where people have a hard time with the message of the Gospel. True repentance admits to something that's hard for sinful human beings to admit: "I was wrong." That's not an easy thing for anyone—no matter how humble—to say. In this case, it's not that you were just a little bit off or got a few things wrong. To repent is to admit that you were completely and utterly wrong about the most important things in life, including yourself. Furthermore, to repent is an act of surrender and submission—a turning from your way, from being Number One in your life, to God's way and making Him Number One in your life.

Confession is the act of admitting your sin condition; repentance is the act of turning away from it in sorrow and humility. Jesus said the truth sets one free (John 8:32). Prior to confession and repentance, you were a hostage to your sin-condition, a hostage to your rebellious nature. After confession and repentance, you are a hostage no longer. You have, indeed, been set free!

TRUST

Repentance includes placing your full trust in Christ and Christ alone for salvation. Jesus told His disciples the night before He was crucified, "I am the way, the truth, and the life. No one comes to the Father except through Me (John 14:6)." A bolder statement has never been made! In the last chapter, the authors established that Jesus did not exhibit either sociopathic or schizophrenic characteristics—he was neither a liar nor a lunatic. Quite the contrary, all the evidence attests to the truth of everything He claimed about Himself. In the above passage in John, Jesus is summing it all up in eighteen words: to wit, He is the one and only means by which salvation can be obtained. Anyone who places his or her eternal trust in anyone or anything other than Jesus is, by definition, lost.

The apostle Peter concluded one of his sermons by testifying that salvation is found in none other than Christ Jesus, "for there is no other name under heaven given among men by which we must be saved (Acts 4:12)." And then there's Paul's statement to a young pastor named Timothy, "For there is one God and one Mediator between God and men, the Man Christ Jesus (I Timothy 2:5)." The conclusion is simple. The only way to get saved is through Jesus Christ. And just to reiterate, Peter and Paul were not profiting in any way by preaching salvation through Christ. They had given up comfortable lives to do so.

But how does getting saved actually happen? You may ask. What does it look or feel like to trust Christ Jesus for your salvation? The paradox here is that this, the most momentous step you will ever take in your life, is also a very uncomplicated step: You simply trust that Jesus' did everything necessary to save you from your sin. He went to the Cross willingly, suffered excruciating pain, and died in order that you might live forever with Him and His Father in Heaven.

Because of the work ethic that is part of America's national character, it may be difficult for you to accept that Jesus took your place on the Cross and did all the work of salvation for you. Therefore, for you, salvation is free. It is a gift of God's grace. You did nothing to deserve it and there is nothing you can do to earn it after the fact. That's what trust, in this context, is all about. It is overcoming the notion that you must *do* something to be saved and place one hundred percent of your faith in what Christ Jesus did for you.

At that point, it is time to give thanks to God for the gift of His Son. Express your confidence in Jesus' saving atonement on your behalf. Consider how the apostle Paul puts this in the book of Romans. He says "if you confess with your mouth the Lord Jesus and believe in your heart that God has raised Him from the dead, you will be saved (10:9)." He goes on to say "For with the heart one believes unto righteousness and with the mouth confession is made unto salvation (10:10)."

Paul is not, however, saying that you need to chatter on and on in thankful prayer. At some point, you may be so overcome with gratitude for the amazing, incredible, mind-boggling thing Christ Jesus has done for you, you may be at a loss for words. In that event, if you just need to kneel and be silent for a time, that's perfectly okay. God hears your heart as well as He hears your voice.

A classic summary of the Gospel message is found in I Corinthians 15:3-4: "that Christ died for our sins according to the Scriptures, and that He was buried, and that He rose again the third day according to the Scriptures." Understand the critical nature of believing this simple yet mind-blowing set of truths, which are at the core of Christian belief. While there are plenty of things Christians can discuss and even disagree about, the essential truth of this scripture is undebatable. It would be a good thing for you to commit 1 Corinthians 15:3-4 to memory and get in the habit of saying it to yourself on a daily basis, maybe even several times a day. Note, by the way, that Paul is careful to point out to his audience—the Christian community at Corinth in ancient Greece—that Jesus is the fulfillment of prophetic writings contained in Scripture (what we today refer to as the Old Testament). In effect, Paul is saying, "If you are familiar with God's Word, you would recognize His Son immediately."

The salvation process, however, is not yet complete. When Paul says that you need to confess and believe he doesn't mean you just need to agree with certain facts. To intellectually agree that Jesus died on the cross and rose from the dead is not enough. The devil and his demons believe those same basic facts. Being truly and unequivocally saved means that your mind, heart, and will are all fully engaged in the act of belief.

This state of complete commitment is what Paul referred to in his first letter to the fledgling Christian community at Thessalonica in northern Greece: "Rejoice always, pray without ceasing, give thanks in all circumstances; for this is the will of God in Christ Jesus for you" (1 Thessalonians 5:16-18).

SURRENDER

Your salvation is completed and ensured when you fully surrender to the Lordship of Christ Jesus in every aspect and area of your life. To be saved is to become a disciple of He who has offered you, through His sacrifice of Himself on the Cross, the gift of salvation and living a life of complete devotion to Him. In other words, salvation is not only a gift but also a responsibility. The transformation in one's heart must be accompanied by a transformation in one's life—identifying and renouncing one's idols, for example. In that regard, you need to accept that as is the case with every unsaved person who has ever walked the planet, your number one idol is *you.* Surrender to the Lordship of Christ Jesus means to stop thinking you know what's best for you and begin taking your life-directions from God's Word. This is the reason why it is so very important that a newly saved person find and begin attending a church that is firmly grounded in The Word (more on this in Chapter 6) and begin reading the Bible with the understanding that it is in effect a manual for living a proper, Christ-centered life (Chapter 7)

Jesus said "he who does not take up his cross and follow after Me is not worthy of Me (Matthew 10:38)." The reference to the cross in this passage is a way of saying that becoming a disciple is an act of death. It is death to wanting things *your* way and surrendering to wanting things Christ's way. Jesus states this principle again directly to His disciples, "If anyone desires to come after Me, let him deny himself, and take up his cross, and follow me (Matt 16:24)."

The secular world wants you to believe that you are master of your own fate. That's a lie. It's an appealing and very intoxicating lie, but despite its lure, it's a lie—it may in fact be accurate to say that it is the single most destructive lie of all time. To become an obedient disciple of Christ means that you accept that God is and always has been sovereign in your life. Even when you were wandering, lost and confused, God was sovereign. Your confused wandering was for a purpose—*His* purpose, not yours. Let go of the seductive illusion that you are in control of your life. That was the empty promise the serpent—Satan, in his first appearance—offered Adam and Eve in the Garden (Genesis 3:4). That belief led to humanity's fall from grace. Leave that behind you and don't look back. God promises you a new life and with that new life comes a new Master of your life, the Lord Jesus Christ.

Before leaving this topic, it is important for the newly saved person to understand that being a disciple of Christ, surrendering to His Lordship in your life, won't be easy. Yes, being saved is a wonderful and joyous thing, but it's easy for a newly saved person to get so carried away with the joy and the promise that he is blind to the flip side of salvation—disapproval, even virulent condemnation by those who will be threatened by your transformation and will do everything they can to undermine your new-found faith. Jesus spoke to this when he warned his disciples "Do not think that I have come to bring peace to the earth. I have not come to bring peace, but a sword. For I have come to set a man against his father, and a daughter against her mother, and a daughter-in-law against her mother-in-law. A man's enemies will be members of his own household" (Matthew 10:34-36). During what is known as the Sermon on the Mount, Jesus issued the same warning: "Blessed are you when others revile you and persecute you and utter all kinds of evil against you falsely *on my account*" (Matthew 5:11, italics added). Luke records the same statement thus: "Blessed are you when people hate you, and exclude you and insult you and reject your name as evil *because of the Son of Man*" (Luke 6:22, italics added). Mind you, Jesus was not saying that a person who becomes His disciple *might* experience hate, slander, rejection, and even persecution; He was saying that a genuinely saved person most definitely *will* experience hate, slander, rejection and persecution from the secular world, even from people he previously counted on as close friends, and even, sadly enough, from family.

If you are not fully prepared for what is coming your way when people learn that you now follow Christ and not those things the world wants you to chase—money, popularity, prestige, material acquisitions—you will be blind-sided and you may begin questioning whether you've done the right thing or trying your best to live with one foot in the secular world and one foot in the Christian life, or both. That never works. Every time someone tries to make that compromise, it fails and they end up with both feet back in the secular world. When churches try to make that compromise—as many so-called "mainline" Protestant churches have done in recent years—they fail. If one does an Internet search of "attendance in mainline churches," hundreds of articles come up that testify to the dramatic decline in regular attendance in secularized churches. These are churches whose local and national leaders just couldn't take the heat that results from standing firm on biblical truth. These are churches that compromise on one hot-button issue after another, from homosexuality to abortion to women preaching to men from the pulpit—in the latter case almost always encouraging them, however subtly, to compromise traditional masculine values and become more like women. And by the way, there is nothing wrong with being a woman, but there is something bad wrong with the notion that men should become more like women. God made two genders with very different physical, mental, and emotional makeups by intention.

The authors do not mean that a Christian should not care what other people think about him. That is nothing but an arrogant form of narcissism. Your character is always an issue. It is even more of an issue after you become saved. Being saved is not merely a gift of God's grace, it is a responsibility that includes conducting oneself in a manner that is above reproach. We simply mean that a saved Christian must not care what non-Christians or in-name-only "Christians" think about the fact that he trusts in Christ Jesus with all of his heart and mind. Paul spoke of the need for Christians to "Put on the full armor of God, so that you may take your stand against the devil's schemes" (Ephesians 6:11), one of which is to employ social criticism and scorn as a means of causing doubt.

WHERE THE RUBBER MEETS THE ROAD

The time has come to put this all together. At this point the authors of this book pray that you have come to believe the truths presented herein. We also pray that you have become convicted of your sin and are ready to trust in Jesus Christ for salvation. If that is the case, then we encourage you to confess to God that you are a sinner. Just come clean and make it clear to God that you admit, humbly, that you cannot save yourself from your sin-condition or its eternal consequences. Confess that Jesus died on the Cross and rose from the dead. Ask God to forgive you of your sins because you believe Jesus offered an acceptable sacrifice on your behalf. Surrender your life to Christ. Do that right now. If you do, and it is a sincere and genuine expression of faith and trust in Christ then you can know that you now possess eternal life. God has forgiven your sins.

There is no fixed formula for confession, repentance, and surrender, but in recent years it has become popular in evangelical circles to encourage new believers to pray what is known as the Salvation or Sinner's Prayer. If nothing else, it provides a template for taking the most important step in your life. It follows, but please know that this prayer is not found in Scripture; therefore, you are free to revise it in any way you see fit:

> *I confess with my mouth that You, Jesus, are Lord, the Ruler over all. You are the Christ, the Son of God. I believe with all my heart that God raised You from the dead and You are alive forevermore, seated on Your throne in Heaven next to the Father. I believe Your blood that was shed on the cross cleanses me of all my sin. I trust in You as my Savior, Lord, King and Commander. I no longer make the vain attempt to try to be in charge of my life. I give it all up to You. I ask for God's forgiveness for my sin through Your sacrifice on the cross. Come make me clean. Restore me to a right relationship as a child of my Heavenly Father.*

WHY DID GOD SAVE ME?

At this point, having humbled yourself before the Cross of Christ Jesus, it's important that you be clear on why God has saved you. We've already established that you did nothing to deserve being saved. In fact, given the enormity of your sin-condition, you *don't* deserve to be saved. You deserve death and eternal punishment. Singer-songwriter Kris Kristofferson asked the same question in his 1972 hit song "Why me Lord?"

> Why me Lord, what have I ever done
> To deserve even one
> Of the pleasures I've known
> Tell me Lord, what did I ever do
> That was worth loving you
> Or the kindness you've shown
>
> Lord help me Jesus, I've wasted it so
> Help me Jesus I know what I am
> Now that I know that I've need you so
> Help me Jesus, my soul's in your hand
>
> Tell me Lord, if you think there's a way
> I can try to repay
> All I've taken from you
> Maybe Lord, I can show someone else
> What I've been through myself
> On my way back to you
>
> Lord help me Jesus, I've wasted it so
> Help me Jesus I know what I am
> Now that I know that I've need you so
> Help me Jesus, my soul's in your hand

Kristofferson admits that given his sin-state, he cannot figure out why God saved him. The answer, for Kristofferson and for you, is two-fold: First, God has saved you because He loves you and wants eternal relationship with you; second, God has saved you not for your glorification, but for His. Now that you are saved, you bear witness to His glory! That means that the words "I've been saved" are all about Him. It will be of inestimable benefit if you keep it in that perspective.

BUT HOW DO I KNOW?

Of course, this leads to one other issue to consider. How do you know that you're truly saved? Do you get goosebumps? Do you begin sobbing uncontrollably? Begin speaking in a strange language? Go around with a perpetual grin on your face? Are you suddenly able to stop smoking or no longer yell at your kids? The truth is that some of the pieces of evidence people look for may or may not be present. To be sure, some people may have an emotional reaction to the Gospel. At the very least there should be true conviction and guilt over sin and a sense of remorse. But there may not be some huge dramatic, emotional moment. In fact, God may work in your heart over months, even years, to fully convince you of these truths. Regardless of how it happens, there will be evidence that someone has experience a life change. The Bible calls this "fruit." Paul lists out this fruit in his letter to the churches of Galatia. True believers will demonstrate, "love, joy, peace, longsuffering, kindness, goodness, faithfulness, gentleness, self-control (5:22-23)." Do not assume that you will demonstrate these qualities perfectly. However, there will be a sea-change in spirit and attitude that results in actions consistent with these qualities. And the longer you live the life of the faith, the more prominent these qualities should become.

But Paul's list is not exhaustive. Closely connected with the fruit mentioned above would be actions consistent with obedience. This could take on different forms. Some people may be in the depths of depravity, struggling with rather significant forms of sin (chemical addictions, sexual immorality, etc.). In that case, the transformation that occurs can be radical. In other cases, it's possible someone was living what they thought was a pretty decent life. They didn't talk ugly, cheat on their spouse, and treat people with disrespect. They tried to be kind and compassionate, love their children, and express a good work ethic. Lost people can demonstrate character and integrity to some degree; some can even demonstrate character and integrity to a convincing degree. In this case, an important act of obedience is one's surrender to the Lordship of Christ and a rejection of the idea that you can save yourself through good works. Whatever the situation, trusting Christ in salvation shows up in the way someone lives. Ephesians 2:8-10 reminds us that both the grace and faith necessary for salvation is God's gift. Our works do not save us. However, as a result of being saved we are "created in Christ Jesus for good works (10)." In other words, good works are the *result* of genuine salvation; they are not the means of obtaining it, nor does one need to perform a yearly quota of good works in order to remain "saved, in good standing."

Another important piece of evidence may seem like a strange sign of salvation. But people who have truly trusted Christ will continue to experience conviction for sin. As we've stated before, sin will still be a reality in the life of the believer. That's not to excuse it. However, you can be certain that if you are truly saved then when you do sin you will experience conviction over that sin and seek to restore fellowship with God through confession. This is not done in order to get saved again. Instead, as a believer you confess and repent in order to continue to cooperate with God's ongoing work of making you more and more Christ-like.

The fact is that sometimes believers struggle with evidence of sin in their lives. As a pastor, Scott has had more than one person come to him concerned that some plaguing sin in their life is evidence that they're not really saved. In almost all cases, these folks are simply dealing with the conviction of the Spirit. If you struggle with sin and seek to deal with it in a godly and biblical way, then sorrow over your sin a good sign the Spirit is at work in your life.

While we're on the subject of the Holy Spirit, The Bible gives assurance that the Holy Spirit works in us to confirm that we are children of God. Paul talks about this at length in Romans 8. After teaching us that children of God are those led by the Spirit and have been adopted by God, he adds, "The Spirit Himself bears witness with our spirit that we are children of God (8:16)." He makes the same basic point in Galatians 4:6 telling us that "God has sent for the Spirit of His Son into your hearts" and that this allows us to declare God is our Father. In other words, the Holy Spirit will confirm our adoption into God's family through Christ.

To all who <u>received Him</u>, to those who believed in His name, He gave the right to become children of God" (John 1:11,12).

CONCLUSION

This is the good news of the Gospel: You can be saved, you can get to Heaven, you can live forever in relationship with God. You can have the assurance that your sins have been forgiven. Colossians 2:13-14 reminds us that even though we were dead in our sin God has made us alive: "And you, who were dead in your trespasses and the uncircumcision of your flesh, God made alive together with him, having forgiven us all our trespasses, [14] by canceling the record of debt that stood against us with its legal demands. This he set aside, nailing it to the cross." This means you can have a relationship with God that begins in this life and continues into the next. Romans 8:38-39 says, "I am persuaded that neither death nor life, nor angels nor principalities nor powers, nor things present nor things to come, nor height nor depth nor any other created thing, shall be able to separate us form the love of God which is in Christ Jesus our Lord." Hallelujah!

    God's love for you is beyond imagination. And God is prepared to express this love to you for all eternity. Philippians 1:6 promises, "he who has begun a good work in you will complete it until the day of Jesus Christ." You can trust God with your life. God can forgive you and cleanse of your sins if you will trust in Him and the work of Jesus Christ. And if you have followed the steps outlined in this chapter then the authors encourage you to find someone and tell them the good news of what has taken place in your life.

    As we conclude, keep in mind that while the information presented to this point in the book is all that is necessary for salvation, this isn't the end of what the Bible has to say on the subject. To be saved is simply the beginning, after which God continues to work in the hearts of believers to make them more and more Christ-like. As believers, we are to cooperate with the work God is doing in us by fostering it. The second part of this book gives some basic instruction on what to do once you've trusted in Christ and surrendered your life to Him. Finding a right church, reading the Bible, and developing a prayer life will put you in a position to continue to grow in your faith.

RECOMMENDED READING

- Klavan, Andrew. *A Secular Jew Comes to Faith in Christ.* Harper Collins, 2016.

- Butterfield, Rosaria. *The Secret Thoughts of an Unlikely Convert,* Crown and Covenant Publications, 2012.

- Chapman, John. *A Fresh Start,* Matthias Media, 1992.

- Greear, J.D. *Stop Asking Jesus Into Your Heart,* B & H Books, 2013.

- Horton, Michael. *The Gospel-Driven Life,* Baker Books, 2012

- MacArthur, John. *Saved Without a Doubt,* David C. Cook 2011

QUESTIONS FOR PERSONAL REFLECTION AND DISCUSSION

1. If you have not yet followed the instruction in this book on how to be saved and ensure that you are going to heaven, what conflict is holding you back? Are you concerned about what certain people will think or how they will react when they learn of your commitment? Do you still have intellectual roadblocks to accepting Jesus as your Lord and Savior? Regardless, what do you think you need to do in order to remove those stumbling blocks from your path to salvation?

2. For purposes of discussion only, let's say that the authors are wrong and everyone's going to Heaven. What, then, would be the consequences to those people who accept the authors' thesis?

3. In looking at the question above from the other perspective, if it turns out that the authors are right, what are the consequences to those who reject their thesis?

4. Why can't you "work" your way to heaven? What is wrong with trying to do more good than bad, believing God will let into heaven based solely on the fact that your moral life is "in the black?"

5. Is there a conflict between believing that Jesus Christ is your Lord and Savior and also believing that you get into heaven by doing lots of good things? If so, describe the difference.

GETTING TO HEAVEN

6

Heaven is Indeed for Real (as is Satan)!

> Creatures are not born with desires unless satisfaction for those desires exists. A baby feels hunger: well, there is such a thing as food. A duckling wants to swim: well, there is such a thing as water.... If I find in myself a desire which no experience in this world can satisfy, the most probable explanation is that I was made for another world. If none of my earthly pleasures satisfy it, that does not prove that the universe is a fraud. Probably, earthly pleasures were never meant to satisfy it, but only to arouse it, to suggest the real thing. – C.S. Lewis, *Mere Christianity*

A spate of books on a certain topic is a sure indication that people are fascinated by it and can hardly get enough. That certainly seems to be the case regarding books written by or about people who claim to have died, gone to Heaven, been given a tour, and then been miraculously restored to life—resurrected, if you will—presumably so they can relate their experience for the benefit of those less blessed. Some of these descriptions have features in common such as a long tunnel with a glowing ball of light at the end, talking with departed family members, and a conversation with Jesus, who usually tells them that their work on Earth isn't complete and they must go back and finish it (which begs the question of why they were transported to Heaven in the first place).

It's often assumed that the similarities from one near-death experience (NDE) to another somehow verify these accounts, but that's making a leap of logic. First, there are certain stereotypical images associated with Heaven—clouds, angels singing, dazzling light—so it's not at all surprising that many NDEs would share certain features, even at the level of small detail. Second, if these celestial travelers are reporting experiences that were contrived by demonic powers (see Ephesians 6:12), that would explain the similarities. In that event, the question then becomes: What would be Satan's purpose?

Deception, of course—he is, after all, the "Great Impostor." In this regard, Satan's purpose would be to convince people that Heaven is egalitarian, intended for an open to anyone and everyone, that the only requirement is death. If that's the case, then Jesus' mortal sacrifice on the Cross was meaningless—He saved us from nothing. If Satan can accomplish that trick, then he has won the battle, hands down.

Chapter 3 of the Book of Genesis opens with a description of "the serpent"—Satan—as, depending on translation, "more cunning" or "more crafty" than any creature God had ever made. His cunning is and has always been directed toward one goal: convincing people that God, not him, is the great deceiver, the liar, the fraud. This is precisely what the serpent beguiles Eve into believing. She falls for Satan's (i.e. the serpent's) temptation and then "passes it on" to Adam. What better way to advance Satan's grand plan than to convince people that Heaven's proverbial gate is wide open to all comers, that a person's beliefs and lifestyle are of no consequence? The idea has obvious appeal as illustrated by the 1998 hit movie *What Dreams May Come* starring Robin Williams. Nonetheless, it is a lie and a very appealing one at that.

"NEAR-DEATH" IS LIKE HORSESHOES... CLOSE DOESN'T COUNT

In 1970 psychiatrist Dr. Elisabeth Kubler-Ross (best known for developing the five stages of grieving paradigm) wrote a best-seller titled *On Death and Dying*. Her initial interest was purely scientific. She was convinced that she could find some rational, natural explanation for the phenomena of NDEs and so interviewed a good number of people who claimed to have had them. Initially, Kubler-Ross believed the standard naturalist position: to wit, once you die, that's it, you cease to exist in any form. But her research convinced her of the reality of an afterlife.

The reader may respond, "Well, that's a good thing," but not so fast. The afterlife in question was a mish-mash of elements drawn from Eastern religions, New Age philosophies, and Kubler-Ross' rather excitable imagination. Kubler-Ross ultimately abandoned a scientific approach to her subject and went off the proverbial deep end, claiming, for example, to have had an out-of-body experience during which she time-traveled at the speed of light. She began experimenting with séances to contact the dead, described face-to-face conversations with ghosts and eventually joined a bizarre religious cult led by a fellow who encouraged his followers to engage in group sex. Ultimately, Kubler-Ross helped found a spiritual healing center in California and became a leading guru in the New Age movement. Unfortunately, when she died in 2004 she realized, in an instant, how terribly wrong she had been, but during her life she attracted lots of followers, including actress Shirley MacLaine.

Kubler-Ross' story is that of an intelligent, albeit gullible, person who fell for Satan's cunning ways. He used her to convince equally gullible people—people drawn to the prospect of unique and exciting "inner" experiences—that he, not God, is the source of all truth. Kubler-Ross was a prime candidate for Satan's guile because she had already embraced the lie of Darwinian naturalism (i.e., atheism). He simply persuaded her—through appeal to her imagination and need to feel important—to exchange one lie for another.

There is no Biblical support for the notion that one can truly die—meaning that all physical processes, including brain activity, ceases—go to Heaven for a look-see, and come back to tell the tale. It's true that Jesus brought at least two people back to life, but the operative difference is Jesus. The authors of "I went to Heaven and came back to tell the tale" books do not claim that a flesh-and-blood Jesus brought them back to life. They simply woke up after being in comas. Nowhere in Scripture do we find God telling a person who has died that He is sending them back to Earth so they can tell everyone what a marvelous place they're eventually going to if they play their cards right. No Biblical character claims to have died, gone to Heaven, and then been resurrected to tell his amazing story to the world. In the absence of clear Biblical support for the validity of the extra-terrestrial voyages in question, the only conclusions available are that (a) these folks are making it all up or (b) they have been deceived into believing something that never happened. Having heard some of them describe their supposed experiences in Heaven, the authors conclude that most of these folks are sincere—they truly believe their own stories. The only remaining conclusion, therefore, is that they have been deceived. And to anticipate the rejoinder: Yes, Satan is capable of deceiving even committed, believing Christians. After all, he deceived Adam and Eve, and they had enjoyed a direct, face-to-face relationship with God Himself!

The fact is that Satan does not want *anyone* to get to Heaven. Once a person gets to Heaven, he is lost forever to Satan, who wants to own every soul that God has ever created and will do whatever it takes to accomplish that goal. Being more cunning than we can even imagine, Satan knows that for his plan to succeed, it must be paradoxical—it must seem to be one thing, for one purpose (liberation, personal autonomy), while actually being the complete opposite (eternal enslavement in Hell). So, he deceives normal, everyday unsaved people into thinking that they've gone to Heaven and have been charged with reporting on it to the rest of us. The clear message is that one really doesn't need Jesus to get to Heaven. Look! So-and-so went there and he's obviously not a committed believer! In this regard, it is significant to note that one of the heavenly tourists in question, an Episcopalian physician, wrote an entire book on his supposed trip to a sci-fi Heaven—which he refers to as the "Core"—in which his only two references to Jesus concern passing references to (a) the theme of someone else's book and (b) an image in a stained-glass church window.[†] It would appear that Jesus does not factor highly into said author's religious beliefs, yet readers of his book are to believe that he went to Heaven. In the estimation of your authors, that is a prime example of Satan's craftiness.

Colton Burpo, the four-year-old boy whose supposed trip to Heaven is chronicled in the 2010 best-seller *Heaven is for Real* (Thomas Nelson), describes encountering a Jesus who rode a rainbow pony and had "red markers" in the center of his palms. In the first place, Jesus' wounds were completely healed when He resurrected; second, nails were driven through his wrists, not his palms. Did Colton believe what he reported? Probably (he continues to insist that everything in the book truly happened), although there is the distinct possibility that the power of suggestion may be at work to some degree. It is, however, highly unlikely that he actually went to

---

[†] Alexander, Eben. *Proof of Heaven: A Neurosurgeon's Journey Into the Afterlife.* 2012, Simon Schuster.

Heaven, talked with Jesus (who supposedly held Colton on His lap while angels sang songs to him), and then returned to the humdrum world of the living. It is significant to note that *Heaven is for Real* has been denounced as misleading and un-biblical by leading Christian theologians including pastor and best-selling author John MacArthur.

In 2004, five-year-old Alex Malarkey was permanently disabled in an automobile wreck. In 2010, Malarkey and his father published *The Boy Who Came Back from Heaven*, an account of Alex's supposed visit to Heaven following the accident and while he was unconscious in the hospital. In 2011, Malarkey began disavowing the content of the book on social media, eventually admitting that the book was a bunch of—sorry, but we can't resist the obvious pun—malarkey. In 2012, after criticizing Christian publishers and bookstores for selling popular "heaven tourism" books, which he said "profit from lies," Malarkey insisted that his book be removed from circulation. When asked about Malarkey's disavowal, Colton Burpo said "People have their doubts about my story" but that he stood by it.

HEAVEN-MINDEDNESS

The church has always encouraged belief in Heaven partly as a means of motivating people to live moral, faithful lives. Such motivation comes straight from the pages of Scripture itself, some examples being

- Matthew 6:19-21 – "Do not lay up for yourselves treasures on earth, where moth and rust destroy and where thieves break in and steal, but lay up for yourself treasures in Heaven, where neither moth nor rust destroys and where thieves do not break in and steal. For where your treasure is, there your heart will be also."
- Romans 8:18 – "For I consider that the sufferings of this present time are not worth comparing with the glory that is to be revealed to us."
- 2 Corinthians 4:16-18 – "So we do not lose heart. Though our outer self is wasting away, our inner self is being renewed day by day. For this light and momentary affliction is preparing for us an eternal weight of glory beyond all comparison, as we look not to the things that are seen but to the things that are unseen. For the things that are see are transient, but the things that are unseen are eternal."

- Philippians 3:20-21 – "But our citizenship is in Heaven, and from it we await a Savior, the Lord Jesus Christ, who will transform our lowly body to be like his glorious body, by the power that enable him even to subject all things to himself."
- Hebrews 13:14 – "For here we have no lasting city, but we seek that city that is to come."

These are merely a sampling of Bible verses that encourage us to think often on the promise of Heaven. According to a rather over-used cliché, however, one can over-contemplate the promise of Heaven: to wit, "You don't want to be so Heavenly minded that you're no earthly good." The reference is to people whose piety overrides their commonsense; people whose eyes are fixed so steadfastly Heaven-ward that they never see the walls with which their faces frequently collide. That undoubtedly describes a few starry-eyed souls, but far more common are people so *earthly*-minded they're not any Heavenly good. As noted above, The Bible encourages the Christian to develop and maintain a Heavenly mindset, not an earthly one. One such verse exhorts, "If then you have been raised with Christ, seek the things that are above, where Christ is, seated at the right hand of God. Set your minds on things that are above, not on things that are on the earth" (Colossians 3:1-2). The fact is, a biblical or Christian worldview is fundamentally a Heavenly worldview, focused on God, His glory, and His purposes. Jesus Himself told us to pray that God's will would be accomplished on Earth as it is in Heaven (Matthew 5:10). In other words, we could all stand to be a little *more*, not less, "Heavenly-minded."

But the question remains: "What is Heaven like?" While The Bible certainly stops short of answering all of our questions about Heaven and giving us a complete picture of what it's like, we do have some important truths to note.

HEAVEN KNOWS

To begin to comprehend what Heaven is, it is necessary to understand what Heaven is *not*. For example, it is not, by a longshot, in any way like the description given by former California First Lady Maria Schriver in her children's book *What's Heaven*: "...a beautiful place where you can sit on soft clouds and talk... If you're good throughout your life, then you get to go [there]... When your life is finished here on earth, God sends angels down to take you heaven to be with him."[†] Setting aside Schriver's stereotypical description, her theology is way, way off the mark. The authors hope the reader is clear by now that one does not get to Heaven by doing good things. One's ticket is nothing more or less than belief in Christ Jesus as Lord and Savior. Finally, dispel the familiar notion that Saint Peter is sitting outside Heaven's pearly gates with what looks like a large ledger open in front of him, admitting some folks while sending others away. There is no biblical verse or passage that describes pearly gates or identifies Saint Peter as Heaven's gatekeeper.

    It's also important to understand that no human language can accurately describe Heaven, the simple reason being that Heaven is unlike anything any living person has ever experienced. Heaven is God's dwelling place, and God is not confined to the four dimensions of length, width, height, and linear time that form the boundaries of our earthly perceptions. According to reputable Christian astrophysicists, God exists in at least ten spatial dimensions and simultaneously in the past, present, and future. Because human beings cannot conceive of a reality that is not limited by the present time and three spatial dimensions, we have not developed words that are adequate to accurately describe what Heaven is like.

    Nearly everyone has developed some imaginative image of Heaven, but not even The Bible says very much about it. Your authors, being sticklers for the sufficiency of Scripture, believe that God has given us scant information for a reason known only to Him. But it must be a good reason. He is, after all, God.

    So back to the topic at hand: What is Heaven like? We do have some Bible passages that give us tidbits of insight, but only enough to whet our

---

[†] Schriver, Maria. *What's Heaven?* 2007, Golden Books Adult Publishing.

appetites. Keep in mind that the people who recorded the following incredible experiences are attempting to use worldly language to describe an otherworldly experience. Their descriptions are rich in symbolism and some aspects of them may even sound downright bizarre but again, that's the case simply because there are not words in the English language (or any other language) that can adequately capture the mind-boggling glory, majesty, and holiness of God's dwelling place.

The Bible tells us that four people, two prophets and two apostles, received visions of Heaven.[†] The prophet Isaiah, for example, tells us that he "saw the Lord sitting upon a throne, high and lifted up; and the train of his robe filled the temple. Above him stood the seraphim. Each had six wings; with two he covered his face, and with two he covered his feet, and with two he flew. And one called to another and said, 'Holy, holy, holy is the Lord of hosts; the whole earth is full of his glory (6:1-3).'" Such a display of glory and majesty resulted in Isaiah's immediate conviction and guilt over sin. In fact, Isaiah thought he was going to be torn apart from the inside out.

Ezekiel, another of God's prophets, was also given a vision of the glorious abode of God though his vision is much more complicated and replete with a fiery storm, sparkling wheels inside sparkling wheels, and winged creatures with four faces (human, bull, lion, eagle) and feet that gleamed like burnished bronze (Ezekiel 1:4-28). At the center of Ezekiel's vision is the glory of God's throne. One finds the same description of holiness, glory and majesty in the Apostle John's vision of Heaven in Revelation, Chapter 4. As do Isaiah and Ezekiel, John describes Heaven as a stunningly magnificent place. John's vision also includes human-like creatures (angels, presumably) seated around God's throne, proclaiming His immaculate splendor.

Unlike the recent descriptions of people who claim to have toured Heaven and then returned to the world of the living, the Bible's descriptions of Heaven are consistent with one another. They all portray Heaven as, in a word, indescribable—a place that exudes the awesome majesty, glory, and holiness of God. That certain elements of these biblical descriptions sound

---

[†] Understand that having a vision of Heaven is not akin to, say, watching a home movie. It may not and probably is not literal. Because a vision, even one that is God-given, is processed through a human brain, it may be nothing more than representational—accurately representational in that it truthfully conveys Heaven's glory, but representational (containing figurative components) nonetheless.

hallucinatory—which skeptics claim they are—simply reflects the limitations of earthbound speech, perception, and understanding. Nonetheless, the consistencies in the several biblical descriptions noted above make it possible to glean several valid observations/conclusions:

- Heaven and the experience of Heaven is centered on God, His throne, His glory, and His worship by winged beings—presumably angels.
- Heaven is not all about encountering departed friends and family members, having discussions with long-dead saints, or sitting down and chatting with Jesus. This doesn't mean there won't be reunions with loved ones. Those reunions, however, as much as we may be looking forward to them, are not the essence of the experience. Heaven is all about God. That's what the Bible wants us to understand.
- All three descriptions (Isaiah, Ezekiel, John) describe Heaven in physical terms. Isaiah talks about a structure like a temple and with foundations. John speaks of a throne surrounded by other thrones occupied by beings robed in garments of white. These biblical descriptions all note the presence of angels (or winged creatures that one assumes to be angels) who have form, substance, and motion. This is significant because it clearly, unequivocally shows that the typical picture of Heaven as a surreal place where a fog machine has clearly gone awry is just plain wrong. Heaven is a real, tangible place where God dwells along with angelic servants and those human souls who have been saved through belief in His Son. It is significant to note that descriptions of Heaven provided by people who have undergone NDEs bear no similarity to the descriptions given by Isaiah, Ezekiel, and John.
- "Heavenly tourism" accounts always focus on the person telling the story while biblical accounts focus on God. Both Ezekiel and Isaiah tremble before God, fearing for their very lives. There's no sitting on Jesus' lap while angels sing.

To this point, we've considered three of the four visions of Heaven contained in Scripture. The fourth account comes from the apostle Paul. His story may well be the most interesting because he refuses to describe it. In fact, he's so overwhelmed by the vision that he doesn't even talk about it in the first person. He says that he knew a man in Christ (presumably Paul) who had been "caught up to the third Heaven (2 Cor 12:2)." The reference to the third Heaven is to the place of God's dwelling. (Note that 2000 years ago, the term "first Heaven" referred to the daytime sky of clouds and sun and "second Heaven" to the nighttime sky of the moon, stars, and planets—that is, the visible universe.) We know that's what Paul is referencing because he goes on to say that this "man in Christ" was "caught up into paradise (v. 3)." Then Paul makes an incredible statement: "and he heard things that cannot be told, which no man can utter (v. 4)." So here we have the greatest Christian missionary of all time, the man whom God commissioned to write nearly half of the New Testament, and yet when it comes to this heavenly vision, he cannot and will not describe it. With all due respect to Colin Burpo, Eben Alexander, and other authors of recent heavenly tourism books, it is obvious that God does not allow just anyone a glimpse into His abode. Some 2000 to 2800 years ago He gave four specifically-anointed individuals all the previews of His heavenly domain that He is going to give, and He only gave permission to three of them to attempt descriptions of what they had seen. In other words, we need no other testimony than The Bible's to be assured that indeed, "Heaven is for Real."

PUT ON YOUR IMAGINATION (BUT DON'T GET CARRIED AWAY)

Thus far, we've covered biblical descriptions of Heaven as a real place defined by and centered upon God, His holiness, His majesty, and His glory. But what about our dear-departed loved ones? What is their experience like? First, it's reasonable to assume that those who have passed on to Heaven can and do experience something akin to what Isaiah, Ezekiel, and John experienced. God allowed the curtain to part quickly and slightly for those three prophets. God is incapable of deceit; therefore, what Isaiah, Ezekiel, and John saw was authentic. Their descriptions, limited as they are by human language and earthbound experience, may not be exact, but what they saw was nothing short of the real deal. That is what believers in and disciples of Christ Jesus can look forward to. And if the reader is still perplexed by images of four-headed flying beings with feet like bronze and the like, well, it will all be made clear once we are there. One's continuing perplexity reflects not something perplexing but rather the limits of human imagination. Our ability to envision Heaven is earthbound—it cannot, without God's direct intervention—make the leap between what is already familiar and what is so mind-boggling that Paul was not allowed to even attempt to describe it.

When all is said and done, we are left with a short list of certainties:
- Heaven is all about God.
- As is God, Heaven is more glorious, majestic, and holy than one can imagine. Or, perhaps it is more accurate to say that one can only imagine how glorious, majestic, and holy Heaven is.
- You, the reader, want Heaven to be your home when you exit this earthly life.
- People who go to Heaven are liberated from the realities of being in fallen flesh and a fallen world. They no longer experience emotional or physical pain. They no longer long for anything. They no longer struggle with their own shortcomings or anyone else's. Their only experience is that of awe and wonder and incredible gratefulness. Their acceptance of the truth of Christ Jesus has, as He promised, set them free.

Before leaving this section, it's important to note that a biblically orthodox view of Heaven is inconsistent with the concept of "soul sleep" espoused by certain denominations. Indeed, there are references in Scripture to believers "sleeping" once they die. Proponents of soul sleep argue from these references that when a believer dies he goes into a period of extended unconsciousness from which he is awakened at the end of historical time and bodily resurrected. The orthodox position, on the other hand, holds that the word "sleep" is merely a euphemism for death. The word is used to denote the fact that the bodies of believers will be resurrected at the end of historical time, upon Jesus' Second Coming. Death is not the end of existence. According to the Bible, it is not even the end of bodily existence.

HEAVEN: NOW, LATER, OR BOTH?

Up until this point, the authors have dwelt exclusively with what the apostle John referred to as the "third Heaven"—God's eternal dwelling place. According to Scripture, that is where believers in Christ Jesus are going when they die. It is what theologians call the "intermediate state"—the Heaven of Isaiah's, Ezekiel's, and John's visions, the Heaven to which people are referring when they say that a friend or relative has "gone to Heaven" or is "in Heaven."

But the Bible also promises another Heaven when God brings human history to a close. Just as there was a beginning when God created the universe and set history in motion (Genesis 1), so a time will come when God will bring it all to a close. At the end of historical time, at the time of Jesus' Second Coming (aka Judgment Day), when He establishes His eternal rule over all creation, the universe as we know it will be radically reformed. In the Book of Revelation, arguably the most mysterious book of The Bible, John writes (describing a vision given to him by Christ Jesus):

> Then I saw a new heaven and a new earth, for the first heaven and the first earth had passed away, and the sea was no more. And I saw the holy city, new Jerusalem, coming down out of heaven from God, prepared as a bride adorned for her husband. And I heard a loud voice from the throne saying, 'Behold, the dwelling place of God is with man. He will be with them, and they will be his people, and God himself will be with them as their God. He will

wipe away every tear from their eyes, and death shall be no more, neither shall there be mourning, nor crying, nor pain anymore, for the former things have passed away (Revelation 21:1 – 4, ESV).

Note that in this passage John refers to both the old Heaven—the Heaven to which believers are bound when they die—and a new Heaven—a second Heaven associated with a new, restored Earth. This second Heaven (not to be confused with the "second Heaven" of moon, stars, and planets to which the apostle Paul referred in 2 Corinthians 12:2) is the Heaven to which believers will be resurrected, in physical bodies, at the end of time, when God draws the final curtain on human history.

The closest one can come to conceiving of this new Heaven and new Earth is the Garden of Eden. Ironically, humanity's first home was, in many respects, very much like its last and lasting home. Again, we are limited in our ability to conceive of this final resting place but every indication is that the new Heaven on Earth will be...

- a physical, literal place;
- a paradise, perfect in every way, in accord with God's original design;
- social, community-based, with human-to-human relationships, and perhaps even vocational responsibility.
- a place where, as was the case with the Garden of Eden, man will be in direct, regular communion with God.

John describes how New Jerusalem reflects "the glory of God (21:10)" and shines with sublime magnificence. The beauty of the walls and gates is beyond description. It is shaped like a giant cube measuring twelve thousand furlongs in height, width and depth. This would equal just over 1400 cubic miles which equates to almost 2 million square miles of ground space, or about half the size of the United States. Imagine a city whose walls extend from the Gulf of Mexico to Canada and from the Atlantic Ocean to the middle of Kansas, keeping in mind that the height of the walls rises to the same height as its length and width.

John uses incredible language to describe how this city was built. The passage is full of references to precious stones used in the building of the walls. There is at least one street that's described as being "pure gold (21:21)." And while the walls are described as forming a cube, it appears that each wall has three gates, each made of "one pearl (21:21)." Unlike cities today that require numerous support services (hospitals, police and fire departments, and so on) New Jerusalem requires only the presence of God and Jesus Christ. They provide all the light necessary. There is "no need of the sun or of the moon to shine in it, for the glory of God illuminated it. The Lamb is its light (21:23)." There is "a pure river of water of life, clear as crystal, proceeding from the throne of God and of the Lamb (22:1)." In terms of food it says "on either side of the river, was the tree of life, which bore twelve fruits, each tree yielding its fruit every month. The leaves of the tree were for the healing of the nations. And there shall be no more curse, but the throne of God and of the Lamb shall be in it, and His servants shall serve Him (22:2-4)." Note that there is sustenance, life, joy, peace, well-being, service and community in this one place—all provided by God the Father, God the Son, and God the Holy Spirit!

John also tells us that "Its gates shall not be shut at all by day (there shall be no night there). And they shall bring the glory and the honor of the nations into it (21:25-26)." The fact that the gates of New Jerusalem will be forever open is highly significant because in John's day, a town's gates were vital sources of protection, especially at night. From sundown to sunup, soldiers were stationed at a town's gate or gates to stand guard. But in New Jerusalem there is no concern, no threat that would require watchful soldiers. As it says in verse 27, "But there shall by no means enter it anything that defiles, or causes an abomination or a lie, but only those who are written in the Lamb's Book of Life." In other words, only those who have Jesus as their Savior—those who have been washed clean of sin by His substitutionary blood sacrifice—have permission to enter and live there forever.

That God will be present tells us that New Jerusalem is a place of absolute perfection. Life there will be free from every form of sin and its corruption. Keep in mind that every atom of the universe deals with the corruption of sin, Adam's fall in the Garden of Eden, on some level. But those who enter into this final state of eternity will enjoy forever a place where death is no longer a word. People won't cry or hurt or mourn.

And now, the most important feature of this final heavenly existence: Since Heaven is a real, physical place, believers will live in it with real, physical bodies. We've already noted the fact that death includes the separation of the soul from the body. The soul of the believer is ushered into the presence of God. At some point in the future, during what are known as the end times, believers in Christ Jesus will be restored to physical bodies. Just as Jesus was resurrected in a perfect body, so too will believers be resurrected. We will be given new and perfect bodies fit for a perfect New Heaven. God will clothe our souls with new physical bodies and it is in this form that we will exist for all eternity.

Consider the Apostle Paul's teaching in I Corinthians 15. "I declare to you, brothers and sisters, that flesh and blood cannot inherit the kingdom of God, nor does the perishable inherit the imperishable. Listen, I tell you a mystery: We will not all sleep, but we will all be changed—in a flash, in the twinkling of an eye, at the last trumpet. For the trumpet will sound, the dead will be raised imperishable, and we will be changed (50-52)." A similar image is taught in I Thessalonians 4:13-18. Paul refers here to the so-called "rapture." Paul is saying that on Judgment Day, at Jesus' Second Coming, "at the last trumpet," (a) believers who have already died will be raised in perfect (imperishable) bodies and (b) the bodies of those believers who are alive at that time will be perfected for eternal life in New Jerusalem.

What will our resurrected bodies be like? The closest The Bible comes to answering that question is found in the apostle John's first letter: "Beloved, now we are children of God; and it has not yet been revealed what we shall be, but we know that when He is revealed, we shall be like Him, for we shall see Him as He is" (3:2). The He and Him referred to in this passage is Jesus. Being "like Him" means that we will be in sinless, perfect and eternal bodies that are invulnerable to disease, decay, or destruction.

FREQUENTLY ASKED QUESTIONS (AND STABS AT ANSWERS)

Q: What will we do in Heaven?
A: This question never fails to elicit imaginative responses. Keep in mind, though, the authors are restricting themselves to only what The Bible says. Because God has chosen to keep Heaven shrouded in mystery, only allowing brief glimpses, the answer to the question is less than complete, but we do have some suggestions as to the activity that takes place in Heaven.

- **Heaven is a place of worship.** Passages such as Revelation 4 and 5, or 19:1-4 or Isaiah 6 depict the worship that goes on unceasingly in

Heaven. This doesn't mean that one will spend eternity singing to God as if Heaven was a never-ending church choir. There are, however, Heavenly beings that do nothing but tend to God's throne through unceasing acts of worship. And there are evidences that the people of God will engage in singing praise to Him.

- **Heaven is a place of rest.** The author of Hebrews says, "There remains therefore a rest for the people of God. For he who has entered His rest has himself also ceased from his works as God did from His (Hebrews 4:9-10)." The image is that of God on the seventh day ceasing from His work of creating the universe. Likewise, God commanded that His people observe a similar "Sabbath rest" on the seventh day of every week. This command was a foreshadowing of the future, eternal rest promised to God's people. To rest is not to cease from all activity; it refers to being free of all physical, emotional, and mental struggle. No unpaid bills looming over your head. No nagging job deadlines. No broken relationships lying heavily on your heart. No anxiety over upcoming doctors' visits. Imagine living every second of every day free of all worry! That's what is meant by Heaven being a place of rest.

- **Paradoxically, Heaven is also a place of activity**. Matthew 19:28 speaks of those who will sit on twelve thrones and be given a place of authority in the kingdom. One can reasonably interpret this to mean there is something about Heaven that requires some form of leadership structure. Also, keep in mind that our final Heaven—New Jerusalem—is described as a "city." That implies activity, albeit refreshing, relaxing activity. Sorry, but you won't be reclining on a divan, eating grapes and listening to angels playing harps. That describes not Heaven, but the depravity of ancient Rome. When God created Adam and Eve, before the Fall, He assigned them the task of tending to the Garden. Work and activity was part of God's initial plan for life on Planet Earth. Work only became a struggle (toil) after sin entered the world. That is precisely what God told Adam: "Cursed is the ground because of you; through painful toil you will eat food from it all the days of your life...By the sweat of your brow you will eat your food...." (Genesis 3: 17-19). In Heaven, that curse is removed and work becomes joy again.

- **Heaven is a place of fellowship.** The Bible tells us that believers will live in relationship to one another, with God, and even with angels. Hebrews describes this community life: "But you have come to Mount Zion and to the city of the living God, the Heavenly Jerusalem, to an innumerable company of angels, to the general assembly and church of the firstborn who are registered in Heaven, to God the Judge of all, to the spirits of just men made perfect, to Jesus the Mediator of the new covenant..." (12:22-24). Note how the passage describes our existence in Heaven in relational terms. It refers to the "general assembly of the church" which implies a festival-like gathering. Furthermore, The Bible talks about there being a meal in Heaven called the marriage supper of the Lamb. Revelation says, "Blessed are those who are called to the marriage supper of the Lamb!" (19:9). Jesus refers to this while eating His final Passover meal with His disciples (the Lord's Supper): "Assuredly, I say to you, I will no longer drink of the fruit of the vine until that day when I drink it new in the kingdom of God" (Mark 14:25).

Q: **Will we see and relate to our friends and family in Heaven?**
A: There is evidence to suggest that even though they (and us) may not look the same, we will know our loved ones in Heaven but that the fundamental nature of these relationships will be different. In 1 Thessalonians Paul offers important teaching on the resurrection of the believer. He does not explicitly state that getting to Heaven involves reunions with loved ones, but that is the implication (4:13-18). But there is also scriptural reason to believe that earthly relationships such as parent-child or husband-wife will not exist. Jesus clearly teaches that there is no marriage in Heaven, other than the marriage between Himself and His Church (Luke 20:27-40). It seems, therefore, that while there will be relationship, that Heaven will be a very social place, that the relationships will be qualitatively different.

Q: **Are my dear departed loved ones looking down on me from Heaven?**
A: Most people probably assume that the answer to this question is yes. People sometimes talk about loved ones "looking down on" or "watching over" them from Heaven. (Some people even claim to have had loved ones

appear to them in visions.) Indeed, there are some passages that could be implied to suggest people in Heaven have some idea of what's happening on earth. Luke 15:7 and 10 both indicate, for example, that Heaven rejoices over news of a sinner who repents. Revelation 6:9-11 says that the martyrs in Heaven want to know when God will judge the rebellious on the earth. Nonetheless, no passage in Scripture indicates that our departed loved ones will truly see those left behind on Earth. Furthermore, there are several problems with believing people are watching from Heaven. First, this carries the potential of creating some rather awkward possibilities. Let's face it, there are times when you want and even need complete privacy from "prying eyes." Second, the assumption that loved ones would want to turn their gaze back to earth contradicts the biblically-based idea that Heaven is God-centric. Third, if Heaven is a place free from all sorrow and pain and yet our dear departed can see us assumes they could see us in adversity without having any kind of sympathetic emotional response. They would be like observers walking through an aquarium, merely observing its denizens but feeling no emotion toward them or on their behalf. So, the answer is probably "no," departed loved ones are not looking down upon us from Heaven. Sorry to burst anyone's bubble.

CONCLUSION

"I've been concerned for some time about a declining interest in Heaven among Christians. Frankly, most North American Christians have things so good right here in this world that they don't know what it is to long for Heaven... There is a danger that we become so comfortable in this life that we forget we are but strangers and pilgrims in this world. Like Abraham, we're supposed to think of ourselves as vagabonds here on earth, 'looking for a city which has foundations, whose architect and builder is God' (Hebrews 11:12))." – John MacArthur, *The Glory of Heaven*.

As Marco Polo, the famous Venetian explorer of the 13th century, lay dying, he was urged by his detractors to recant—to withdraw the fantastical stories he had told about China and the lands of the Far East. But he refused, saying, "I have not told half of what I saw."

Like Polo, God has not revealed to us even half of what Heaven is like. He has given us but glimpses that are tantalizing, mind-boggling, and even perhaps a bit frightening at times. Whatever His reasons, the glimpses promise a place that is mind-boggling in every respect. We can be assured of one thing, and one thing only, that Heaven is waiting for the believer in Christ Jesus and that God is looking forward to us being there as much, or more, than we are.

RECOMMENDED READING

- Alcorn, Randy. *Heaven*, Tyndale House Publishers, 2004.
- Enns, Paul. *Heaven Revealed: What Is It Like? What Will We Do? And 11 Other Things You've Wondered About*, Moody Publishers, 2011.
- Lutzer, Erwin. *One Minute After You Die*, Moody Publishers, 2015.
- MacArthur, John. *The Glory of Heaven*, Crossway, 2013.
- Sanders, J. Oswald. *Heaven: Better by Far: Answers to Questions About the Believer's Final Hope*, Discovery House, 2013.

QUESTIONS FOR PERSONAL REFLECTION AND DISCUSSION

1. Can you think of reasons other than those given above (see Conclusion) why God has given us nothing more than a few brief glimpses of Heaven?
2. Using The Bible as your reference point, is there the slightest possibility that a person who claims to have been to Heaven and back during a near-death experience is telling the truth?
3. What aspects of these "heavenly tourism" reports identify them as untrue without a shadow of doubt? Clue: How do they all differ from Biblical descriptions of Heaven?
4. Identify four characteristics of the New Jerusalem, the Heaven-on-Earth referred to in The Bible.
5. Complete the following sentence: The primary reason believers in Christ Jesus are going to Heaven when they die is so that they may _____. Is it to reward them for the good things they did while they were alive? Is it to restore them to loved ones who died before them? Is it so that they can finally meet Jesus face-to-face? Is it to prove to them that cloud-walking is a reality?

Section Two

What Do I Do Now?

7

Go to Church, but Not Just Any Church!

Now that Christ Jesus is in your life and you're saved, you are assured of getting to Heaven. You're on your way! The remaining chapters deal with the things you should do to grow in spiritual maturity and thus grow closer and closer to your one-and-only Lord and Savior.

The next step in your journey is to begin regularly attending a church that will advance your faith development. Becoming an active member of the Body of Christ will move you from being a mere believer to being a disciple—one who not only follows Jesus, but is a living witness to others of His salvation and grace.

In other words, being a believer is not a one-way street where good stuff is constantly coming your way. You need to take that good stuff out into the world. The more actively you share with others the good news of Christ's redemption and offer of salvation, the more of a model you become of His grace, the stronger and more joyous your faith will become. That "giving back" begins with you receiving the teaching and discipleship essential to being a proper witness for our Lord.

People who fail to "activate" their own salvation with regular church attendance are very likely to slip back into the counterproductive habits of their former, non-believing lives. The somewhat tragic truth, however, is that not all Christian churches (or churches that claim to be Christian) are equal. Some will further your Christian journey and some, quite frankly, will lead you away from Heaven—and as you should know by now, away from Heaven is Hell. The churches in question engage in various forms of scripture-twisting and false teaching and fail in various other ways to properly address discipleship needs. They also fail to develop the sort of fellowship bonds that are necessary to resist the temptations of Satan and stay on the Christian path. In making your choice of church, the most important variables to be considered are:

- Denomination
- Fellowship
- Worship
- Teaching
- Preaching
- Counseling
- Mission Work

As we consider these church features, one at a time, the authors want the reader to keep in mind that both of us are Southern Baptists, and SG is the pastor of Tabernacle Baptist Church in New Bern, NC. No doubt about it, we are biblical fundamentalists, albeit we do differ with respect to two or three non-essential biblical matters—that is, matters that do not affect one's salvation. Concerning theological essentials such as the virgin birth, Jesus' divinity, the Trinity, and Jesus' redemptive sacrifice on the Cross, we are squarely in accord and in solid agreement with reform theology. No doubt about it, we are biased concerning the issue of choosing a church home, and we make no apologies concerning that bias.

DENOMINATION

In the United States, the two major Christian classifications are Protestant and Roman Catholic. Less-prominent "stand alone" churches include Greek Orthodox (also known as Eastern Orthodox), Russian Orthodox, Anglican Catholic, Coptic, and Armenian Christian, all of which spun-off at some point from either the Church of Rome or the Eastern Orthodox Church but still share many liturgical and doctrinal characteristics.

Up until 1517, the Roman Catholic Church was "it" in Western Civilization—the "only game in town," as goes the contemporary saying. That was the year Martin Luther—at the time, a German Catholic monk and well-known professor of theology at the prestigious University of Wittenberg—mailed his so-called *Ninety-Five Theses* (actually titled "Disputation of Martin Luther on the Power and Efficacy of Indulgences") to his presiding bishop. In the *Theses*, Luther challenged several Catholic Church teachings and practices, most notably the unbiblical belief that freedom from God's punishment for sin could be purchased with money—a practice known as "indulgences." The following year, several of Luther's like-minded friends paid to have his *Theses* printed and distributed. In short order, Luther and his writings were the talk of Europe. In 1520, both Pope Leo X and Holy Roman Emperor Charles V (the Pope's secular counterpart in Medieval Europe) demanded that Luther retract his writings. He refused, and was subsequently excommunicated by the Pope and designated an outlaw by the Emperor.

Luther continued to teach and develop his "new" theology, the word requiring quotes simply because Luther was attempting to do nothing more than restore the beliefs of the First Century church patriarchs. Luther advanced four fundamental theological precepts or doctrines, all of which were at the time and still are in direct opposition to Catholic doctrine:

- Salvation is not earned by good deeds but is received as a free gift of God's grace through faith in Christ Jesus (thus challenging the Catholic doctrine that salvation could be purchased through indulgences or earned through charitable works). In Protestantism, this is known as the doctrine of *sola fide* or "through faith alone"

- Christ Jesus is the *one and only nly* mediator between God and man (thus challenging the Pope's authority, the authority of priests, bishops, and cardinals, and the Catholic practice of praying to Jesus' mother Mary and various other "saints"). This is known as the doctrine of *solo Christo* or "through Christ alone."
- The Bible—Old and New Testaments—is God-given and is the one-and-only source of divinely-received knowledge (thus challenging the authority of extra-biblical papal works such as the so-called Magisterium). This is known as the doctrine of *sola scriptura* or "by Scripture alone."
- All baptized Christians are co-equal members of a Holy Priesthood (thus challenging the notion that certain knowledge, functions, and sacraments are invested in the Catholic priesthood alone).

Luther didn't stop there, however. His translation of The Bible into German vernacular made it accessible, for the first time, to the common man and led to the first English translation known as The Tyndale Bible. The many hymns he wrote helped establish the practice of congregation-wide singing in church (as opposed to all singing being performed by choirs only) and his marriage opened that institution to Protestant clergy.

Luther's radical (for the time) teachings were the impetus for the Protestant (as the word indicates, a protestant is one who opposes and *protests* the abuses of the Roman Catholic Church) Reformation, which is without doubt one of the Top Five Events in the history of Western Civilization. The first followers of Luther called themselves *Lutheran* and eventually formed the Lutheran Church in Germany. Shortly thereafter, other Protestant denominations began forming in Europe. In 1534, the English Parliament passed the Act of Supremacy which vested King Henry VIII as "Supreme Head on Earth of the Church of England." From that point, despite several intra-European wars, the Protestant Reformation was unstoppable.

The authors are unabashed in encouraging the reader to choose a church home that is Protestant and incorporates the features discussed below.

FAITH-STRENGTHENING FELLOWSHIP

When picking a church, resist the temptation to base your decision primarily on where lots of people you know, including close friends, are attending. Oftentimes (but not always), the most popular churches in a town are those that do a good job of entertaining or simply making people feel good about themselves and the good works they are doing but a mediocre to downright bad job of properly teaching The Bible.

    A right and proper church experience will and should strengthen fellowship, true. The issue is the quality or nature of the fellowship. In short, like all Christian churches are not equal, all Christian fellowship is not equal either. Early on in our Christian walk, for example, Willie and I (JR) attended a church where fellowship was strong, but we eventually came to the realization that it was the wrong sort of fellowship; to wit, church members would get together on a regular basis and party. Generally speaking, a good time was always had by all. The adult beverages flowed, people told jokes, and the food was always recommendable. Except for Sunday sermons, no one ever talked about The Bible, however, much less Jesus. In fact, it seemed that on the rare occasion when those subjects came up, people—including, at times, the minister—became noticeably uncomfortable. And most of the folks who kept bringing up those subjects came to be regarded as extremists who lived out on the religious fringe. Mind you, church fellowship can and should involve get-togethers where people have a good time. But when having a good time overshadows supporting one another's faith-walk, something is wrong.

WORSHIPFUL MUSIC

These days, a significant number of highly popular churches feature loud guitar-driven bands that play what's called contemporary Christian praise music. That's a euphemism for rock 'n' roll with themes that are at least nominally Christian. Don't misunderstand me on this point. I happen to love good rock 'n' roll, most of which I believe was done between 1955 (Elvis' first ground-breaking recordings at Sun Studios in Memphis and Chuck Berry's recording of "Maybellene" at Chess Records in Chicago) and 1980 (Led

Zeppelin disbands following the tragic death of their drummer, John Bonham). Sometimes, upbeat contemporary music can be an effective means of inspiring worship, but in a properly grounded church the music is secondary to the message, the teaching, and compliments it rather than being a stand-alone. In many of the churches in question, that relationship is inverted for the purpose of attracting young people who all too often come to the church in question, hear the music, and go back home with little memory of the message that was delivered, if in fact it was even memorable. Furthermore, I've belatedly come to the conclusion that the most meaningful "church songs" are the traditional ones like "How Great Thou Art" and "Just a Closer Walk with Thee." Done properly, they can bring one to tears of gladness and joy. Maybe I'm just getting crotchety in my old age, but I think something is amiss when the words to a song are less important than the rhythm, the instrumentation, and the volume. There are few experiences as moving as a full church choir performing "Amazing Grace" *a cappella*. Rock 'n' roll just can't compete.

TRUTHFUL TEACHING

The term *orthodoxy* refers to church doctrine, teachings, and practices that are based on reasonably accurate interpretations of accurate (inspired) Bible translations. Unorthodoxy, therefore, refers to doctrine, teachings, and practices that are biblically incorrect and, therefore, misleading. Unorthodoxy has been a problem in Christianity from its beginning. The apostle Paul forcefully addresses the issue of false doctrine and teachings in his two letters to the Christian community at Colossus. He warns against Christians falling under the sway of "deceitful philosophies" that are contrivances of man's own tendency toward self-serving thought. This does not mean that orthodoxy makes no room for debate on matters that are not central or essential to the very existence of Christianity, because it does. For example, there is ongoing debate going back nearly five hundred years concerning whether salvation is predestined or an act of free will. This debate, which may never be resolved, does not threaten the integrity of the Church, the Body of Christ itself; therefore, one can be orthodox and believe either way.

If a pastor's teaching on essential matters (Jesus' divinity, His virgin birth, the Trinity of Father, Son, and Holy Spirit, salvation by faith alone, the inerrancy and sufficiency of God's Word, Jesus' redemptive sacrifice on The Cross and His literal resurrection) is not securely grounded in Scripture—God's Word—then it does not come from God; and if a church's teaching on a certain essential subject is not of God, then it is of Satan. There is no middle ground on that matter. Without exception, false teachings lead people away from Christ, which has been Satan's sole purpose since his first appearance in the Garden of Eden (Genesis 3).

Paul's warning is as relevant today as it was in the first century. Then, the controversies centered on the issue of Jesus' divinity and whether he was corporeal or simply a spirit. Today, many if not most false teachings tend to be politically-correct corruptions of or even downright departures from fundamental biblical principles and teachings concerning gender and sexuality. Most commonly, they deny sin and embrace postmodern "tolerance" (i.e., unequivocal acceptance) of homosexuality, transgenderism, and the ever-growing list of sexual aberrations. In 2003, for example, the Episcopal Church ordained an openly homosexual male bishop who subsequently "married" his male lover in 2008 (they divorced in 2014). Since that ground-breaking ordination, several other denominations, including the Presbyterian Church USA, have ordained openly homosexual clergy.

In and of themselves, incorrect teachings do not automatically disqualify a denomination as authentically Christian. Certain departures from orthodoxy (regarding the seven *essentials* above), however, do constitute such disqualification. The number of false teachings is also relevant to this determination.

Catholicism off the rails

Without doubt, more than a few Roman Catholic doctrines cannot be supported by a clear reading of Scripture. In this regard, a significant number of Protestant theologians have asserted that Roman Catholicism, because of both the nature and number of such doctrines, is a cult.[†] That

---

[†] Many people believe that a cult, by nature, is a small, insular group. In fact, a cult is defined by inerrancy, lack of orthodoxy in essential matters, not size. In the author's view,

may or may not be true, but the assertion, especially coming from respected theologians, certainly raises serious questions. The unbiblical teachings in question include:

- **Transubstantiation,** or the belief that the bread and wine of the Eucharist are transformed into the actual body and blood of Christ. It is obvious from a correct reading of Scripture that at the so-called Last Supper, Jesus was using the terms "my body" and "my blood of the new covenant" metaphorically, not literally. For one thing, Jesus' disciples were all Jews and Talmudic law, which Jesus said He came not to destroy, forbids the ingestion of blood. The disciples would have been repulsed and adamantly uncooperative if they thought Jesus was asking them to drink His blood. Furthermore, it is relevant to note that the doctrine of transubstantiation was not adopted until the Fourth Lateran Council of 1215. In other words, the early church fathers did not believe in transubstantiation, and it was *not* Catholic doctrine for longer than it has been doctrine.
- **Works-based salvation,** or the belief that salvation is a matter of both faith and good deeds. A proper reading of the New Testament reveals that good works are the "fruit" of salvation, not a means by which it is obtained.
- **Purgatory,** an intermediate state after physical death in which certain souls ultimately destined for Heaven must first undergo purification of a remaining sinful nature. This unbiblical doctrine (neither the Old nor New Testaments speak of Purgatory or any sort of similar place) denies the sufficiency of Jesus' redemptive sacrifice on The Cross. The concept of Purgatory was a matter of esoteric debate until its formalization at various Councils from 1245 to 1563.
- **The Assumption of Mary,** referring to the Catholic belief, unsupported by any verse of Scripture, that Jesus' mother was bodily taken to Heaven at the end of her earthly life.
- **Mary's supposed perpetual virginity,** which denies numerous references in the New Testament to Jesus' brothers and sisters. The Catholic Church insists that such references refer to cousins, but the

---

for example, the Mormon church (Church of Latter-Day Saints) is a cult by virtue of its many false teachings, which are reviewed in this chapter.

distinction between cousin and sibling is clear in Greek, the original language of the New Testament.
- **Mary's supposed sinlessness**, which contradicts several scriptures that clearly say that the only sinless individual who has ever lived was Christ Jesus (1 John 1:8, Romans 3:23) and the words of Jesus Himself who responded to a man who had called him "good teacher" that "No one is good except God alone" (Mark 10:17-18).
- **Relics**, which are supposed body parts (bone, teeth, hair, and so on) or possessions of so-called saints. The idea that these objects—even if their genuineness could be unequivocally determined—possess some spiritual power is a complete fabrication and once again denies the sufficiency of Christ's redemptive sacrifice on the Cross and that as the Apostle Paul clearly stated, He is our one-and-only mediator.

Arguably, the most egregious of official Catholicism's theological errors is the doctrine of **papal infallibility**—formalized at the First Vatican Council of 1870—which holds that the Pope is *incapable* of doctrinal error. Said differently, this means that any theological statement made by a Pope is correct. (The Catholic Encyclopedia—an official Catholic source—defines papal infallibility as meaning "more than exemption from actual error; it means *exemption from the possibility of error*" [italics added for emphasis].)

The doctrine of papal infallibility has put the Catholic Church into some interesting predicaments, ultimately compromising its theological integrity. In December 2015, for example, Pope Francis publicly asserted that Muslims and Christians worship the same god. This is clearly a doctrinal assertion; therefore, must be accorded unquestioned authority by the Catholic Church.

As is the case with a significant number of Catholic dogma, the doctrine of papal infallibility is an example of circular reasoning: *The Catholic Church says it is not possible for the Pope to commit doctrinal error; therefore, it is not possible for the Pope, who is the most exalted representative of the Catholic Church, to commit doctrinal error.* So, because the issue of God's character is most certainly doctrinal in the highest degree, when the Pope says that Allah and Yahweh/God are one and the same, Catholics are obliged to accept that the assertion is true.

But it is not true. The Koran describes a supposedly supreme being who is a liar and believes lying is justified when it achieves Islamic objectives;

who prescribes the murder of homosexuals; who authorizes the murder of Christians, Jews, and anyone else who does not believe in "Allah and his messenger"; who frequently changes his mind; and who is clearly not triune. The Bible, by contrast, describes a Supreme Being who is incapable of deception, is constant in every aspect and expression of His character, and Who is simultaneously One God and the Holy Trinity of Father, Son, and Holy Spirit. Therefore, Allah and Yahweh/God are not one and the same. Period.

Pope Francis is not the only Pope in recent history to embrace or downplay Islam—a religion whose holy scripture, the Koran, calls for the execution (without even a shred of due process) of homosexuals, Jews, and Christians. In addition, Islam denies to women the most fundamental of rights and prescribes death for a woman who has been raped by anyone but her father, husband, or brother. In 1999, Pope John Paul II publicly kissed the Koran and proclaimed that Muslims were equal to Catholics in their qualification for eternal life in Heaven. There is no doubt but that the doctrine of papal infallibility applies to such an absurd, not to mention dangerous, pronouncement. Pope John Paul II might as well have kissed *The Satanic Bible* (Anton LeVay, 1969).

Protestants accept that their church leaders are fallible. That is why, unlike the Catholic Church, orthodox Protestant churches invest infallibility not in any person, but in Scripture only (sola scriptura). To a Protestant, The Bible is the final authority concerning all matters, but especially church matters. That protects against the sort of doctrinal error that has plagued the Catholic Church since at least the Middle Ages. The Catholic Magisterium consists of a series of official pronouncements that have come down over the centuries from popes and committees of bishops and cardinals. Not one of the pronouncements in question stands on a solid biblical foundation. That is precisely why the Magisterium exists. Effectively, it is a man-contrived addendum to Scripture. It exists because the *Catholic Catechism* says that God's Word is "living"—the same word liberals use concerning the United States' Constitution. In both cases, "living" means that the original document is nothing more than a guide that is open to revision and amendment as times change. In the case of Scripture, the *Catechism* says that Christ, the eternal Word of the living God, must, through the Holy Spirit, "open our minds to understand the scriptures." That is nothing more than an official endorsement of theological relativism. It essentially means that if at any time Catholic Church leaders decide that scripture is insufficient or no longer relevant concerning a certain issue and should be amended vis-à-vis official pronouncement, the pronouncement in question is justified because Christ, through the Holy Spirit, inspired it—again, circular reasoning.

Mormonism is NOT Christianity

The Mormon church—also known as the Church of Jesus Christ of Latter-Day Saints—is another toxic environment in which false teaching abounds. Mormons tend to become very defensive when one challenges their claim to being Christian, but the undeniable fact is that despite their protests to the contrary, they do not believe in the God of The Bible or the Jesus of the New Testament Gospels. Prominent Mormons have admitted to exactly that.[†]

Gordon B. Hinkley served as the 15th President of The Church of Jesus Christ of Latter Day Saints from 1995 until his death at age 97 in 2008. He was the oldest individual to ever hold that highest of LDS offices and was regarded by Mormons as a prophet, seer, and revelator. In 1998, Hinkley publicly proclaimed that the Jesus of The Bible "is not the Christ of whom I speak." He went on to refer to Jesus and God's supposed conjoint appearance to sixteen-year-old church founder Joseph Smith in 1820, after which, according to Hinkley, Smith "knew more of the nature of God than all the learned ministers of the gospel of the ages." That's certainly a boastful claim, especially in light of the fact that there's no Biblical support for *any*—that's right, not one—Mormon belief concerning Jesus or God.

Mormons believe, for example, that Jesus was the result of (presumably) sexual relations between God the Father and his goddess wife—known only as the heavenly Mother or Mother in Heaven—both of whom were originally non-deities from another world or sphere of existence who somehow attained the status of supreme beings (Mormon doctrine is understandably fuzzy concerning the precise origin of God and the Heavenly Mother). Both the Mormon god and his goddess have bodies of

---

[†] In fairness, it must be noted that as is the case with many Catholics and mainline Protestants, significant numbers of Mormons do not recognize the un-Christian nature of most if not all Mormon teachings because they are sufficiently literate scripturally, a condition that renders them vulnerable to teachings that lead away from Christ (see Colossians 2:8). In short, many Mormons do not realize they are being deliberately misled.

flesh and bone and together they produce spirit-children in Heaven who go on to inhabit human bodies on Earth. Jesus is the spirit-brother of Satan as well as the authors and the reader—that is, everyone. Yes, you read that right.

Mormons claim that Mormonism is Trinitarian, but they do not believe that God, Jesus, and the Holy Spirit are One. Jesus and the Mormon god—both of whom inhabit separate physical bodies—are two separate personages of the "Godhead," which also includes the non-corporeal Holy Spirit. In a very loose sense, Mormonism is monotheistic but does not recognize that Jesus is co-equal with God the Father—which, the reader will recall, He clearly said He was. Furthermore, according to Mormon doctrine, Jesus atoned for the sins of mankind both in the Garden of Gethsemane and on the cross, in which case, His crucifixion was effectively irrelevant—had He not been put to death, He would still have atoned sufficiently.

That is but the short list of doctrinal differences between orthodox Christianity and Mormonism. Mormons claim to be Christian, but their corruption of centuries-old understandings concerning the nature of God, Jesus, sin, and salvation qualifies The Church of Jesus Christ of Latter-Day Saints as a cult. LDS President Hinkley was correct—the God and Jesus of Judeo-Christian Scripture are not the god and Jesus of Mormonism, not by a long shot.[†]

There are those who contend that Mormonism and orthodox Christianity are "close enough" in beliefs and maintain that the doctrinal differences are insignificant to the larger issue of salvation. Do not be deceived! That simply is not true. Jesus said that He and the Father are one and the same, that to know Him is to know God, and that no one comes to the Father (gets into Heaven) except through Him. The simple fact is that Mormon belief and doctrine precludes knowledge of the True Christ. It promotes a Christ who is a mere facsimile of the Christ of the New Testament. Subscribing to this pseudo-Christian denomination, therefore, prevents authentic salvation. Close counts in horseshoes; it does not amount to anything when it comes to getting to Heaven.

Keep in mind, dear reader, that Satan's one goal—not his primary goal, but his one-and-only goal—is to prevent YOUR salvation, to *own* you,

---

[†] http://www.christianpost.com/news/what-do-mormons-believe-ex-mormon-speaks-out-part-two-58494/

body and soul. To accomplish that, he must and will do all that he can to prevent you from coming to know the True Jesus, the True Christ. Mind you, the authors do not imply that the cult-denominations in question are satanic or that they secretly worship the devil. Nonetheless, they have unwittingly been seduced into his devious service.∞

Mainline Protestant churches and sexual deviance

Since the 1970s, many mainline denominations—specifically, Presbyterian (USA), Methodist, Lutheran, American Baptist, and Episcopal—have recanted or are in the process of "reconsidering" a biblical position concerning homosexuality. They have embraced the fiction that homosexuality is determined by inborn biological factors beyond a person's control—a theory that is not supported by any compelling scientific evidence and is clearly inconsistent with God's many statements concerning the issue. In 2003, the Episcopal Church USA went so far as to ordain an openly gay bishop, prompting a precipitous drop in Episcopal membership. When Episcopal spokespeople were confronted with the fact that The Bible specifically proscribes homosexual relations, their response was that The Bible only "mentions" the ban against homosexuality eight times, Jesus never mentioned it at all, and many of The Bible's teachings only applied to early Jews and have since expired. In this regard, it is significant to note that Jesus did not "mention" sexual abuse of children or animals, incest, bestiality, or rape either. According to the perverse "logic" of the contemporary Episcopal Church, those behaviors must be perfectly okay. And the idea that God must say something at least nine or more times for it to be binding and that anything He has said is subject to a statute of limitations is beyond absurd.

The false teachings from many mainline Protestant pulpits are becoming legion as the individuals occupying those pulpits become more concerned with appearing to be open-minded (tolerant, inclusive, embracing of diversity) than they are with dispensing unadorned Truth, which Jesus Himself said would divide families and friendships. One of the authors once attended a Sunday morning service in a well-populated

---

∞ The term "cult" is generally associated with a sect that is relatively small in number; therefore, it may challenge one to think of Catholicism and Mormonism—both of which enjoy large memberships—as cults. Numbers do not tell the story—teachings do.

mainline church where the pastor announced—presumably to the relief of many—that not believing in the Virgin Birth or Jesus' divinity did not disqualify one as a Christian. That essentially means that Christianity is anything anyone wants it to be. That's very inclusive, embracing, tolerant, and all those other characteristics of postmodern political-correctness, but it is simply not true. Jesus said the way to salvation was narrow, not wide. There are, in other words, boundaries to Christian belief and behavior. Any church that operates outside of those boundaries is "of the world," not of Christ. Period.

Oneness Pentecostalism

The "oneness" in Oneness Pentecostalism refers to the belief that God is not Trinitarian and that Jesus became the Son of God only at the moment of His birth. This belief simply does not square with Jesus' words in John 17:24 that God the Father loved Him "before the foundation of the world," or before the Creation. In other words, Jesus pre-existed time and space, which confirms that He is the eternal, ever-living Son of God. Furthermore, Jesus' promise to His disciples that He was leaving the Holy Spirit behind to guide, inspire, and help them build His church confirms the Trinity.

Whereas most Pentecostals and evangelicals believe that faith in Jesus Christ and repentance from sin are the only essentials for salvation, Oneness Pentecostalism defines salvation as consisting of repentance of sin, baptism in Jesus' name, and receiving of the Holy Spirit with the evidence of speaking in "tongues." There is no reasonable reading of Scripture that would support this works-based salvation doctrine.

Jehovah's Witnesses

If you talk with a Jehovah's Witness, you will undoubtedly be told that the accusation they are a cult is unfounded. You will be told that their beliefs are biblical. In fact, you will be told that the Jehovah's Witness Bible—the New World Translation of the Holy Scriptures—is the only true and accurate translation; that other translations deliberately mangle the original wording because the translators wanted to promote the absurd idea that Jesus was both fully God and fully Man, which he was not.

Jehovah's Witnesses do not believe in the Trinity of God the Father, Son, and Holy Spirit. They believe Jesus was divine while he was in heaven—their official website, Watchman's Post says Jesus was "a god" during that time—but "... while Jesus was on the earth he was not a deity. He was a man."[†]

Hello? A mere human being is not capable of bringing people back from the dead, walking on water, turning water into wine, multiplying bread and fish to feed thousands of people, or perform any of the other miracles Jesus performed during his active ministry.

Without doubt, the Jehovah's Witness church (officially, the Watchman Bible and Tract Society) qualifies as a cult. Witnesses do not believe in the Trinity. They have their own unauthorized Bible, they discourage their members from associating with people who are not JW and have been known to excommunicate them if they do. That's a cult. Do not go within 200 yards of a Jehovah's Witness church.

Christian Scientists

According to Christian Scientist doctrine, the material world is an illusion, illness is caused by improper thinking, and Jesus was a highly-developed human being who had the ability to harness the healing power of the Christ, a power that is ultimately available to anyone who has mastered proper self-discipline. Enough said. Do not go within 200 yards of a Christian Scientist Church or Reading Room.

(**Note**: The churches mentioned above are not the only ones currently engaged in false teaching. They are merely the most prominent and likely the most familiar to the reader. Hopefully, a summary of their heresies will suffice to attune the reader to false teachings in other religious environments and from other "religious" persons.)

[†] www.jw.org

PREACHING

One of a pastor's most important responsibilities is that of composing and delivering sermons that enlighten God's Word, The Bible, such that it guides listeners toward developing an informed Christian worldview and living a proper Christian life. Studies confirm that good quality preaching is of critical and often primary importance to people who are looking for a church home, as well it should be. For example, when Willie and John Rosemond moved to New Bern, North Carolina, in 2014 and were seeking a church home, John's first question of Pastor Scott Gleason was "Tell me about your preaching philosophy."

Unfortunately, the criteria that some people use to evaluate a pastor's preaching is often misplaced. Some folks are primarily interested in sermons that are entertaining and full of interesting anecdotes. Others are less interested in content than they are in style—they're attracted to a preacher who is full of energy and gets people "fired up." And then there are those folks who are primarily interested in pastors for whom conveying a proper understanding of the Word is less important than telling their flocks how to live a moral life—often, unfortunately, defined in terms of the pastor's socio-political perspective.

None of these criteria have any biblical merit. Granted, a preacher who can hold your attention is preferred over a preacher who's not a good public speaker, but it's also true that the latter may be adhering more steadfastly to the Word. What matters the most in preaching is not the preacher but the source from which the sermon is drawn. To put simply, you want someone who preaches from The Bible. Consider the apostle Paul's words: "All Scripture *is* given by inspiration of God, and *is* profitable for doctrine, for reproof, for correction, for instruction in righteousness, that the man of God may be complete, thoroughly equipped for every good work" (2 Timothy 3:16-17). The reason you want a pastor who faithfully teaches The Bible is because The Bible is the means God uses to equip you to live the Christian life.

But let's get a bit more specific. Plenty of people may preach with a Bible in hand or a verse on their lips, but looks can be deceiving. The preacherz in question may or may not actually be delivering sermons that are biblically-based, true to God's Word. Sermons that are true to the Word, that enlighten Scripture, are called "expository," meaning they teach what The Bible says in a way that properly explains a portion of Scripture—its historical context, its original meaning, and its present-day application to our lives as Christians. Other forms of preaching may, at times and from the mouths of certain pastors, be more entertaining, even interesting but they will not feed your faith as will expository preaching.

Phillip Nation, adult ministry publishing director for LifeWay Christian Resources, gives five preaching styles:

1. **Pulpitainment,** in which being clever and funny replaces stating truth plainly.
2. **Pulpiteering,** in which the pastor and his life experience are the point of the message.
3. **Over-sharing,** referring to generally well-intentioned sermons that are so full of personal confession that listening to them becomes awkward.
4. **Exegete-Only,** or sermons that are biblically-based, but academic and dry.
5. **Passage-Driven Exposition,** in which the preacher, says Nation, sets about "engaging people with the power of The Bible" and "exposes the truth about God in the Scriptures to people in desperate need of transformation."

In other words, the pastor's personality, personal experience, and punditry are less important than his faithfulness to God's Word. The expository preacher spends most of his time in the pulpit teaching through books of The Bible (or large portions of The Bible). While he may from time to time tackle a hot cultural or theological issue, most of his preaching is spent unpacking Scripture passages. This affords you the best opportunity to cooperate with the work of the gospel in your life.

MISSION WORK

Another important aspect of church life is what church insiders call mission, meaning the way in which a church shows concern for spreading the gospel to the ends of the earth. Such church efforts are driven by Jesus' parting instruction to His disciples: "Go therefore and make disciples of all the nations, baptizing them in the name of the Father and of the Son and of the Holy Spirit, teaching them to observe all things that I have commanded you; and lo, I am with you always, *even* to the end of the age" (Matthew 28:18-19). Thus, our Lord gave His church her "marching orders." Our purpose as members of the Body of Christ is to spread the Good News (gospel) of the work He did on the Cross for all mankind. In effect, once a believer's eventual place in Heaven is assured, he or she is charged with helping others attain the same assurance.

The church is not a "holy huddle" where Christians can keep themselves safe from all the non-Christian dangers of the world. That is, unfortunately, the seeming purpose of some church bodies. For example, JR sometimes relates a story of visiting a church where the preacher explicitly warned the congregation against having dealings with people who were not "members of the covenant." It was obvious that this was not a church; it was a cult, or at least bordered on being one. Its mission was less about the gospel than it was the pastor.

Not surprisingly, when Jesus created His church, He gave it a mission statement: Take the Good News to the ends of the earth! This work takes many forms. A church could

- adopt a particular Christian church or mission group somewhere in the world and give focused time to praying for them, engage with missionaries working in that area, sponsor mission trips to aid the missionaries, and otherwise give as much support and encouragement as possible;
- be involved in planting other churches both in the USA and abroad;
- provide essential financial support for young churches that need aid to get themselves "off the ground" as well as mission work around the world;
- and, needless to say, works within its own local area to bring people to discipleship in Christ Jesus.

In short, a church that recognizes that the mission field begins where the property line of the church ends and extends to the farthest reaches of the planet. To put it simply, God's mission of redeeming people to Himself in Christ is the church's mission. And this should play a critical role in the life of the church.

COUNSELING

One of a church's most important functions is that of providing counseling to members who are experiencing emotional, ethical, moral or relationship difficulties of one sort or another. Without exception, counseling done within a church should be firmly grounded in biblical principles. The only counseling form that Christians should expose themselves to is biblical or what is also known as *nouthetic* counseling. Churches that host or refer individuals to so-called Christian psychologists—individuals who make the vain, albeit sincere, attempt to blend biblical teaching and psychological theory and therapeutic techniques—are, in effect, denying the sufficiency of Scripture as a basis for counseling, encouragement and correction.

Psychology is a secular ideology that promotes a secular, humanistic worldview. Without exception, the major theorists in the history of psychology—Freud, Jung, Rogers, Maslow, Skinner, and so on—were atheists. Not one major psychological figure was a believing Christian. The worldviews of orthodox Christianity and psychology are in opposition. Furthermore, they cannot be reconciled, period. Therefore, there is no such thing as an authentic Christian psychologist. There are only psychologists who are trying to market themselves to Christians. The authors recommend against joining churches that affiliate with psychologists, regardless of the modifiers they may use.[†]

[†] To put these remarks in proper context, keep in mind that John Rosemond is a psychologist, licensed since 1979 by the North Carolina Psychology Board. His psychological bona fides uniquely qualify him to understand the irreconcilability of Scripture and psychology. He makes clear that he is not a Christian psychologist; rather, he is a believing Christian who happens to possess a license to practice psychology. In his counseling, however, he does not use psychological principles but sticks squarely with Scripture.

CONCLUSION

When searching for church you will discover no shortage of websites and church-related material delineating any given church's or denomination's mission or purpose. These statements are carefully crafted and usually the result of months of group discussion. In many cases these efforts to find a fresh "vision" for the church can distract from the biblical expectations for God's people.

In the final analysis, one can summarize the authentic church's fundamental purpose using straightforward language: *God has designed the church to be a fellowship of Christians who seek to glorify God in all they do as they grow in Christ-likeness and seek to make disciples of all nations.* Consider the picture presented of the first church in Acts where we learn that the very first church "continued steadfastly in the apostles' doctrine and fellowship, in the breaking of bread, and in prayers" (Acts 2:42). Verses 46 and 47 go on to say, "So continuing daily with one accord in the temple, and breaking bread from house to house, they ate their food with gladness and simplicity of heart, praising God and having favor with all the people. And the Lord added to the church daily those who were being saved." You can see in these verses the presence of the ideas mentioned above. The very first church was committed to those actions which would encourage worship, growth in Christ-likeness, and the sharing of the gospel with others.

When you look for a church you want to look for a place that offers you the opportunity to truly worship God. The music should be God-glorifying, focused on the gospel, and theologically rich. The preaching and teaching, both in the pulpit and classroom, should be centered on Scripture and help you grow in maturity in God's Word and, therefore, faith. Finally, the church should be concerned with the obligation given by God to make disciples of all nations. In other words, the church should be committed to sharing the gospel with those who have not yet believed in the gospel.

RECOMMENDED READINGS

- Dever, Mark. *9 Marks of a Healthy Church*, Crossway, 2013.

- MacArthur, John. "What Should I Look for When Choosing a New Church Home" (http://www.gty.org/resources/questions/QA121/what-should-i-look-for-when-choosing-a-new-church-home).

QUESTIONS FOR PERSONAL REFLECTION AND GROUP DISCUSSION

1. What does history demonstrate concerning the consequences to the Christian church of teachings that are not firmly grounded in God's Word?

2. What are the potential consequences to the integrity and effectiveness of a local church that makes loud, guitar-driven contemporary praise music the centerpiece of its worship?

3. Why is expository preaching preferable to the other four preaching styles identified by Phillip Nation? What are the potential pitfalls of each of those four preaching styles?

4. Some prominent theologians, including Dr. Bill Jackson of Association of Fundamentalists Evangelizing Catholics (AFEC), believe Roman Catholicism qualifies as a cult.[†] Others, including Hank Hanegraaff of the Christian Research Institute, maintain that although certain Catholic doctrine are un-biblical it is not a cult. What do you think and why?

5. Jesus warned His disciples that toward the end of the age, many false prophets would come claiming to represent Him (Matthew 24:4-5). Do you take Jesus' warning seriously? Are there false prophets operating in the church today? Who are they? Do you think that the presence of false prophets means we are in the end times?

[†] For an excellent summary of this position, see either http://www.eaec.org/cults/romancatholic or htmhttp://www.rapidnet.com/~jbeard/cath/isitcult.htm.

8

Reading and Studying The Bible

The purpose of this chapter is two-fold: First, the authors intend to convince you that The Bible is more than just another book; it is God's Word, intended especially for you; second, we want to provide beginning instruction on how to get the most out of reading The Bible. You've never read a book like The Bible; therefore, you shouldn't read it like any other book either.

By this point you've embraced God's plan of salvation and are ready to move ahead in your Christian faith. That means that the Holy Spirit—God's spiritual representative or "agent" on Earth—is working within you and will provide you with (a) guidance and resolve for proper Christian living and (b) Christian insight. By reading The Bible, God's Word, you begin the process of activating and energizing that insight. As His Word comes alive for you, you will begin to sense God's presence and will in your life.

God has given us two revelations concerning His nature and character, two means by which one can come to know Him: His physical Creation and His Word. Not *or*, but *and*. To know God as fully as possible, one must study and contemplate both His Creation and His Word—known respectively as His general and specific revelations.

God's Creation: As God created, He marked the end of each of His six creation periods by pronouncing that what He had done was "good." Some three thousand years later, God's Only Son Jesus said that "No one is good – except God alone" (Mark 10:18). Jesus never used a word loosely. In this case, Jesus is saying that if one wants to know God, who is good in every sense of the term, and penultimately so, one must know His Creation, which He pronounced "good" (in this context, *good* means perfect, without flaw, as it was prior to the Fall).

God's Word: When God, through Moses, liberated the Israelites from bondage in Egypt, He designated them His Chosen People by giving them the first five books of the Old Testament—what Jews refer to as the Torah. This momentous event took place, depending on one's source, sometime between 1500 and 1250 BCE. Since then, God has added another sixty-one books to The Bible, the last being the Book of Revelation, written in the latter half of the First Century A.D. Up until the philosophical revolution of the late Seventeenth and Eighteenth Centuries, commonly referred to as the Enlightenment, there was no debate in Christendom concerning The Bible's authorship. But as science and secularism began to displace faith in Western Civilization, that debate began, quickly became contentious, and has been heating up ever since. Today, for one to admit belief that God did in fact author The Bible, that it is "God-breathed" and inerrant, is to invite scorn and ridicule. Secularists are convinced that no intelligent person would believe such a fantasy.

Therefore, the reader is hereby cautioned: The authors intend to convince you in this chapter that what secularists believe is entirely subjective nonsense, mythology, fable—that The Bible is the very Word of God and as such is in fact the truth, the whole truth, and nothing but the truth. (Yes, he had human co-authors of a sort, but God's co-authors did not contribute their own ideas to The Bible; they simply wrote what the Holy Spirit inspired them to write.) We believe—and we claim to be reasonably intelligent people—that God created the Universe and everything in it, including mankind, that He gifted mankind with language and writing, and that He gave us The Bible in order that we may come to know Him and His Plan for mankind's redemption.

Think of it this way: If, when you were a child of, say, ten, your parents came to you one day and handed you a book, saying, "We wrote this book for you, so that you might understand yourself and us as much as possible and come to know our plan for you," you would waste no time in reading it from cover to cover, right? Right! Well, that's exactly what God, your Heavenly Father, has done. He has written a book for you so that that you might understand yourself and Him as much as possible and come to know His plan for your life. You best read it. Even if you possess doubt concerning The Bible's authorship (which we hope to dispel by the end of this chapter), you would do well to give benefit of doubt to the claim that The Bible is God talking directly to you.

What is it about The Bible that gives confidence that it comes straight from God? That very pertinent, all-important, life-or-death (literally) question can be answered by considering six facts:

- The Bible testifies on its own behalf
- The Bible is internally consistent (it does not—as does the Koran, for example—contradict itself) and a reliable source of truth
- From beginning to end, The Bible is one unified story as opposed to a collection of random stories
- Biblical prophecy has never failed to be fulfilled
- Time and time again, archeology has confirmed The Bible (unlike the case with the Book of Mormon)
- The Bible's verified impact on people's lives is unequalled in the history of literature

SELF-VERIFICATION

One reason to believe that The Bible is God's Word is because it claims to be. Some would object that the previous sentence amounts to circular reasoning: to wit, The Bible says it comes straight from God; therefore, The Bible comes straight from God. So then, why should one believe that the claim of The Bible's divine authorship is a special case, unlike, say, the Book of Mormon which was obviously the product of Joseph Smith's imagination (and probably helped along by a demonic being who claimed to be an angel named Moroni).

Right from the beginning, the reader of The Bible encounters a God who not only speaks, but a God who also speaks truthfully about Himself (and everything else). In Genesis 2, God instructs Adam on life in the Garden of Eden. The Bible does not say that these thoughts came to Adam in a dream or after he ate some plant he found in the Garden. It says God told Adam, in words, face-to-face, the things in question. This pattern continues with other biblical figures including Noah, Abraham, and Moses. The prophets of the Old Testament claim that God spoke directly to them. Some people—including most psychiatrists—would say that the prophets were more than a tad deranged; that they were undiagnosed schizophrenics. Two considerations are relevant to that judgment:

1. That bias currently exists because long ago (more than 2500 years, or around 500 BCE) God stopped using prophets as His spokespeople. Indeed, people who today claim ongoing personal

communication from God are, most likely, unbalanced. But way back in the prophetic period (1500 BCE – 500 BCE) certain people who made such claims were not regarded as slightly wacko, much less dismissed. It is likely, by the way, that even in the days of Isaiah and Jeremiah not everyone who claimed to be receiving messages directly from God were regarded as legitimate.

2. The Old Testament prophets may be fired up, but they do not come across as raving lunatics, by a long shot. Raving lunatics are not capable of coherent, sequentially logical, and often poetic writing of the sort in question. And raving lunatics do not correctly predict major future events, but we get ahead of ourselves. In every instance, when God speaks through an OT prophet, His words are critical to well-being of the Jewish people (e.g., Ex 17:14; 21:1; 24:4; Deut 31:9; Joshua 24:26; Isaiah 8:1; Habakkuk 2:2; Revelation 1:9-11, 19).

One of the most compelling statements in The Bible about the value, power, influence, and sufficiency of the Word of God is Psalm 19:7-11. After beautifully describing how all of creation (God's first revelation of Himself) testifies to the glory of God, King David turns his poetic pen to the Word of God (God's second revelation of Himself). He strings together several pearls that aptly describe The Bible.

> The law of the LORD *is* perfect, converting the soul; The testimony of the LORD *is* sure, making wise the simple; The statutes of the LORD *are* right, rejoicing the heart; The commandment of the LORD *is* pure, enlightening the eyes; The fear of the LORD *is* clean, enduring forever; The judgments of the LORD *are* true *and* righteous altogether. More to be desired *are they* than gold, yea, than much fine gold; Sweeter also than honey and the honeycomb. Moreover by them Your servant is warned, *and* in keeping them *there is* great reward.

The first thing to consider is that David, whom you may remember as the greatest hero of Old Testament Israel (defeating the giant Goliath with a slingshot) and who rose from shepherd to become Israel's greatest king, believed deeply in the reality of God. He also believed that the Jewish scriptures (at the time no more than the first seven books of the Old Testament) were authored by God Himself. It is beyond preposterous to think the Jewish people would have made a madman their ruler.

Second, notice how David follows a pattern throughout this description. He uses synonyms like "law", "testimony," "statute," and "commandment" to describe The Bible, which he clearly understands is the holy Word of God. Then he uses terms that emphasize its truthfulness such as "perfect" or "sure." Finally, he highlights the impact of Scripture on someone's life. It "converts the soul" and makes "wise the simple." David beautifully describes God's Word as not only perfect but effective. It possesses the ability to correctly govern the lives of those who put their faith in it. This one passage is enough to cause anyone to think carefully about the truth claims made in The Bible. As King David clearly and unequivocally believed, God's Word is not to be taken with a grain of salt.

Consider also a striking statement in the New Testament about Scripture:

> But you must continue in the things which you have learned and been assured of, knowing from whom you have learned *them*, and that from childhood you have known the Holy Scriptures, which are able to make you wise for salvation through faith which is in Christ Jesus. All Scripture *is* given by inspiration of God, and *is* profitable for doctrine, for reproof, for correction, for instruction in righteousness, that the man of God may be complete, thoroughly equipped for every good work. (2 Timothy 3:14-17)

In other words, The Bible tells us all that we need to know about how to obtain salvation through Christ Jesus and live a proper Christian life. The apostle Paul also asserts that The Bible's message comes to us directly from God Himself. In some Bible translations the phrase "given by inspiration" is actually stated as "God-breathed"—a term that is in fact closer in meaning to the Greek word used in the passage. This is important is because it helps us understand how God communicated the words of The Bible to the human authors. Theologians use the word "inspiration" to describe this process.

However, in this context the idea that something has been inspired doesn't mean that certain men drew inspiration from God as an artist might draw inspiration from nature to paint a landscape in some interpretive manner. Rather, God moved in the minds and hearts of the writers in such a way as to ensure that His message was accurately communicated, while at the same time allowing those authors to use contemporary style so that the result might be easily understood by the people.

The Bible uses unequivocal language when talking about itself. Throughout both the Old and New Testaments we read that God not only communicated with and through certain individuals, but that He did so such that the individuals in question were moved to accurately record what God had told them.

SELF-RELIABLE

Another piece of evidence that points to The Bible as God's revelation is its reliability—meaning its internal consistency, historical accuracy, and dependability. It has become popular sport among liberal academicians to characterize The Bible as nothing more than a collection of myths and legends of the sort found in the historical records of all ancient cultures. Native Americans have their fantastical myths concerning the origins of daylight (a talking crow brought it to the people) and the rainbow (two playful bluebirds accidentally painted it in the sky). One of the many gods of Viking lore had been born of nine mothers. Another cultivated apple trees that were the source of eternal life. In Chinese mythology, Fuxi and Nuwa, who were siblings as well as husband and wife, were the half-snake, half-human ancestors of all of mankind.

The stories contained in the Old and New Testaments are in no way comparable to the myth literature of ancient cultures. Myth is populated with talking animals that teach men how to grow food, giants the size of mountains, sharks that transform themselves into humans, and the like. Myth is self-evident—it has little if any grounding in any objective reality. It is even likely that the people of the ancient cultures in question knew that the stories their elders told and re-told weren't true; that they were creative and entertaining ways of explaining events and natural phenomena that they did not comprehend and could not explain otherwise. That is not the case, by a long shot, with The Bible. For example, Twenty-First Century Native Americans do not insist that the story of a shark transforming itself into a human to win the love of a beautiful maiden is true, but Twenty-First Century Orthodox Jews are absolutely convinced that God did in fact part the Red Sea to allow their ancestors to escape Pharaoh's pursuing army. That remarkable story, by the way, has not changed one iota in more than 3,500 years, and as time unfolds, it gains more and more believers, many of whom are highly intelligent, verifiably rational individuals!

Moving forward historically, the New Testament's stories concerning Jesus—his teachings, his many miracles, his resurrection—are indeed incredible, amazing, even unbelievable from a modern, scientific point of view. And yet, liberal academicians who make a living by denying the divinity of Jesus have yet to come up with a plausible explanation for the fact that many of Jesus' followers were willing to die rather than recant their claims to have seen him, fully healed, within days after His prolonged torture and excruciating death on The Cross. In recent years, numerous Christians in the Middle East have chosen death when told by Muslim fanatics that their lives will be spared if they renounce Jesus. There has never been credible evidence to the effect that any of these martyrs, past or present, were raving lunatics, deluded, or just plain stupid. By contrast, no present-day Scandinavian of sound mind would give his life rather than publicly denounce Thor, the Norse thunder god. Furthermore, not one of the myths of any ancient culture has ever been verified with archeological evidence. By contrast, the more archeologists dig in the Middle East, the more evidence they uncover confirming that The Bible is accurate history.

Another characteristic of myth is its lack of continuity over time. Every generation adds new material to a culture's myths, putting its own "stamp" on them. As a result, the mythology is clearly identifiable as simply a collection of fanciful tales. By contrast, The Bible's stories, which cover a historical period of approximately 3000 years, are internally consistent. The sixty-six books of The Bible (39 in the OT, 27 in the NT) hold together. They do not contradict one another. Furthermore, the New Testament's authors reference the older stories as if there is no doubt but that they are true. Jesus, for example, refers in this fashion to Adam and Eve, Moses, Noah, and Jonah. Furthermore, it is obvious that He is not referencing whimsical children's stories but rather referring to actual historical events.

Finally, mythological heroes are generally presented without major character flaws. They make mistakes, they fall for deceptions, and in some cases, they are killed. But through it all, they remain heroic. The Bible's heroes, on the other hand, are presented warts and all. Abraham, arguably the most important person in Jewish history, ignores God's promises and sires a child with his wife's slave. Moses disobeys God and consequently is not allowed to enter the Promised Land with the people he's courageously and self-sacrificingly led for forty years. King David has an affair and then, to cover it up, conspires to have his paramour's husband killed in battle by one of his own soldiers. (And that's just one example of David's many character flaws, all of which are laid bare in The Bible.)

The New Testament contains similar examples. Following Jesus' arrest by Roman authorities, His disciple Peter is portrayed as a coward. Three times, he denies that he knows Jesus. And Peter is not alone in his weakness. When Jesus is taken into custody, the same disciples who had sworn their allegiance to Him go into hiding like scared rabbits. Only one of them, John, has the courage to be present at Jesus' crucifixion. After Jesus' death and entombment, His eleven remaining disciples (Judas, unable to live with his betrayal, has committed suicide) are huddled in a locked room, each fearing that there is a cross with his name on it. There are more examples of New Testament figures being presented as less than ideal, but the two examples just given will do to make the point that if the New Testament was fabricated, these same fellows—several of whom contributed to its writing—would have made every effort to portray themselves in a good light.

In fact, the gospels sometimes present the *women* who followed Jesus as more courageous and faithful than the men. On the morning of the Resurrection, it is the *women* who risk exposure and arrest to go to Jesus' tomb for the purpose of completing His burial ritual (interrupted by sundown on the beginning of the Sabbath). Lest the significance of this be lost on the modern reader, to say that women in first century Palestine were second class citizens is an understatement. Women had no say in anything. They were not even allowed to testify concerning legal matters because they were regarded as incapable of being credible witnesses. The mere fact that First Century Jewish male authors portray Jesus' female followers in such a positive light is all the proof necessary of the Gospels' veracity. The Gospels' authors even present Jesus with His full humanity showing. They present His healings and other mind-blowing miracles right alongside descriptions of Him sleeping, eating, crying and even, on one occasion, going on somewhat of a rampage, turning over tables, yelling, and chasing moneylenders from the temple, His Father's House.

The New Testament is not propaganda cleverly constructed by public relations experts to put a positive spin on the fledgling Christian movement. If that was the case, the PR folks would have presented the movement and its leaders in the best possible light. Much ink would have been spilled to underscore the righteous cause of a band of unblemished heroes struggling against the wrongs of the world. But that was clearly not the purpose. Rather, it was to tell a story as truthfully as possible, knowing that the story was incredible enough without embellishment.

Bible deniers also point to the fact that no original copy of any book of The Bible—either Old or New Testament—exists. All we have are what are known as "autographs"—copies of copies of copies. In no specific case does anyone really know exactly how many copies preceded the existing one. The deniers further assert that the existing copies are full of scribal errors.

That all we have available to us are copies of copies is undeniable. And because a human copier, unlike a Twenty-First Century copy machine, is prone to error, it is also undeniable that these copies contain errors. Nonetheless, there's a wealth of evidence to the effect that the copying errors in question do not alter the meaning of the text one iota. Without exception, they are the equivalent of someone changing "I am proud to say that I own one of the first so-called 42-line Bibles to come off Johannes Gutenberg's printing press in 1455" to "I am proud to say that I *am* the owner of one of the first 42-line Bibles to come off Johannes Guttenberg's printing press in 1455." Although the two sentences are slightly different, it does not matter if someone reads the former or the latter—they will obtain the exact same meaning. The same is true of biblical autographs. And mind you, the scribal errors in question do not even approach the changes in that second sentence, above. Although it's undeniable that we do not have any original manuscripts, the evidence confirms that we have a reliable Bible. No other book of antiquity comes close to having as many old manuscripts as The Bible. When we read The Bible today we can be certain that we are basically reading what was originally written, and that is true of both the Old and New Testaments.*†

NO HODGE-PODGE HERE

The Bible presents the reader with one grand and solidly unified story from beginning to end—from Genesis through Revelation. A good number of people think The Bible is nothing more than a bunch of manuscripts written over a span of approximately 1500 years by men who in most cases did not know and could not have known one another, and that other men chose (in keeping with their biases) what manuscripts to include and not include and sequenced them in a manner that suited their rather pragmatic objectives. According to this contemporary academic explanation, the resulting book does nothing but provide the reader with an insight into the religious mythology of an interesting but otherwise insignificant and relatively tiny Middle Eastern culture that was destroyed by the Romans in 70 A.D. But while that's the view of lots of self-impressed university professors—even, believe it or not, professors of religious studies at prestigious places like Duke University—that's not an accurate understanding of The Bible by a long shot. There's lots of truth to the idea that someone can be too smart for their own good.

When one reads The Bible with an unjaundiced eye, a marvelously unified story emerges. One step at a time, God tells the story of His plan for humankind's redemption from the sin and brokenness Adam and Eve purchased in their deal with the devil made in the Garden of Eden. The Bible begins with a scientifically accurate description of creation—a description, mind you, that lines up perfectly with the most current scientific findings

---

† *We don't want to get bogged down in stuffy academic footnotes. But we do want you to know that there's plenty of resources you can read that backs up what we've said. For example, in an essay titled "The Historical Reliability of the New Testament" (contained in *Reasonable Faith: Christian Truth and Apologetics* by William Lane Craig) respected theologian Craig Bloomberg argues "97-99% of the NT can be reconstructed beyond any reasonable doubt..." He also says, "The texts of the NT have been preserved in far greater number and with much more care than have any other ancient documents." We could keep listing out book after book. But here's the bottom line: For every attack on The Bible's exactitude from a clever liberal there is a successful parry from an equally smart and more well qualified orthodox theologian.

and conclusions. It then moves on to the story of man's creation and quick fall from grace. When God exiles Adam and Eve from the Garden of Eden and into a hardscrabble life, things quickly go south. Right off the bat, one of their children murders his brother. One sin leads to another until the entire earth is in a state of self-indulgent moral anarchy. God gets really upset at the state of His creation and ends it with a worldwide flood, preserving the one truly righteous man on Earth, Noah, and his family. Shortly thereafter, He chooses Abram, soon to become Abraham, to sow the first seeds of what will eventually become the nation of Israel. God's redemptive plan unfolds through the early history of His Chosen People, His instructions for living (the Law), and the post-flood history. At that point, the prophets—God's specifically chosen spokespersons—begin proclaiming the coming of a Messiah who will save not just Israel, but all of mankind. And then, once the stage has been fully set, Jesus steps into the scene, and the discerning reader realizes that the entire Old Testament was a prelude to His momentous arrival.

God's story continues in the New Testament with the story of the Christ as the one who restores and frees us from the eternal consequences of our inescapable sinful nature—the fulfillment of God's promise related to the future and ultimate defeat of sin and death. The Bible is remarkable in the way the Old and New Testaments' books unify around this one central theme. While many of these books are very different from one another in style and format, they come together to form a brilliant tapestry of God's story of redemption.

Consider some interesting facts about The Bible:
- It was written over a period of more than 1500 years and spanned some sixty generations.
- At least forty different authors coming from all walks of life can be identified. Moses, who wrote the first five books of The Bible, was a political leader, trained in the universities of Egypt, turned outlaw and shepherd. Peter, who authored two New Testament epistles (letters) was a fisherman. The prophet Nehemiah was a Jewish exile and a cupbearer to the king of Persia. Daniel, whose prophetic gift was amazingly accurate, was also an exile but served at the highest level of the Babylonian and Persian empires. Matthew, one of the four gospel authors, was a tax collector before becoming one of the twelve disciples. And then there's Paul—an upper-class Jew and a

zealous persecutor of the first Jewish Christians—who encounters the risen Christ, repents, and goes on to author half of the New Testament.
- The various books of The Bible were written from what were far-flung geographical locations. Books were composed on three different continents; Asia, Africa, and Europe. Some were authored in remote places like the wilderness and even prisons. Other books were written in palaces or while the authors were on the road.
- The original manuscripts represent three languages; Hebrew, Aramaic (acquired during the Babylonian exile), and Greek. Consider the fact that The Bible contains hundreds of subjects that are hotly debated and controversial, yet The Bible's many authors write with a consistency and unity of worldview that would be impossible to produce were not for one important truth: The Bible was inspired by God—its human authors, as they would all admit, were mere agents. No other explanation accounts for such symmetry in a book composed over such a long time by so many authors writing under varying circumstances in different languages.

PROPHETIC VALIDITY

Another important piece of evidence to consider is the fulfillment of prophecy. If someone you know has a habit of making promises, then breaking them, you eventually come to distrust him. If, on the other hand, the person consistently keeps his word, your trust grows over time. Likewise, we can place full trust in The Bible because of its many kept promises and fulfilled predictions. This is also known as prophecy. A significant portion of Scripture, both OT and NT, contains material that points to the future. Much of the prophetic material in Scripture has come to pass. It is estimated that about 2500 prophecies appear in the pages of The Bible. An incredible number—2000—have been precisely fulfilled, and that is a conservative estimate. The probability that just one of these prophecies would be accurately fulfilled is less than one in ten; the odds that 20 out of every 25 of these prophecies would be fulfilled is less than one in 10 to the 2000th power. In addition, those prophecies that have not been fulfilled are those that point to a time that is beyond the publication date of this book. In other words, not one biblical prophecy has ever failed to come to pass!†

As one might expect, the most notable prophecies pertain to the life and ministry of Jesus Christ. Every major element of Jesus' life can be found in some OT prophecy (Chapter 4 of this book provides a table that highlights these prophecies). Turning our attention to the crucifixion itself, it's first important to note that this form of death does not appear in history until the 6th century BCE when the historian Herodotus records the practice among the Persians. It was subsequently picked up and practiced by Alexander the Great and then the Romans. However, sources indicate that the practice was not found in Palestine until Hellenistic times or the period between the OT and NT (See Josephus Ant. Xii 240-41; I Macc 1:44-50). Why does this matter? Because David in Psalm 22:16 prophetically says of the Messiah, "They have pierced my hands and my feet." The context makes inescapable that David is writing about the Promised One. Mind you, these words were written about 1000 years before the time of Christ which was 500 years before the first historical appearance of crucifixion!

Several chapters in the prophecy of Ezekiel (25-27) record proclamations of judgment against cities that engaged in wicked behavior toward the Hebrew people. The city that receives the majority of Ezekiel's attention is Tyre—a coastal city of great wealth and power, not unlike a major contemporary metropolis like New York or Los Angeles. The people of Tyre regularly oppressed the people of God. Therefore, God pronounced a judgment upon her. Consider Ezekiel 26:4-5:

> And they shall destroy the walls of Tyre and break down her towers; I will also scrape her dust from her, and make her like the top of a rock. It shall be a place for spreading nets in the midst of the sea, for I have spoken,' says the Lord God; 'it shall become plunder for the nations."

---

† Hugh Ross, Reasons to Believe, accessed 8.12.15 - http://www.reasons.org/articles/articles/fulfilled-prophecy-evidence-for-the-reliability-of-the-bible

Three years after this prophecy, the city was attacked by Nebuchadnezzar and laid to waste by the Babylonians. Many of Tyre's inhabitants, however, survived by moving off shore to a nearby island. Three hundred years later, in 332 BC, Alexander the Great conquered the second Tyre and added considerably to its destruction, but it wasn't until the Twelfth Century AD—fifteen hundred years after Alexander—that the city would fall once and for all. One secular historian has the following to say:

> [Tyre] never regained the place she had previously held in the world. The larger part of the site of the once great city is now bare as the top of a rock—a place where the fishermen that still frequent the spot spread their nets to dry. (Philip Myers, *General History for Colleges and High Schools*, Boston: Ginn and Company, 1889, pg 55).

Note the precision with which the prophecy was eventually fulfilled. Such examples further illustrate that The Bible is God's Word and as such, should be taken with utmost seriousness.

CONFIRMED BY ARCHAEOLOGY

Up to this point the evidence we've considered has largely been dependent upon the text of Scripture itself. It is reasonable to ask if there is information outside of The Bible that verifies its content. In fact, there is a whole field of study devoted to this issue: biblical archaeology. Many of the archaeologists who have pursued this area of study—members of liberal faculty at secular universities—have done so with the assumption that at some point their findings will disprove Scripture. And yet no such evidence has been uncovered. Quite the contrary, in fact. One of the greatest archaeologists of the modern era, William Albright, has said, "Discovery after discovery has established the accuracy of innumerable details, and has brought increased recognition to the value of The Bible as a source of history."[††] A similar assessment is given of the New Testament by renowned scholar F.F. Bruce. He said, "... it may be legitimate to say that archaeology has confirmed the New Testament record." He goes on to say that archaeology demonstrates that the works of the New Testament reflect a first century background.[∞] This is significant because it shows that the books of the New Testament were not written, as some prominent liberal professors claim, one hundred or so years after Jesus was crucified but within one generation of His death on the cross and reflect eyewitness testimony.

Throughout the Old Testament the reader is confronted with numerous geographical locations as well as the people who inhabited those areas. In the 19th Century, progressive academicians began to dispute the historicity of The Bible, pointing to the lack of evidence for these places and people. Subsequent archeologists, however, have been able to verify their existence. Consider, for example, the Hittites, a Semitic tribe referred to in both Genesis and 2 Samuel 11. According to Scripture, the Hittites interacted with both Abraham and David. In the elite intellectual circles of the 19th Century, it was vogue to pooh-pooh the Hittites as people of myth. And then, in 1906, a team of archeologists digging in Turkey discovered the ruins of an ancient Hittite capital replete with historical records indicating a flourishing civilization in the mid second millennium (circa 1500 BC).

A critically important feature of biblical history is the return of the nation of Israel to Jerusalem after spending 70 years in captivity in Babylon. This important event is referenced in 2 Chronicles 36:23 and Ezra 1. What's significant about these texts is that Cyrus the Great, after conquering Babylon, decreed this return. Again, two centuries ago it was assumed that such an act on the part of a pagan king would have been impossible. Archaeologists, though discovered a nine-inch clay cylinder at Babylon from 539 BC which describes Cyrus' policy of permitting Babylonians captives to not only return to their homes but rebuild their temples. This is the exact story recorded in the Old Testament.

These are just a couple of examples from dozens more that verify the historical record of Scripture. Such outside verification provides further

---

[†] William F. Albright, *Archaeology, Historical Analogy, and Early Biblical Tradition.* Baton Rouge: LSU Press, 1966, 127-128.
[∞] F.F. Bruce, "Archaeological Confirmation of the New Testament," in *Revelation and The Bible*, ed. by Carl F.H. Henry (Grand Rapids: Baker, 1958): 331.

encouragement that the text of Scripture is trustworthy. To cite but one significant contrast, whereas the Book of Mormon, supposedly discovered by Joseph Smith in 1823, describes numerous events occurring in North America including warfare between expatriated Hebrew tribes and American Indians, not one archaeological discovery has been made to even hint that these stories are anything more than complete fabrications by someone with a genius for fiction if, nonetheless, sociopathic.[†]

AFFIRMING IMPACT

Millions of people trust The Bible because of the impact it has had on their lives. As God, by His Spirit, brings the truth of His Word to bear on people's lives, the Word has a powerful and profound influence. In the very first Psalm, the author testifies to the applicability of God's Word. He says,

> Blessed is the man who walks not in the counsel of the ungodly, nor stands in the path of sinners, nor sits in the seat of the scornful; But his delight is in the law of the Lord, and in His law he meditates day and night. He shall be like a tree planted by the rivers of water, that brings forth its fruit in it season, whose leaf also shall not wither, and whatever he does shall prosper (Psalm 1:1-3).

Notice how this passage promises a life that is constantly nourished by God's Word. It guarantees that the one who faithfully reads and applies God's Word will have a productive life. What other book written from 2000 to more than 3000 years ago is still so highly regarded as instructive for 21st century living? Of course, some may counter with the idea that people have used The Bible to do horrible things. History certainly bears witness to such abuses. But that's only because sinful human beings misused and abused The Bible. There are many more examples of people being inspired to do

---

[†] The curious reader who would like to further explore the issue of biblical archaeology is referred to *Biblical Archaeology Review* and the website of the Associates for Biblical Research website at www.biblearcheology.org.

great things because of the influence of The Bible. Some of history's greatest advancements in education, healthcare, economics, civil liberties, and even science have been motivated in some part by beliefs arising from The Bible.

Then there's what is called the internal testimony of the Holy Spirit. One of the most compelling reasons to trust The Bible comes as the Spirit of God confirms in the heart and mind of the reader the truthfulness of The Bible. As people read The Bible prayerfully and thoughtfully, they often discover The Bible's ability to direct thoughts and actions. Through this process, God confirms that the words of The Bible can be equated with the words of God Himself. To use another phrase, this is the way in which God speaks to His people; He speaks through The Bible.

There is a story from the gospel of John that illustrates just how important the Word of God is for life now and life forever. By the time the reader gets to John 6, Jesus has amassed a huge following. Through a combination of teaching and miracles, thousands of people have been touched by Jesus' ministry. But then Jesus begins to reveal to them who He really is. In no uncertain terms, He makes it clear that He is not only divine but the means to eternal life. In response, many of these supposed followers exclaim that Jesus' words are too hard to understand. John 6:66 says, "From that time many of His disciples went back and walked with Him no more." At that critical juncture, Jesus turns to his twelve disciples and asks, "Do you also want to go away?" Peter responds for the group with a stunning confession. "Lord, to whom shall we go? You have the words of eternal life. Also we have come to believe and know that You are the Christ, the Son of the living God (6:68-69)." Peter's words reflect the very heart of this book. Where else can we go to find the truth about eternal life? Only God has this information and God has only communicated this information in the pages of The Bible.

HOW TO READ THE BIBLE

Hopefully this chapter has encouraged you to give your full attention to Scripture. You can begin every day of your life for the rest of your life by reading words that come to you from God Himself. However, there is still one issue to address. Most people who read The Bible find it difficult, so we're going to conclude this chapter by giving you a few tips on how to start reading and studying The Bible.

Pick a time and place. First, choose a time each day and a location where you will devote a certain amount of time to Bible reading. Make this a priority in your schedule like everything else. Reading The Bible is a discipline and requires focus. If you want to get the most out of Scripture then you've got to be willing to put time in to it. At first it may require a good amount of time, but the more you read The Bible on a consistent basis, the more you will find yourself understanding what's being said.

Choose an accurate translation that is relatively easy to understand. While the New International Version is touted as the most readable, the authors recommend either the English Standard Version or the New American Standard Version as better options. They stick more closely to the original text of Scripture. Whichever translation you choose, we recommend purchasing what is called a Study Bible. A Study Bible is unique in that someone has included alongside the text of Scripture an introduction to each book and study notes that help to clarify any given passage. One of the best Study Bibles available is the MacArthur Study Bible which comes in an English Standard Version. The one caveat we stress is that only the text of Scripture is infallible. Any comments made in a Study Bible are interpretations and should therefore be understood as such. However, especially if you are new to The Bible, having a trustworthy Study Bible can help you navigate the more difficult passages you come across.

Choose a book. The next tip helps with an issue most people encounter when they first sit down to read The Bible. Where do I start? That's a great question. And it's understandable that someone's first foray into Bible reading is intimidating. You have sixty-six books from which to choose, so let us help you with this issue. First, pick a book of the New Testament—we suggest that you begin with one of the four gospels. While these are some of the longer books in the NT, because they center on Jesus as the fulfillment of the OT and the means of salvation, they will prove particularly beneficial as you start your journey of faith.

Read and re-read a passage. The next step may seem obvious but this is the part of the process that separates good students of The Bible from great ones. The people who best understand The Bible are those who read it the most. This is where a lot of people really get tripped up. They read through a passage once and either don't understand it or fail to recall any of the words they just read and assume they've failed. Again, The Bible's not like any other book. But if you read the passage over and over again you will find yourself gleaning more and more. Spend the first few days reading through the book you've selected as many times as you can. Have a pen and paper handy to jot down questions, note patterns, and record thoughts that may jump out as you read.

Ask the right questions. Then you'll want to work through the book again taking it a passage at a time. A good rule of thumb is to let the headings in The Bible be your guide. Those headings are put there by translators to help you follow the flow of the book. While they are not original to the text of scripture, they are a helpful way to break up the book. A good study Bible will help with this as well because it will give you an outline of the book. Once you've turned your attention to a particular passage you can then ask important questions.

1. *What does the passage say?* At this point you are simply working through the details of the passage. If you are reading through a Gospel you would begin by making sure you understand the story, the facts about the story, and the location of the story in the overall flow of the book. You may even read the passage a couple of times and then try and write a synopsis of it.
2. *What does the passage mean?* Once you've got a handle on what the passage says, you then want to begin to interpret what it means. At this point you are identifying key theological ideas that are either stated or illustrated in the passage. You are trying to understand the grammar of the passage, identifying the audience, and determining how the original audience would have heard the story. With the gospels you want to determine what a given passage tells you about Jesus and about those who follow Him. Of course, there may be plenty of situations where you have lots of questions without answers. Make sure you write them down and then talk with your pastor or a mature believer on the meaning of the text.
3. *How does the passage apply?* Finally, you want to consider the way the passage impacts Christian living. In some cases there may be direct commands to obey. Other passages may provide truths to be believed, sins to be confessed and avoided, examples to follow, or expressions of

worship. And still other passages may simply provide historical and theological insight. The important idea is that you look at the passage as a means by which God through the Holy Spirit shapes your thinking and thus your life.

Don't do it alone. As we already stated in the chapter on selecting a church, the Christian life was not meant to be lived in isolation. Healthy relationships with mature believers are essential to your own personal growth. One important aspect of reading The Bible is reading it with other believers. You may already have a relationship with two or three other believers. If so, get together with these Christians and read The Bible together. You could set a time and place each week where you sit down and talk about the passage or passages you read the previous week. This not only helps you develop a better understanding of the passage but offers accountability in your efforts to read The Bible.

CONCLUSION

As you continue in your relationship with Christ, know that God will work in concert with The Bible to make you the Christian He wants you to be. Just as self-effort is unable to save you, self-effort will not produce growth. Consider the Apostle Peter's admonition in I Peter 2:1-3, "So put away all malice and all deceit and hypocrisy and envy and all slander. Like newborn infants, long for the pure spiritual milk, that by it you may grow up into salvation— if indeed you have tasted that the Lord is good." The "spiritual milk" to which Peter is referring is the life-giving truth of God's Word. Just as an infant requires milk to not only sustain life but grow, so does the child of God need The Bible. God has given you all that you need for life and godliness, it's just a matter of taking advantage of it.

RECOMMENDED READING

- Fee, Gordon & Douglas Stuart. *How to Read The Bible for All Its Worth*, Zondervan, 2014.

  Hanegraaff, Hank. *Has God Spoken? Proof of The Bible's Divine Inspiration*, Thomas Nelson, 2011.

- Helm, David. *One to One Bible Reading*, Matthias Media, 2010.

- Jones, Timothy Paul. *How We Got The Bible*, Rose Publishing, 2015.

- Lutzer, Erwin. *7 Reasons Why You Can Trust The Bible*, Moody, 2015.

- MacArthur, John. *How to Get the Most from God's Word*, Thomas Nelson, 1997.

- McDowell, Josh. *God Breathed – The Undeniable Power and Reliability of Scripture*,

  Barbour Books, 2015

QUESTIONS FOR PERSONAL REFLECTION AND GROUP DISCUSSION

1. What distinguishes the stories in The Bible from the stories of other faith traditions?
2. Why should one believe that The Bible is truly God's Word and not simply a collection of fictional stories?
3. What are the possible consequences of ignoring The Bible or taking it lightly?
4. The Mormon church claims that the Book of Mormon is "sacred." Why isn't it?
5. Why is the story of Jonah being swallowed by a great fish any different from the traditional Native American stories of a shark transforming itself into a man in order to woo an Indian maiden?

9

Get Down on Your Knees (or stand, if you prefer)

"The proper way for man to pray," said Deacon Lemuel Keyes; "The only proper attitude is down upon his knees."

"Nay, I should say the way to pray," said Reverend Doctor Wise, "Is standing straight with outstretched arms with rapt and upturned eyes."

"Oh, no, no, no," said Elder Snow, "such posture is too proud." A man should pray with eyes fast-closed and head contritely bowed."

"It seems to me his hands should be austerely clasped in front. With both thumbs pointing to the ground," said Reverend Doctor Blunt."

"Last year I fell in Hodgkin's well headfirst," said Cyril Brown. "With both my heels a-stickin' up, my head a-pointing' down; And I done prayed right then and there; best prayer I ever said, The prayin'est prayer I ever prayed, a-standin' on my head."

Some years ago, a now-defunct site called NewPrayer.com popped up on the web. Its stated purpose was to "send prayers via radio transmitter to God's last known location," identified as star cluster M13, believed to be one of the oldest of its kind in the universe. Crandall Stone, 50, a Cambridge, Massachusetts, engineer and freelance consultant, set up NewPrayer after an evening of sipping brandy and philosophizing with friends. The conversation turned to the Big Bang (see Chapter One), and someone suggested that if all the matter contained in the universe was in one place at the time of the "bang," then God must have been and may still be there. They further theorized that if the bang's cosmic location could be identified, a radio transmitter could then send a message to God. After consulting with NASA scientists, the friends settled on cluster M13. They chipped in about $20,000, and launched NewPrayer. At one time Stone claimed it transmitted about 50,000 prayers a week from seekers around the globe. One sent a prayer to God by typing it into the website, clicking SEND, and—voila!—the prayer was on its way.

It's hard to tell if Stone and his friends were truly serious or engaging in chicanery. Regardless, NewPrayer's success attests to the fact that most people not only believe in a God/god of some sort but also assume that communication with Him is possible. Every religious tradition incorporates some means of communicating or "getting in touch" with whomever or whatever the religion in question worships. For Druids and Wiccans, it's communing with nature. For Buddhists, it's meditation. Christians, talking to God is done through prayer, which takes two forms:

Group prayer: In group settings, prayers are either recited in unison or the group leader prays out loud while everyone else participates silently. In the former case, the prayers are "standard"—that is, they are printed or memorized (e.g. the so-called "Lord's Prayer") and spoken out loud by everyone in the group. When only the leader prays out loud, the prayer is usually improvised. Group prayers are usually very general in nature—thanking God for His many blessings, asking that He bring about world peace, and so on.

Individual prayer: As the name indicates, individual prayer is done privately (although there may be witnesses) and is usually improvised. The content and purpose of any given prayer depends on the individual's circumstances at that time in his or her life. A person who has fallen ill prays for healing, for example; or, someone prays for another person's healing.

Most practicing Christians engage in both group and individual prayers. In either case, prayer is not so much about form as it is about content (although it's undoubtedly true that during memorized or recited group prayers some folks are simply "going through the motions" without much if any sincerity).

WHY PRAYER IS IMPORTANT

When you meet someone for the first time, the two of you explore forming a relationship by talking to one another—engaging in conversation. As conversation develops, it deepens as the two individuals move beyond the superficial and begin to reveal more and more about themselves to one another. Eventually, one of them may begin telling the other person things he's never told anyone else and even confiding in and seeking counsel from him concerning highly personal issues.

Two people cannot have relationship without conversation vis a' vis some medium. It would be absurd for someone to say, "So-and-so and I are good friends, but we've never communicated with one another." Likewise, it's impossible for a person to have full relationship with God without talking to Him. Another way of saying the same thing: To truly *know* God, you must talk with Him; otherwise, you will only know *about* Him. In this regard, group prayers alone are less than optimal. God certainly hears them, but individual prayer engaged in on a regular basis is essential to a personal, intimate relationship with one's Creator and Sovereign.

When you surrender your life to Christ, the Holy Spirit takes up residence within you. He begins to "walk" with you everywhere you go, providing protection, spiritual sustenance, and direction. Two thousand years ago, Jesus ascended to Heaven in front of several of His disciples, but God's Spirit, the third person of the Holy Trinity, remained (John 14:15-31, Acts 1:9-11). When a Christian prays, he does so through (invokes) the power of the Holy Spirit; likewise, God acts in his or her life through that same power. The Holy Spirit, therefore, functions as an intermediary in the believer's relationship with God.

As is the case when two people participate in conversation, the more one talks to God through prayer, the stronger one's relationship with God becomes. Over time, that relationship deepens and becomes increasingly intimate. When someone says they "know" God or claim to have a personal relationship with Jesus, they mean they communicate on a regular basis with God and therefore His Son through the Holy Spirit. As such, prayer involves all three persons of the Holy Trinity.

Prayer not only expresses faith; it feeds it as well. It's a form of spiritual food that is a medium for one becoming a believer of strong conviction. The more a person prays, the stronger his faith becomes, and the stronger his faith, the bolder will be his confession of faith to others. Prayer, in other words, strengthens relationship with God, strengthens faith, and slowly transforms the believer into a bold witness for our Lord and Savior, thus spreading the Good News (gospel) of His redemptive sacrifice on the Cross and triumph over death on our behalf (see Matthew 28:16 - 20).

Sometimes, one will hear a Christian say that prayer is not his gift or strong suit or words to that effect. He undoubtedly believes that about himself, but there is great likelihood that "I'm not good at praying" actually means "I don't pray often enough to become good at it." Praying is like any other skill—one's prayer ability strengthens through practice. Very few people truly have a gift for prayer in the sense that from the get-go their prayers are creative, fluid, impassioned, and—when these folks are leading group prayer—inspiring to others. But almost everyone can become reasonably good at prayer and any committed believer can pray adequately—the Holy Spirit will see to that. The key—like the key to developing a good golf swing—is practice; and as in golf, the more one practices prayer, the more "natural" it will become. That's how one becomes a "prayer warrior" or, if not a warrior, at least a worthy foot-soldier in Christ's army of believers.

WHAT PRAYER IS AND A BEGINNER'S GUIDE TO HOW

Prayer, whether spoken aloud or silently, is *intentional*, meaning that it is done with specific purposes in mind. These include

- praising God, acknowledging His supremacy over all things,
- thanking God, showing appreciation for His grace, mercy, and many blessings,
- humbling oneself before the Almighty,
- making confession and asking God's forgiveness for one's sinfulness or specific sins,
- contemplating the mysteries of the divine,
- Inspiring stronger faith,
- making general requests, and
- making specific requests.

There's no firm set of prayer prerequisites. If you feel like communing with God concerning some issue in your life or the life of someone else, simply find a reasonably quiet place and begin talking to Him, silently or out loud. If a quiet place is not convenient, pray anyway. Solitude will help you stay focused but your prayer environment does not affect God's ability to hear you. The important thing is not where you pray or even the words you use, but simply that you have a desire to speak with God. Even if you fumble over how to express yourself, God will know what you mean to say. Don't worry about form, in other words. Just start talking. The Holy Spirit will take over from there.

While the basic act of prayer is easily defined and uncomplicated, the subject of prayer raises several theological questions, including:

Question: Is God more likely to listen to someone who is in prayer than to someone who is addressing Him but not "prayerfully"?

Answer: *Yes, definitely. God hears every single thing a person says and knows all of a person's thoughts (Psalm 139), but He is, according to The Bible, more inclined to truly listen to a prayer than to, say, a spontaneous outburst (e.g. 1 John 5:14).*

Question: How does prayer actually work?

Answer: *The question actually misses the point, which is that God works in the world and in any given person's life according to His will, whether the individual is praying (or even a believer) or not. He is Sovereign, in control of all things. Prayer is somewhat akin to making an appointment with your company's CEO to talk to him about a work issue. If you simply walked up to the CEO rather randomly and impulsively and began talking to him, he would almost surely say "This is not the time or place for this; please call my secretary and make an appointment and I'll be glad to discuss these issues with you" or words to that effect. In the same way, approaching God properly requires making an appointment, but whereas your boss' secretary may tell you that the earliest available appointment is tomorrow, you can make an appointment with God at any time, even right now, right where you are at this very moment. If you feel like praying and you're in a situation where it's possible for you to get down on your knees, close your eyes, and bow your head, then by all means do so, but keep in mind that Jesus specifically said that a person in prayer should not attract undue attention to himself lest the act simply be a means of proclaiming one's piety to the world (Matthew 6:6). In other words, getting down on your knees and bowing your head is good prayer form because that posture puts you in an attitude of reverence and humility, but it's not necessary. You can pray anywhere, at any time. You can even pray when you're driving down the road (but don't close your eyes or bow your head). But let's say you're behind the wheel of your car and you suddenly feel the need to connect with God. Just turn off the radio and start talking out loud to your Heavenly Father. Count on it, He's listening.*

Question: If God is all-knowing why do I need to pray to Him in the first place?

Answer: *Prayer is not about God getting to knowing you. He has known you since before the Creation (e.g. Ephesians 1:4). Prayer is primarily about YOU developing a fuller relationship with HIM. As you begin to connect with God through prayer you will eventually begin to experience His activity, His movement in your life at a mental, emotional, and even sensory level. Prayer will calm you and cause you to feel a sense of peace and well-being. As this takes place, you will begin also to fully accept God's will in your life, regardless of the direction it takes at any given moment concerning any given issue. You'll eventually come to realize that even a "bad" event in your life is* *ultimately for good (for more on this seeming paradox, read the story of Joseph and his brothers in Genesis 49 and 50).*

Question: Can my prayers change God's plan or will?

Answer: *There are several instances in The Bible when it appears that through the prayers of certain individuals God took, did not take, or postponed certain actions (e.g. Jeremiah 26:3). Such instances do not mean however that God somehow changed His mind because someone so persuaded Him. God is not in the process of working out, by trial-and-error, His plan for mankind's salvation. His plan has been in place since Day One (Genesis 1: 1 – 5). The future is set and already known by God, its author. Prayer does not, will not, change any aspect of that Divine Plan. Making specific requests of God is fine and encouraged in Scripture, but one should always come to prayer with humility, seeking to understand His will, even when His will is counter to one's own desires. When all is said and done, it will become clear that everything God does, He does for an ultimately glorious and perfect purpose.*

Question: How can God hear thousands, if not millions, of prayers that are occurring simultaneously?

Answer: *Because God is not restricted, as we are, by the three dimensions of space (length, width, and height) and time. God occupies dimensions that are unavailable to us.*[†] *These divine dimensions constitute Heaven. The Bible is clear that God hears not only the speech of every single person, but also their thoughts. The actual "how" of this will remain a mystery until one gets to Heaven, if even then.*

The Bible tells us that God is in complete control of everything; that He knows when a sparrow falls to the ground and has numbered every hair on your head (Matthew 10:29 – 30). Furthermore, The Bible tells us that God "works out everything in conformity with the purpose of His will" (Ephesians 1:11). Nonetheless, God desires that we pray to Him. Because Jesus prayed and taught his disciples to pray, there is no doubt but that prayer is vital to a proper relationship with God. So even though it's true that God knows what you need and want and even knows your thoughts—He knows you infinitely better than you know yourself, in fact—prayer is an important

---

[†] Christian astrophysicist and author Hugh Ross, arguably the best authority on this topic, says that God occupies at least ten dimensions, and perhaps more (Beyond the Cosmos, Navpress, 1999).

aspect of a full Christian life. Always keep in mind that the purpose of prayer is not to make requests of God, but to thank Him, praise Him, and have relationship with Him.

PRAYER BASICS

The seven questions most often asked concerning prayer are: when, where, why, how, for what, how often, and for how long? The answer to each of those is "it depends." The general rule of thumb is *if you feel like praying, then pray*. With rare exception, it doesn't matter where you are, what your immediate situation might be, or what time of day it is. You certainly don't have to and shouldn't wait until you're in church on Sunday morning to honor your Heavenly Father with prayer.

Folks also want to know the proper words with which to begin and end a prayer. There's no absolute rule governing these two issues either, but beginning with something along the lines of "Lord God, Heavenly Father, I give you all thanks and praise..." and ending with "I offer up these thanks and petitions for your blessings in the Holy Name of Your Son Jesus Christ...Amen" is appropriate and sufficient.

When all is said and done, the bottom line concerning prayer is simply this: To grow in your new-found faith and come to know God better and better with every passing day, you need to make prayer a regular—preferably daily part of your life. As you will see in the next chapters, however, prayer is not the *only* thing a Christian should do to come to develop a deep relationship with God and His Son.

What prayer is not and should NOT be

There are Christian leaders who teach what is known as "contemplative prayer," which involves achieving a meditative state akin to that practiced by New Agers and Buddhists. The growing popularity of contemplative prayer is a prime example of the influence relativism and philosophical progressivism are having on the contemporary church. Relativism holds that all standards, and especially standards concerning right and wrong, are arbitrary; therefore, all such attempts to define morality are equally valid (which logically means that none of them are valid). The central tenet of philosophical progressivism is that new ideas are better than old ideas. Put those two ideas—relativism and progressivism—together and you have postmodernity, the interesting and imperiled times in which we currently live (and have been living in since the mid-1960s). Make no mistake, orthodox Christianity and postmodernity are in polar opposition. Christians believe that (a) The Bible is Ultimate Truth and, as such, the single most valid source of moral definition and guidance and (b) in the realm of ideas, old (traditional, Biblically-based) trumps new. Because contemplative prayer reflects a postmodern, New Age worldview, it poses a distinct threat to the spiritual welfare of its practitioners. In the same way that smoking marijuana is a "gateway" for many people to harder drugs, contemplative prayer can eventually lead one's faith completely astray.

Contrary to the popular and erroneous notion that all religions worship the same God or "lead to the same place," Christianity is unique, one of a kind. It is, for example, the only faith that offers a real, flesh-and-blood Savior, and that flesh-and-blood Savior said He was "the Way, the Truth, and the Life." It is important to note that He did not say he was "a" way; rather He made it clear that he was THE way, as in the One-and-Only forever and ever. Orthodox Christianity is the One True Faith. All other faiths are un-true; they are not the way or the truth, and they do not lead to eternal life. They are facsimiles, imitations, counterfeits, impostors, frauds. In effect, because they are without the True God, they are literally atheistic. Incorporating the practices of other faiths into Christian prayer may be in keeping with the postmodern emphasis on tolerance and diversity, but it is a sure way of going off on a wrong path that leads, ultimately, into a dead end. In short, Christianity cannot and should not be "mixed" with any other faith or its practices. The practices in question—meditation, contemplative prayer—are also distinctly contrary to Jesus' own instructions concerning prayer.

JR once found himself in conversation with a good fellow who was on the ministerial staff of a mainline, liberal Protestant church and who led contemplative prayer groups as part of his ministry. When JR asked him to explain contemplative prayer, he described it as a form of meditation where one "stills the mind" and "lets go of preconceived ideas" concerning God, thereby allowing God "to reveal Himself in whatever form and manner He chooses." Presumably, God might reveal Himself as a long-haired and bearded old man to one person, as a beautiful woman to another, and as a shimmering ball of light to yet another. Preconceived ideas concerning God only get in the way, the good fellow said. He was very passionate about all of this, but none of it's true. In the first place, if one studies The Bible and comes to know God through His written revelation, then said individual's ideas concerning God will be right on target. God is Spirit. One may sense God's presence during prayer, but He does not take various forms so as to "meet people where they're at" or some such relativistic nonsense. In the second place, on those occasions when God did in fact take form so as to reveal Himself to certain people, the people in question were not meditating and the God they saw was not an image projected onto the backs of their eyelids from inside their own heads. The God they saw was God, the Real Deal.

One such occasion is described in Exodus when God appears to Moses as a burning bush, telling Moses that He is the God who led the Hebrews out of bondage in Egypt. When Moses asks His name, God replies, "I am Who I Am" (Exodus 3:14)). This story does not mean that God revealed Himself to Moses as a burning bush because that image best suited Moses' spiritual needs at the moment. Quite the contrary, Moses was scared to death (as well he should have been) precisely because he could not in his wildest imaginings have anticipated encountering God in that fashion. That God manifested as a burning bush had absolutely nothing to do with anything about Moses. It was God's doing, a clear means of letting Moses know that he was in the presence of unimaginable power and holiness. Earlier, in Genesis, God appears to Jacob, one of the patriarchs, as a man. They wrestle all night long, a contest that leaves Jacob alive but with a permanent physical affliction (Genesis 32:25 – 30). And then we have Jesus, God incarnate, born of a virgin, whose three-year ministry is described in detail in the Gospels of Matthew, Mark, Luke, and John.

With due respect, the good fellow's understanding of God was way, way off the mark and the contemplative prayer groups that he led were leading people astray into what is called *syncretism*—an understanding of God that is not based on His Word but is based rather on an arbitrary synthesis of different beliefs and faith practices—Eastern, pagan, and New Age. As such, it is a serious and truly life-threatening error (Deuteronomy 12:31 – 32, James 3:11 – 12)).

Beware also pastors representing the "name it and claim it" or "prosperity gospel" movement. These charlatans tell their flocks that a person of adequate faith can, through prayer, make materialistic requests of God that He's—we're talking about God, mind you—then obligated to satisfy. They assert that God not only wants the true believer to be happy and wealthy, but has in fact *promised* material wealth to the authentic believer. This false belief rests on a misinterpretation of Bible passages such as Malachi 3:10 which says "'Bring to the storehouse a full tenth of what you earn so there will be food in my house. Test me in this,' says the Lord All-Powerful. 'I will open the windows of heaven for you and pour out all the blessings you need'" and Matthew 25:14-30 (the Parable of the Talents). The prosperity gospel message has obvious appeal to our sinful natures but has resulted, paradoxically, in a fair amount of unhappiness, especially among folks who don't end up "claiming" the material goodies for which they have prayed. The implication, of course, is that God did not bestow wealth upon them because they do not possess adequate faith or their sins outweigh their faith. It should not surprise the reader to learn that prosperity gospel pastors tell their congregations that in order to get what one wants from God, one must give a lot of money to the church, a good amount of which goes toward supporting lavish lifestyles—even personal jets—for the pastors in question. The god these pastors believe in is more like the wish-granting genie in the story of Aladdin and His Magic Lamp than the God of Judeo-Christian Scripture.

    Keep in mind that God is all-knowing. He does not, therefore, need you to tell Him what your or anyone else's needs are. On this point, we have no less an authority concerning God than God Himself. During the Sermon on the Mount, Jesus tells His followers, "...your Father knows what you need before you ask Him" (Matthew 6:8). It is adequate, therefore, to simply thank God for the many blessings in your life, including the hardships and challenges (which, if you allow, are strengthening), thank Him for another beautiful day in His creation (regardless of the actual weather), ask that His will be done in your life and the lives of other people you name, and end with "In your Son's (or Jesus') name, Amen." God is no more likely to listen to a long prayer than a short one or one with lots of emotion behind it than one delivered straightforwardly. In the gospel of Matthew, Jesus is recorded as saying "And when you pray, do not keep on babbling like pagans, for they think they will be heard because of their many words" (6:7).

    It is paradoxical but truthful to say that prayer is more fulfilling when the person who is praying *expects* absolutely nothing. That doesn't mean you shouldn't ask for anything from God; rather, you simply shouldn't *expect* whatever it is you ask for. If you expect God to say "yes" to a prayer request, you set yourself up for possible disappointment, disillusionment, and even anger. It's true that God hears all prayers. And He *answers* all prayers as well—the idea that if one doesn't get what one asks for from God means God wasn't listening or chose to ignore the request simply isn't true. The fact is, God's answer to any given prayer may (in effect) be "Sorry, but not at this time" or "I have other things in mind for (that situation or the individual in question)." Remember, God's ways are and will forever remain a mystery to us (until, that is, we get to Heaven at which point much, but certainly not all, will be revealed). Through His Creation, His Word (Scripture), and His Son Jesus God has revealed as much about Himself as He is going to reveal, for the time being at least. We're not supposed to figure Him out completely, including understanding why He chooses to seemingly answer some prayers with "yes" and answer others with "sorry, no."

Having said all that, it is necessary to point out that God may and probably will "ignore" the prayer of someone who, perhaps without realizing it, was praying to a different god than the One God of The Bible, Author of the Universe. The person may have been praying to a genie-in-a-bottle god whom the person misconceives as a cosmic waiter of some sort—a god the individual in question "made in his own image." Or, the person may simply be unwilling to accept that his or her prayer request represents a self-centered desire, a "coveting." God is unlikely, for example, to see to it that a person gets a promotion and a big raise or that the horse he put a lot of money on wins the Kentucky Derby. In other cases, people's requests, even though they aren't self-centered, even though their fulfillment would benefit lives other than their own, may not fit with God's plan. The satisfied, happy Christian always keeps in mind that man's plan and God's plan are not the same any more than a child's desires will always fit with his parents' plan for him.

It may in fact be helpful to illustrate the difference between man's plan and God's plan using that very child-parent analogy. A seven-year-old child may want nothing more than a certain new bicycle for his birthday. He begs his parents for it and they say no, telling him that the bicycle he has is perfectly adequate, that he does not need a new one. Nonetheless, the child continues to harbor hope that they will surprise him with the bike of his dreams on his birthday. But they don't. What the child doesn't know and wouldn't be able to appreciate even if he did know is that his parents are putting every spare penny they have into his college fund so that he can eventually enjoy the advantage of attending one of the best colleges in the country. If his parents told him, "The money we would spend on a new and unnecessary bicycle is going into your college fund," said seven-year-old would not glow with gratitude toward his parents. Being a child, he would probably sulk. Why? Because at age seven, he has no appreciation for the value of a good college education. But when he's twenty and in his second year at Apex University and thanks his parents for the sacrifices they made to send him there and they say, "You know, one of the reasons you're here is because we didn't buy you the bicycle you wanted for your eighth birthday, to name but one request of yours we did not meet because there were more important things in our plans for you," he's going to thank them for not giving into his childish entreaties.

The same applies to our relationship with God. He may well "ignore," "not listen to" or deny a request someone makes today to bring something even better into that person's or someone else's life later on. A wife dies at a young age, but her organs save the lives of three other people. A child comes down with a rare and permanently debilitating illness that shortens his life considerably but the research his disease enables results in treatments that save thousands of children from similar fates. A person loses a job and is forced to declare bankruptcy but the energy-saving invention he works on while he looks for new employment is eventually bought by a large corporation for a huge sum.

So, despite what some people think or have heard, God hears everyone's prayers. If every Christian in the world were to pray to Him at the same time (Greenwich Mean Time), He would hear every single prayer clearly. He would hear *your* prayer as if you were the one and only person praying to Him. That's an amazing concept to try and wrap one's head around, but that's what being all-knowing, all-seeing, and all-powerful means. It means God is capable of ANYTHING and EVERYTHING. His physics and our physics are not the same, by a long shot.

Prepping for Prayer

Let's start with some of prayer's figurative nuts and bolts. As mentioned above, nothing arcane, much less odd, is required, but there are several tips that will make your prayer time more successful, fulfilling, satisfying, and productive.

- *First, pray regularly.* While you can and should pray spontaneously whenever and wherever you feel like it, it is helpful to set a daily "prayer appointment" with God—a specific time and place when you're going to talk to God. Mind you, this is not to say that from that point on you should only pray at that appointed time. Ideally, conversation with God should happen throughout the day, spontaneously. The apostle Paul advised that believers "pray without ceasing" (1 Thessalonians 5:16 – 18). That does not mean one should have head bowed and eyes closed in prayer every waking minute. Paul is referring to a prayerful awareness that God is always with us, actively involved in our lives—an attitude of unceasing consciousness of and gratefulness toward Him. But even if you prefer to pray spontaneously, whenever the inspiration strikes, it will still be helpful for you to have a specific time set aside each day that you devote to *purposeful* prayer and Bible study (not necessarily in that order). The purpose is to bring prayer discipline into your life and relationship with God.
- *Second, pray often.* It's a fact that God *wants* relationship with us. We are, after all, his most beloved creation. The more one prays to God (talks to Him), the more God likes it. (That does not mean, however, that He listens or "gives" more to someone who prays thirty times a week on average than He does to someone who prays seven times a week or even only once or twice.) At this point, the question nearly everyone asks is when they're going to find the time in their already too-busy lives for a daily prayer appointment with God. The corresponding complaint is "I just don't have the time!" The person so complaining believes that's true, but it's not. The problem is not the amount of time one has in his or her life; the problem is how one manages that time, the priorities one sets. Someone who has time for Facebook, golf, crossword puzzles, music, power walking, a favorite hobby, watching puppy videos on

YouTube, and so on most definitely has ample time to talk to the LORD of the universe, the Almighty I Am. For example, instead of lying awake worrying about the next day, consider instead talking to God for three to five minutes every night between the time your head hits the pillow and you fall asleep, thanking Him for all the many blessings He has bestowed upon you (i.e., show some gratitude), and asking Him to help you bring peace to your thoughts, to help you stop worrying so much, so that you can enjoy His creation more joyously and love Him more steadfastly. You have the time and by the way, when JR began doing exactly that, he suddenly found himself falling to sleep more quickly and sleeping much more soundly through the night. The voice that says you don't have time to pray is the voice of your rebellious, sinful nature, helping you make excuses for putting God less than first in your life.

- **Third, be proactive concerning distractions.** It's uncanny how easily distracted one can become when praying, how easily one's mind can drift off into worldly thoughts. As mentioned above, the idea of praying out loud or writing down what you want to say to God before you pray will help you stay focused. That's different, by the way, from writing a prayer and then reading it. The authors strongly encourage you to get in the swing of improvisational prayer. Sure, write down some notes concerning what you want to say, but then put your list aside, close your eyes, bow your head (or lean back), and just pray. You're going to find that as you're praying, additional things you'd like to say to God will come to mind. If there are things going on around you, block them out as well as possible. If you lose your place, open your eyes, consult your notes, close your eyes again, and pick up where you left off. The Holy Spirit is going to help you with this, and so you're going to eventually discover that noise that would really bother you in most situations doesn't bother you nearly as much if at all when you're in communion with God. Again, prayer is like anything else you do—the more you pray, the better you're going to get at it.

The bottom line: Accept that getting good at praying, like any other skill, takes time and practice. But unlike other skills—golf and chess, for example—prayer has benefits beyond this earth-bound life.

"LORD, TEACH US TO PRAY"

In Luke's gospel and then again in Matthew we find the story of the one and only time Jesus' disciples made a specific request of Him. He is praying (most likely silently or inaudibly) and an unidentified disciple asks, "Lord, teach us to pray, just as John [the Baptist] taught his disciples." Jesus proceeds to give them what has become known as the Lord's Prayer.

Consider the significance of that disciple's request. Jesus' twelve disciples accompanied him constantly for three years, listening to Him teach, witnessing Him perform many miracles, and watching huge crowds flock to Him and hang on his every word, yet this is the only time on record that a disciple make a specific request of Him. This is all the more significant because when First Century Jews prayed, they did so only in group settings, at synagogue, and only men were allowed to pray. Furthermore, the prayers in question were usually read. It's safe to say that Jesus' Jewish disciples are not familiar with the idea of an individual praying silently without the aid of a parchment. But the disciples know that John the Baptist taught his disciples to pray and they've seen Jesus in prayer on numerous occasions. Jesus had a habit of getting up early in the morning to pray and there were even times when Jesus talked to His Father through an entire night. They know, therefore, that prayer is important, but they don't know how to properly go about it. So, they ask Jesus to teach them how. And He says, "When you pray, say:

> Our Father in Heaven,
> Hallowed be Your name.
> Your kingdom come.
> Your will be done,
> On earth as it is in heaven.
> Give us day by day our daily bread.
> And forgive us our sins,
> For we also forgive everyone who is indebted to us.
> And do not lead us into temptation,
> But deliver us from the evil one." (Matthew 6:9-13)

Note two significant aspects of this prayer:

First, its brevity. In this translation (New King James Version), it consists of ten lines, fifty-nine words. It may well be that Jesus did not mean for those ten lines to be an entire prayer but only a model for *beginning* prayer. It may be that He is simply telling His disciples, "Begin prayer in the following manner." Nonetheless, He gives the disciples a means of saying a lot in relatively few words.

Second, its focus on spiritual rather than material needs. Jesus begins by praising God's name. Then he asks that God's kingdom be established on earth, that God's will be done (in all things), that God forgive sins, and that God provide protection from Satan. The only request that comes close to being "material" in nature is the request that God provide daily bread, but in so doing Jesus is not asking for something out of the ordinary much less extravagant. He's simply asking God to provide the basics—bread, not an opulent meal. Furthermore, the phrase "daily bread" refer not just to food, but to basic necessities of all sorts. He's asking God to provide nothing more than life's essential requirements.

Jesus was a master at compressing a point into the fewest words possible. Most of your prayers are probably going to be more than fifty-nine words long, but the point is, they don't have to be. Here's an example:

Lord God, Heavenly Father,

Thank you for the many blessings of this life,

Including the blessing of eternal life extended to me

Through the sacrifice and resurrection of your Son, Jesus.

I confess my sinful inclinations, which trouble me constantly,

And ask Your forgiveness as well as your help in controlling my sinful nature.

May I come to completely accept Your will in all things,

In the Holy Name of Your Son, Jesus Christ, I pray.

Amen.

That's seventy-seven words, eighteen more than are in the Lord's Prayer, and it is perfectly sufficient. By the way, the authors feel it is counterproductive and perhaps even somewhat inconsiderate for someone leading group prayer to pray for more than a minute—two at the most. By our calculations, a one-minute prayer is going to be approximately three times as long as the Lord's Prayer, and that's quite enough. Any longer and people are going to begin drifting off or silently praying, "Lord, make him stop." In this regard, one should keep in mind that Jesus compared long, drawn-out prayers to pagan babblings (Matthew 6:7).

CONTENT OF PRAYER

Once a place and time for regular prayer have been established, it's time to consider the issue of content. And again, there's no better model than what Jesus set forth in the Lord's Prayer, found in the gospels of both Luke and Matthew (the latter may simply be a somewhat "fleshed out" retelling of Luke 11). In spite of the fact that some religious traditions merely repeat this prayer as some kind of mantra (generally in a group context), Jesus never intended such. Instead, before offering his disciples this model prayer Jesus says, "In this manner, therefore, pray." The phrase "in this manner" implies a basic outline or template that offers prayer points, not an actual prayer to merely be memorized and repeated. Jesus actually discourages such a formulaic approach to prayer when He warns His disciples not to "use vain repetitions (6:7)."

Considered, then, simply as a model, the Lord's Prayer contains several important features:

- ***Reverent approach and attitude:*** Jesus begins his prayer in a very clear and intentional manner, addressing "Our Father in Heaven." Right off the bat, Jesus tells His disciples that they should approach God as a child should approach a loving parent—reverently—but the parent in this case is spirit, not flesh, and "resides" (if that is an accurate term) separate and apart from His creation in a "place" (if that is an accurate term) known as Heaven. Immediately following that opening phrase Jesus' model prayer honors God's very name as holy, thus acknowledging that there is nothing about God, not even His name, that is not sacred. In this regard, Orthodox Jews believe the name of God to be so holy that they are forbidden to speak it, and when they write either Yahweh or God, they do so by substituting dashes for the vowels, as in Y-W-H-W or G-d. The next phrase in Jesus' model prayer—*Your kingdom come, your will be done on earth as it is in heaven*—continues the "hallowing" (honoring) by praising God's boundless authority over the universe, His creation. One does not have to begin personal prayer with the first lines of the Lord's Prayer, but every prayer should begin with words that reflect a formal, reverential approach that acknowledges God's majesty and dominion over all things. Beginning prayer with statements of that sort puts one into a proper frame of mind.

- *Humility:* Most people associate prayer with asking God for things—thus, the ubiquity of the phrase "I prayed for...."—and even though that purpose, in and of itself, reflects a very narrow view, prayer does indeed provide the necessary context for asking God's providence concerning certain aspects of our lives or the lives of others. In fact, The Bible explicitly instructs us to make requests of God. Philippians 4:6 says, "Be anxious for nothing, but in everything by prayer and supplication, with thanksgiving, let your requests be made known to God." In other words, one can ask God to intervene in situations in your life (or the lives of others). At the very least, one can ask God to provide direction and guidance for handling problematic situations, to reveal His will. That said, it is important to keep in mind that when Jesus is teaching his disciples to pray, He asks only that His Heavenly Father provide necessities. Jesus is in effect saying that if all God does for you is provide you with your "daily bread," the absolute rock-bottom essentials of life, then He has done enough and deserves your praise and gratitude.
- *Confession and forgiveness:* The next lines in the Lord's Prayer (a) request God's forgiveness for sin and sinfulness and (b) "pass it on" by extending forgiveness to neighbors who have sinned against us. The word "debt" as used in some translations refers to moral, not financial, debt. Because sin is what separates us from God, it is man's greatest enemy and biggest problem. All sin is offense to both God and neighbor. Thus, the sinner requires the forgiveness of both and must be as willing to extend forgiveness to the same degree that it is desired. Make no mistake, however, God's forgiveness of us and

our forgiveness of others are two different kinds of forgiveness. When God forgives, He removes the penalty for sin. When we forgive, we choose to no longer hold someone's offense against them, but if that individual wants freedom from the ultimate penalty of their sin, they must ask forgiveness of God.
- **Request for deliverance:** Following His words about forgiveness Jesus segues rather logically into a request for God's protection from the enticements of the flesh. Jesus says "And lead us not into temptation but deliver us from evil." This does not imply that God would actually lead a person to sin by setting a moral trap for him. Jesus is asking God, on His disciple's behalf, for moral fortification, that they would have knowledge, insight, and power to deal with the various temptations to evil that exist in the world.

PRAYER IS FOR JUST ABOUT ANYTHING AND EVERYTHING

While Jesus' model is a helpful outline we can follow as we develop the discipline of prayer, Scripture has more to say about the topic. Consider other important prayer purposes:

- **Pray for people in positions of leadership.** I Timothy 2:1-2 says "Therefore I exhort first of all that supplications, prayers, intercessions, and giving of thanks be made for all men, for kings and all who are in authority, that we may lead quiet and peaceable life in all godliness and reverence." Notice how Paul not only offers the general exhortation to pray for all people but to direct some time in prayer to those who are in positions of authority. After all, we should all want our leaders to be involved in forming a society which allows us to pursue our faith in peace.
- **Pray for other people to grow in their relationship with Christ.** As in the above example, the Apostle Paul is one of the best sources to which you can turn to gain insight into prayer. Several of his letters indicate the way he prayed for the various early Christian communities with which he was involved. Paul's prayers are pointed

petitions for the ongoing growth of believers. For example, Philippians 1:9-11 says, "And this I pray, that your love may abound still more and more in knowledge and all discernment, that you may approve the things that are excellent, that you may be sincere and without offense till the day of Christ, being filled with the fruits of righteousness which are by Jesus Christ, to the glory and praise of God." Other examples include Ephesians 1:15-21, 3:14-19, and Colossians 1:9-14. If you find yourself uncertain what to pray for people then just let these words form the content of your prayer. These are also helpful prayers to guide the way you pray for yourself.

- **Pray for evangelistic endeavors.** As we pray we should pray that we and others would be able to effectively communicate the gospel to others. In Ephesians 6, Paul asks for these believers to pray for him and all the saints, "that utterance may be given to me, that I may open my mouth boldly to make known the mystery of the gospel." He asks for essentially the same thing in Colossians 4:2-4. Not only can you pray for your own ability to share the message of Jesus, but also pray for others including missionaries around the world.
- **Pray for those with physical, emotional, and relational needs.** For lots of folks, praying for those who are in sickness and adversity is their primary prayer form. Indeed, God's Word clearly encourages us to pray in this manner. James 5:14 says, "Is anyone among you sick? Let him call for the elders of the church, and let them pray over him, anointing him with oil in the name of the Lord." Needless to say, as one prays for the physical needs people are facing, one should also pray for the spiritual ramifications of such trials. People who are facing serious health crises also endure mental and emotional stress. In many cases, God uses sickness to bring people to a deeper understanding of Himself. Do not discount the ways God can work in someone's life through the infirmities they are called upon to endure.

GOD'S BOOK OF PRAYER

The authors would be grievously remiss if we did not point out that there is arguably no better resource for prayer than the Book of Psalms, which consists of poems/songs of worship written by King David (1040 – 970 BCE). For prayer exercise, read a psalm and then, using it as a model, compose your own prayer to God. (Give an example or two?)

CONCLUSION

It is indeed one of the great privileges of the Christian life that a believer can go before the Sovereign King of the Universe with our requests. Hebrews 4:16 says, "Let us therefore come boldly to the throne of grace, that we may obtain mercy and find grace to help in time of need." Not only can we come before God but we can do so with complete confidence (boldness) in Him, confident that His love for us is deep and wide and the assurance that His Plan for history will turn out well. For a Christian, prayer is a responsibility. God requires relationship with us and until we encounter Him in Heaven, prayer is the primary means of initiating and developing that relationship. There is no better time to begin developing a prayer life than right now.

RECOMMENDED READING

- Bennet, Arthur. *The Valley of Vision: A Collection of Puritan Prayers & Devotions*, The Banner of Truth Trust, 1975.
- Carson, D.A. *Praying with Paul*, Baker, 2015.
- Keller, Timothy. *Prayer: Experiencing Awe and Intimacy With God*, Penguin Books, 2016.
- Miller, Paul. *A Praying Life: Connecting with God in a Distracting World*, NavPress, 2009.
- Ryle, J.C. *A Call to Prayer*, Banner of Truth, 2005.
- Whitney, Donald. *Praying the Bible*, Crossway, 2015.
- Valley of Vision: A Collection of Puritan Prayers – Arthur Bennett

QUESTIONS FOR PERSONAL REFLECTION AND DISCUSSION

1. What are some of the common hindrances to prayer? Which of these do you identify with? What can you do to overcome these barriers?
2. Scripture encourages us to pray with "all kinds of prayers and supplications" (Ephesians 6:18). What do you think this means? What kinds of situations are you facing but have yet to pray about them?
3. Why are memorized, formulaic prayers potentially problematic?
4. Of what significance to all Christians is the fact that when Jesus prayed to His Father to spare Him from death on the Cross (Luke 22:42), God did not spare Him.

10

Spread the Good News!

> "I've always said that I don't respect people who don't proselytize. I don't respect that at all. If you believe that there's a Heaven and a hell, and people could be going to hell or not getting eternal life, and you think that it's not really worth telling them this because it would make it socially awkward—and atheists who think people shouldn't proselytize and who say just leave me alone and keep your religion to yourself—how much do you have to hate somebody to *not* proselytize? How much do you have to hate somebody to believe everlasting life is possible and not tell them that?" – Avowed atheist Penn Jillette on the topic of evangelism

Up to this point we've covered some profound, powerful, and life-changing truths. We've worked our way through the essence of the Bible's message concerning how someone can be certain he or she is going to Heaven, and we've considered some important ways we can grow in faith as we worship with God's people, study God's Word, and pray. We turn now to what is for many Christians one of the most difficult aspects of our earthly responsibilities: the command, from Jesus Himself, that we share the message of His gospel with unbelievers.

The 2016 presidential election demonstrates that Americans are not generally hesitant when it comes to speaking their minds. We'll readily engage in argument over politics, food, sports, philosophy, and even certain features of theology. But at the suggestion that believers in Christ Jesus need to intentionally develop relationships with people who don't know Him and then share Him gospel with them, lots of otherwise outspoken folks suddenly clam up. No longer is there the boisterous bravado of opinion concerning "safe" topics. Suddenly we become concerned about offending someone. Or, we worry that we may not say the right thing or be able to give proper answers to the inevitable questions.

There are at least three reasons why this is often the case. First, some folks may not know exactly how much and what aspects of the gospel to share. Second, some become anxious that they may be asked hard questions they can't answer. The third and perhaps the most important reason is because the stakes involved in sharing the gospel of Christ Jesus are huge. It is, after all, a life-or-death matter. For that reason, there is a unique approach-avoidance conflict that goes on in the mind and heart of many a believer when an opportunity to share the gospel presents itself. And yet, as the quote that begins this chapter indicates, to refuse to share the gospel is ultimately an act of hatred toward unbelievers. If we who are followers of Christ Jesus truly love other people then it is imperative we share His vital message with them. Therefore, this final chapter will help you take what you've learned and share it with others.

That act of sharing is known as *evangelism*. The root word in evangelism, "evangel" (Greek: euangelion), simply means "good news." The word evangelism has therefore been used to refer to the proclamation of the good news. Given the fact that we are talking about evangelism in a Christian context we can define evangelism as the act of declaring the message of the gospel with the hopes that the individual who hears it will be moved by the Holy Spirit to listen, understand, and believe. Keep in mind, though, that whereas leading a person to belief in Christ Jesus is our evangelical hope, we are powerless to make that happen. We can act as catalysts to an act of faith, but only the Holy Spirit can enable someone to understand their sinful condition and place their faith in Christ. Nonetheless, the first part of the process sits squarely on our shoulders. Our task is to faithfully and accurately share the gospel with those who have not yet heard it, or have heard it but for whatever reason(s) don't believe it. Provided you are sharing the gospel's essential features as outlined in Scripture (and described herein) then the only way you can fail at this responsibility is by not sharing. You are not required to make anyone believe anything. You don't have to know the answers to each and every one of the questions a non-believer might ask. (In that regard, it's perfectly okay to answer a difficult question with "I don't really know the answer to that, but it's a good question. I will ask my pastor and get back to you.") You don't have to convict someone of their sin. God simply wants and even commands us to share the message He's given to us in His Word. He will take care of the rest.

THE COMMAND TO SHARE THE GOSPEL

Now that you have a basic understanding of what evangelism is, let's turn our attention to the Bible's command to engage in such work. The most well-known evangelical scripture—called the "Great Commission"—is found at the end of the New Testament book written by the apostle Matthew. While Matthew doesn't call it the Great Commission (or any other name for that matter), Christians have long considered it as such because of its significance for the purposes of the church.

The story line up to this point: Jesus has been crucified and resurrected. For several weeks He has been appearing to His disciples (and others) and offering further instruction to them concerning the establishment of His church (not a denomination, mind you, but the body of believers, often referred to as the Body of Christ). The time has come for Jesus to ascend to Heaven, to return to His Father. Right before He physically leaves planet Earth, He says to His disciples, "All authority has been given to Me in Heaven and on earth. Go therefore and make disciples of all the nations, baptizing them in the name of the Father and of the Son and of the Holy Spirit, teaching them to observe all things that I have commanded you; and lo, I am with you always, *even* to the end of the age." Those were His last earthly words to His disciples. Needless to say, they are central to the Christian mission.

Note, Jesus first declares His authority to issue the command that follows. It is, in fact, a boundless authority. He possesses absolute sovereignty and lordship over all things. Having established His bona fides, Jesus then articulates the central mission of His church—"go...and make disciples." He then explains what "making disciples" involves: purposefully seek out new believers, baptize them, and teach them. Christians are to seek out the lost with the intention of converting them and then, through baptism and teaching, helping mold them into genuine followers of Christ. In summary, the Christian church's primary purpose is to grow by sharing the gospel with lost people with the intention of helping them become disciples of Lord Jesus.

If one follows the New Testament story as it unfolds beginning with the four gospels and then segueing into the book of Acts, we see how this disciple-making takes place in the life of the church. We see in Acts, Chapter 2 that the Holy Spirit comes upon the disciples (at the Feast of Pentecost), many people are saved through the preaching of the gospel, and the church begins to grow—by leaps and bounds. In fact, Acts 2 closes with an account of how the disciples—now known as apostles—go about making converts by teaching, praying and worshipping with them as a body. The story goes on to tell us how this first group of converts not only grow in their own faith but continue to reach people in the city of Jerusalem. Shortly thereafter, this new movement begins to threaten the Jewish establishment. As persecution begins, the church moves out of Jerusalem and into "the nations." Acts 8:1 tells us that believers began to flee Jerusalem (where hostility and persecution were most intense) and scattered throughout the regions of Judea and Samaria. But they do not cower in fear. Rather, they immediately begin to spread the Good News! The result is a massive growth of the church throughout the region and into other countries. In other words, a case can be made that Jesus' command to "go and make disciples" is more than a bit prophetic. It almost seems as if the early believers are forced out of their ancestral homes so that the gospel can be preached beyond the national boundaries of Israel and eventually to the ends of the earth.

ACTS 1:8

A second evangelical passage, Acts 1:8, is similar in context and wording to Matthew 28 (and may be a retelling). Jesus has gathered His followers together for final instructions. Unbeknownst to them, He's going to ascend into Heaven right after this last meeting. Clearly these words bear significant weight. The disciples want to know if Jesus is finally going to usher in His kingdom. They're ready to see the dynasty of King David rise again. But that's not the plan. Instead, Jesus tells them to not concern themselves with such worldly things. He says, "But you shall receive power when the Holy Spirit has come upon you; and you shall be witnesses to Me in Jerusalem, and in all Judea and Samaria, and to the end of the earth." While these words bear some similarity to the Great Commission, they also provide more clarity on the exact nature of Jesus' mission to His followers. Note some important features of this scripture:

- **First**, Jesus informs His disciples of the means by which they will accomplish sharing the gospel—they will be empowered by the Holy Spirit. This promise is fulfilled one chapter later as the Holy Spirit suddenly shows up during a sermon Peter is preaching. As Peter preaches the Good News of Christ Jesus, a miracle occurs: people hear his message in their respective languages. (Keep in mind that Jerusalem lay at the intersection of vital trade routes and was both cosmopolitan and, of necessity, multi-lingual.) The result is that thousands of people are saved on that auspicious day. From this story, we know that when a person is saved, the Holy Spirit begins to dwell in him. This doesn't mean one begins to do weird or supernatural stuff. It simply means that God through His Spirit (the third person of the Trinity) enables the new believer to begin acting in accord with His will, including being empowered to share with others the truths about Jesus Christ.
- **Second**, Jesus says that the disciples will be empowered to serve as "witnesses." This is an important word in evangelism because it summarizes the essence of the process. To witness is to testify to something, to give verbal assent to certain events. An important implication of being a witness is that you are a firsthand recipient of

the information you are being expected to communicate. Jesus expected his followers to accurately teach what they'd experienced, first-hand, while He was with them. In other words, a witness of Christ Jesus isn't free to alter, edit, or offer his own opinion or perspective. Think of the witness stand in a court of law. It is in this setting that one offers "testimony" regarding the case at hand. One's sole obligation is to tell the truth, the whole truth, and nothing but the truth. Evangelism, at its core, is surprisingly simple. You are commanded by God to clearly and plainly state the truths of the gospel to those who have not yet believed.

- **Third,** Jesus spells out a specific evangelistic plan. He says that his apostles will witness in Jerusalem, Judea, Samaria, and then take the Good News to the ends of the world. The disciples will begin evangelizing in Jerusalem, the capital of the Jewish homeland. Then they are to take the gospel into the countryside of Judea, then beyond the borders of Jewish orthodoxy to Samaria, and finally, "to the ends of the earth." Jesus has a long-term view in mind. He's obviously addressing generations of believers who live centuries in the future. The phrase "to the ends of the earth" means not only "all over the world" but also "until the end of historical time."

It's important at this point to add some clarification. The Bible never encourages believers to only share the gospel. The specific command is always in the context of "making disciples." This means that we share the gospel not only to see someone become a Christian but to also help them continue to grow in the faith—become disciples of and evangelists for the most important person who's ever lived and the most important message ever given. While we may end up sharing the gospel with total strangers that we will never see again, many of our evangelistic efforts will be directed at people we know. This means we bear some responsibility to continue to aid them in their growth as Christians.

SHARING THE GOSPEL

The Bible makes clear that all believers are responsible for sharing the gospel with others. But that is often—more often than not, in fact—easier said than done. At least at first, and more often than not, the new believer feels a tad (or more than a tad) awkward about doing something so intimate. He asks himself what he's supposed to say, what to do if someone asks him a question he can't answer, and so on. He's expected to be a spiritual salesperson of sorts, but there's no evangelism school that prepares one for this undertaking. Searching Amazon, one can find a good number of books on the subject, pastors tend to talk it up a fair amount, and church members talk about it among themselves, but it's probably the case that the reading and talking far outdo the actual practice. That's perfectly understandable. Evangelizing with the wrong person or at the wrong time in his or her life can ruin a friendship. Yes, the Holy Spirit will be there with you as you make the attempt; nonetheless, the attempt may fall flat or even end in disaster. Then again, it may bear fruit years later.

Shortly after being saved, JR reconnected with a college buddy and worked up the courage to begin talking to him about God, Jesus, and Heaven as they were zig-zagging around a golf course—of all places! The old friend seemed receptive, but not all that enthusiastic. Ten years later, the same friend told John that he had been instrumental in leading him back to Christ (he'd been raised Catholic and began, upon his salvation, to attend a Protestant church). So, you never know. The moral of the story is that the effect of one's attempt to spread the good news may not be known immediately. On another occasion, with another old friend, JR asked, "Can I talk to you about Jesus?" The friend's answer: "I'd rather you didn't." And that was that. As they say, win a few, lose a few. JR also understood that this same friend may accept Christ at some later time in his life. On yet another occasion, a close relative (JR's hope is that he reads this book with an open mind) became agitated to the point of anger at JR's attempt to bring up the subject of Christ. In this regard, it is healthy, always, to keep in mind that YOU do not ever save someone; only Jesus can do that, and with any given person, He will do it in His way, in His time.

With the uncertainties in mind, here are some tips that may (and sometimes, with some folks, may not) increase the possibility that any given attempt at evangelizing someone will be successful, or at least received with grace:

- **DO YOUR HOMEWORK.** Before taking the plunge into the waters of evangelism, it can helpful to do some prep work. One way of overcoming some of the fear and intimidation associated with sharing the gospel is to make sure you know the message to begin with. The good news is that the book you are presently reading can help you become prepared. Work your way back through the first five chapters, highlighting and underlining as you go. Maybe even develop an outline of essential points in each. You don't have to memorize all that material, but make sure you have established in your mind the essential features of the gospel. It would even be helpful to memorize a few essential verses of Scripture. Focus attention on the sinfulness of man, our need for salvation, the meaning of the crucifixion and resurrection of Jesus, and the fact that salvation can be obtained in no other way but through surrendering faith in Christ Jesus. The disciple Peter exhorts us to "always be ready to give a defense to everyone who asks you a reason for the hope that is in you" (1 Peter 3:15). God expects His people to be prepared to articulate the essential truths of salvation—why we all need it and how we can obtain it. Peter's exhortation does not mean we are obligated to succeed at convincing everyone we attempt to convince. It only demands that we be prepared to share and defend our faith.
- **MAKE IT PERSONAL.** Along with developing a firm knowledge of the essential elements of the gospel, think about how you might weave your own story into your evangelical message. Share how you came to become a believer, and then share how the gospel and faith in Christ has changed you—your heart, your work, your entire life. The message should never be that as a believer, you occupy some superior position, but that you were once lost as well, struggling with addiction to sin (you don't have to be specific). Try your best to help the person to whom you're witnessing identify with the "old" you. As you share the truth that Jesus died for sin and conquered it for all

mankind by rising fully-healed from literal death you can talk about the time you heard that message and were moved to accept it.
- **PRAY.** Ask God, through prayer, to provide you opportunity to witness for Christ. Ask Him to cause your path to intersect with that of others who need the gospel in their lives.
- **TAKE THE LEAP!** Look for openings in conversations with family, friends, and even strangers. Granted, there may be situations where these people may not be open to hearing the message—at least they may not be open to it at that point in their lives. The bottom line is that you never know until you give it a try. The situation here is analogous to a writer who is trying to get a book published. He sends his manuscript to publisher after publisher and is met with nothing but polite rejection. And then, just as he's about to accept that he's not destined to become a published author, a publisher responds to his submission with enthusiasm. Likewise, you may just have to keep at it until you experience success. By all means, do not take "rejection" personally. Keep in mind, always, that you are a messenger, nothing more. Your responsibility ends with delivering the message. The Holy Spirit takes over from there.
- **DON'T GIVE UP.** Make a list of people in your life that are not believers. Begin to pray for them. Begin to pray for opportunities to share the gospel with them. With any given individual, this process may take some time. It may require that you share portions of the gospel and your personal testimony several times before it begins to "stick."
- **SHARE THIS BOOK.** Finally—and at the risk of seeming to self-promote—use this book as an evangelistic tool. We recognize the challenges involved in confronting another person with the truths of the gospel. We've been there, done that. There's nothing easy about telling someone else that they are sinners and will face judgment unless they trust in Christ. For sure, that message must come across non-judgmentally. One reason we wrote this book was to provide believers with another tool to help in this effort. Consider giving this book to an unbeliever and then meet with him or her once a week, going over it chapter by chapter. Granted, there could still be difficult questions asked and even moments of confrontation. But although it's a dwindling pastime, most people in our culture still like to read.

And now, an **EVANGELISM WARNING**: It can be easy to convince ourselves of a lesser form of evangelism. The Christian world is rife with people who want to broaden the definition of evangelism to include just about any word or act that hints at Jesus. So, some people think it is enough to tell people that Jesus loves them. While that is certainly a great message, it is not the full gospel. People need to know why Jesus loves them, why they need His love, and how He has demonstrated that love for all mankind. Another popular "method" is for people to assume that they are being evangelistic when they live a faithful Christian life. In support of such an effort people will offer a quote often attributed to Francis of Assisi. "Preach the gospel at all times and when necessary use words." While there's no evidence Francis ever actually said those words, the statement has been used by many a believer to justify never sharing the gospel with anyone else and simply live a life filled with good works. The authors certainly commend living a faithful Christian life. Furthermore, a person's commitment to Christ in every aspect of life is a powerful evangelistic tool. But people do not get saved by merely observing your good works. People are saved through Jesus Christ when they hear and believe the gospel. In other words, when you preach the gospel you absolutely must use words. And the more you do it, the better your words will become.

CONCLUSION

The task of evangelism, though not easy, is essential to Christianity. It is the means by which God has chosen to spread the message of the gospel from one generation to the next. In this regard, it has been said that the church is only one generation away from extinction. Theologically speaking, the adage fails to fully appreciate God's sovereignty over such matters. However, on an emotional and motivation level, the statement has more than a ring of truth. How many important movements and ideas and philosophies have died off because the next generation did not pick up the ball and run with it? Christianity has demonstrated incredible endurance for 2000 years. Its endurance can rightly be attributed, at least in part, to the fact that pure,

Bible-grounded, orthodox Christianity is the truth, the whole truth, and nothing but the truth. Now the task has been delivered to us to continue to boldly proclaim the hope of Christ as found in Scripture. We do not know who will be saved, but we know God is in the business of saving. Famed British pastor Charles Spurgeon put it best, "I would sooner bring one sinner to Jesus Christ than unravel all the mysteries of the divine Word, for salvation is the one thing we are to live for."

Amen to that!

RECOMMENDED READING

- Coleman, Robert. *The Master Plan of Evangelism*. Revell, 2010.

- MacArthur, John. *Evangelism: How to Share the Gospel Faithfully*. Thomas Nelson, 2011.

- Jamieson, Bobby. *Reaching the Lost: Evangelism*. Crossway, 2012.

- Pippert, Rebecca Manley. *Out of the Salt Shaker & into the World*. IVP Books, 1999.

QUESTIONS FOR PERSONAL REFLECTION AND DISCUSSION

1. What are some of the barriers or hindrances you might experience when trying to share the gospel? Which hindrances come from within and which come from others? What are some ways you could deal with or overcome those barriers?

2. We know from both the Bible and history that Christianity spread rapidly in the first century. To what do you attribute such a rapid growth? Given the fact that these early believers faced immense persecution and opposition, what made them so effective? How does that compare with evangelistic efforts today? Why does it seem more difficult today than 2000 years ago?

3. Who are some people in your life who have yet to become Christian? Take time and think of at least five people. Pray for opportunities to share the gospel with them. What are some ways you can begin to introduce the truth of the gospel to their lives?

The Authors

John Rosemond: John is a family psychologist who has completely rejected the teachings of his profession and embraced the sufficiency of Scripture. He has written a nationally-syndicated newspaper column since 1976, is the author of 18 books on parenting and family issues, and is the most in-demand speaker in his field. He and his wife Willie have been married since 1968. They have two 40-something children and seven grandchildren. John and Willie are members of Tabernacle Baptist Church in New Bern, North Carolina.

Dr. Scott Gleason: After receiving his Master of Divinity and doctorate in Christian Theology from Southeastern Baptist Theological Seminary, Scott served in several pastoral positions in Tennessee and North Carolina. Since 2009, he has been Senior Pastor of Tabernacle Baptist Church in New Bern, North Carolina. Scott and his wife Bekah have three boys who keep them busy and entertained.

The brief story behind the book: John and Willie moved to New Bern, North Carolina, in 2014 and began attending Tabernacle Baptist Church. They were immediately impressed with Pastor Scott's ability to bring Scripture to life through his riveting expository preaching and teaching style. Having wanted to write a theological book for several years, John approached Scott with the idea for this one. And there you have it!

GETTING TO HEAVEN

Made in the USA
San Bernardino, CA
14 April 2018